CRITICIZING ART

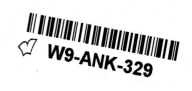

CRITICIZING ART

Understanding the Contemporary

TERRY BARRETT
THE OHIO STATE UNIVERSITY

Mayfield Publishing Company
Mountain View, California
London • Toronto

Library of Congress Cataloging-in-Publication Data

Barrett, Terry Michael.
    Criticizing art: understanding the contemporary / Terry Barrett.
        p.   cm.
    Includes bibliographical references and index.
    ISBN 1-55934-147-5
    1. Art criticism—United States—History—20th century.   2. Art, American.
3. Art, Modern—20th century—United States.   I. Title.
N7476. B38   1993
701' . 18—dc20

                                                                93–27241
                                                                CIP

Manufactured in the United States of America
10   9   8   7   6   5   4   3   2   1

Mayfield Publishing Company
1280 Villa Street
Mountain View, California 94041

Sponsoring Editor, Janet M. Beatty; production editor, Sondra Glider; manuscript editor,
Carol Dondrea; text designer, Jeanne M. Schreiber; cover designer and production artist,
Jean Mailander; manufacturing manager, Martha Branch; cover image, Elizabeth Murray,
Truth, Justice and the Comics III, 1990, oil on two canvases, photo by Lee Fatherree.
Courtesy of Paula Cooper Gallery, New York. The text was set in 10½ × 12½ Times
Roman and printed on 50# Finch Opaque by Malloy Lithographing.

For Mom

CONTENTS

PREFACE

The primary goal of this book is to bring readers inside the immensely fascinating world of contemporary art. I have written it to help readers operate more comfortably and knowledgeably within the field of contemporary art criticism in a manner as much like that of professional critics as possible.[1] More specifically, I have written it to enable readers to write and talk about art better than they now can.

The book is built around the practices of contemporary critics writing about contemporary art. Most of the critics are American, mostly writing about American art. Their writings have been gathered from an intentionally wide variety of publications, from newspapers and newsmagazines to international journals of art criticism. A constant supposition of the book is that variety is healthy. Thus, you will find a wide sampling of critical publications, each geared to a different audience and written in a distinct tone of voice with its own vocabulary.

The book uses the thoughts and words of dozens of critics about the works of dozens of artists. The selection of critics and artists was somewhat arbitary. Sometimes I chose the critics I wanted to include first, and the art they wrote about was not the deciding factor. In most cases, however, I selected the artists first and then read published criticism about the art they made. The criteria I used to select the artists was also arbitary but carefully considered: I wanted diversity of media and messages, the influences of Modernity and Postmodernity, ethnic variety, females as well as males, and socially activist artists as well as those more concerned with formal issues.

To help in the selection of critics and—especially—artists, I polled several friendly colleagues[2] at Ohio State University and nationally who are knowledgeable from a variety of perspectives and professions about recent art and criticism, asking them which artists and critics should be considered for a book such as this one. They responded with over 250 different artists[3] and 72 critics.[4] I then made my final choices based on my own preferences, their recommendations, and my goal of inclusivity. The group I finally chose is broader than it would have been without my colleagues' generous advice. Nevertheless, I could not, of course, accommodate all the artists and critics working today; thus, the exclusion of any particular artist or critic should not be construed as being based on a negative appraisal.

A number of years ago, the aesthetician Morris Weitz[5] undertook a study of what critics did when they criticized literature. Among his conclusions were that critics engaged in one or more of four central activities: They described, interpreted, judged, and theorized. This book is organized around these categories of critical activities. The categories are sufficiently general as to provide direction without being overly specific and limiting thinking. Neither Weitz nor I, however, offer these critical activities as the steps to take in doing criticism or as a method of criticism. In this book, I have derived principles of description, interpretation, and judgment from the writings of published critics, and discussed aspects of theory in relation to art and criticism. If readers understand these principles, they can think independently of methods, developing their own to suit their ways of working.

Description, interpretation, judgment, and theory overlap in the writings of critics and in this book, even though separate chapters are built around each. It is difficult to write about art without describing it. Consciously and unconsciously held theories of art affect all criticism, and for that reason the reader may want to read the chapter on theory before the chapters on description, interpretation, and judgment. Not all critics engage in all four activities in the same piece of writing, and some critics choose to write primarily interpretive criticism while others insist that judgment is the most important activity of criticism. I think that interpretation is the most important critical activity in that, if one fully understands a work of art, judging it becomes easy—and may not even be necessary. Judgments without interpretations, however, are irresponsive to the artwork and perhaps irresponsible to the reader.

The book is based on several other suppositions as well. First, art critics are generally and most often interested in contemporary art rather than old art. When they deal with older art in contemporary exhibitions, they are likely to discuss what that art means to present-day viewers rather than what it might have meant to the viewers in the past for whom the art was originally made.

In addition, criticism is generally positive; it puts the experience of art into language to interest and inform readers. Criticism is usually not written for the artists whose work the critic is discussing. Rather, critics are usually trying to increase the public's thoughtful appreciation of art.

Good criticism is careful and engaging argumentation that furthers dialogue about art and life; dogmatic and terse pronouncements of good or bad are antithetical to fruitful critical dialogue.

Artworks generate different interpretations, and to interpret an artwork is to generate meaning.

In the process of writing criticism—that is, by carefully articulating their responses to art so they may communicate them to their readers—critics enlighten themselves about art and their own reaction to it.

Critical plurality—a variety of voices—is a welcome phenomenon of contemporary art criticism. A diversity of critical voices, even though they sometimes contradict each other, is healthy for the art community because it gives readers of criticism more to think about regarding works of art and the world from which it emerged.

A plurality of critical voices may help readers find their own voices, allowing them to identify with some, disagree with others, and eventually formulate their own positions.

Viewing art and reacting to it and reading criticism and reacting to it can provide self-knowledge as well as knowledge about art.

Critics criticize criticism as well as art; criticism itself can and should be criticized.

Critical discourse is interesting in itself, as well as a contribution to knowledge about art and the world. Through this book, I hope to encourage the reader to join the discussion.

ACKNOWLEDGMENTS

I thoroughly enjoy working with Mayfield Publishing Company—particularly my sponsoring editor, Jan Beatty, and my production editor, Sondra Glider. I also wish to thank Carol Dondrea, Jean Mailander, Martha Branch, Julie Rovesti, Jeanne Schreiber, Patricia Smith, and Pam Trainer.

I want to thank the following reviewers of my initial proposal and of subsequent drafts of the manuscript: Don Bacigalupi, University of Texas at Austin; William Bradley, The Pennsylvania State University; Liana Degirolami Cheney, University of Massachusetts at Lowell; Mark Gottsegen, University of North Carolina at Greensboro; Paul Eli Ivey, University of Arizona; David William, University of Pittsburgh; and Joseph F. Young, Arizona State University; and especially Sally Hagaman, Purdue University.

I also want to thank Judith Koroscik and the College of the Arts, and the Office of Research, The Ohio State University, for partial funding of the research for this book; Christine Huntley, a research assistant, for valuable hours in the library and at the copy machine; the many students who have read and used the book in manuscript format and found mistakes and offered valuable suggestions; Elizabeth Garber of Pennsylvania State University, for a careful reading of the section on feminism in particular and for general help with Chapter 5; colleagues at The Ohio State University, Sydney Walker and Patricia Stuhr, for help with Chapter 5; and Michael Parsons, for a careful reading of the entire manuscript and his thoughtful suggestions throughout; Linda Himes for her proofreading and compliments; my son Jesse, for his encouragement; and especially Pam Reese, for her constant and loving support.

CRITICIZING ART

1
ABOUT ART CRITICISM

This chapter is an overview of contemporary art criticism. It is a cross section of a broad spectrum of current critical practice—not a careful history of art criticism in the twentieth century. It includes critics who hold varying and sometimes disagreeing points of view about a wide variety of artworks. It is a sampling of critical voices, some soft and others shrill. It samples critical writings from daily newspapers, national popular newsmagazines, regional art journals, sophisticated academic journals, and national and international art publications written in English. Some of the critics have overt political motivations that they directly identify; others leave their politics, or lack thereof, implicit. The chapter views criticism as a lively, ongoing, interesting, valuable, and complicated conversation. It—and indeed the whole book—has been written to encourage readers to join the discussion.

LOVE AND HATE

"You presumably write about works of art because you love them. I don't write out of hate. I write out of love, and that's what I think criticism should primarily be."[1] These are the comments of Robert Rosenblum, a critic living in New York. His sentiments are echoed by other critics. Rene Ricard, a critic and poet, stated in *Artforum* that "in point of fact I'm not an art critic. I am an enthusiast. I like to drum up interest in artists who have somehow inspired me to be able to say something about their work."[2] Of her desire to spend time with art, Rosalind Krauss, a founder of the critical journal *October,* says: "Presumably one gets involved with this rather particular, rather esoteric form of expression because one has had some kind of powerful experience with it—and that presumably this powerful experience then makes you want to go on and think about it and learn about it and write about it. But you must have at some point been ravished, been seduced, been taken in."[3]

These statements by these critics serve to offset the popular misconception that the criticism of art is a negative endeavor. In ordinary language, the term *criticism* does connote disapproval and fault finding: thus, it is quite natural for those who are unknowledgeable about art criticism to associate it with negativity toward art. In aesthetic discourse, *art criticism* neither denotes nor connotes a negative activity. But unfortunately the term continues to be confusing to the public—and some, like Ricard, do not even want to be called critics. Lucy Lippard, a very prolific art critic, also distances herself from the label *critic:* "I never liked the term anyway. Its negative connotations place the writer in fundamental antagonism to artists."[4] She and other critics do not want to be thought negative about art or antagonistic to artists because they are not. Certainly critics sometimes do make negative judgments about art (critical judgment will be thoroughly considered in Chapter 4), but most often critics' judgments are positive. As Ricard says, "Why give publicity to something you hate?"[5]

The attitudes expressed in this book are positive about art and art criticism. In general, critics choose to spend their lives thinking and writing and talking about art because they love it and see it as a valuable phenomenon in the world. Most are grateful to be professionally associated with art and art criticism. They do not always agree with the art that is made, but they enjoy thinking about it. Rosenblum summarizes their attitudes: "We just want to write about art and look at it and talk about it."[6]

CRITICAL ARROGANCE AND HUMILITY

Sometimes critics are accused of arrogance and pomposity. They are often portrayed as snobs in popular culture. And perhaps they are. Neither critics nor artists are necessarily nice people. In one of his critical essays, Jeremy Gilbert-Rolfe reminds us that the Greeks who gave us concepts of democracy and aesthetics were slave owners.[7] Janet Malcolm, in a lengthy, informative, and gossipy two-part series of articles on the editing of the influential critical journal *Artforum,* says that Krauss "is quick, sharp, cross, tense, bracingly derisive, fearlessly uncharitable—makes one's own 'niceness' seem somehow dreary and anachronistic. She infuses fresh life and meaning into the old phrase about not suffering fools gladly."[8]

Many critics express humility about being critics. Peter Plagens is a critic and an artist who currently writes art criticism for *Newsweek* magazine. Before moving to New York some years ago, he lived and worked in California. In a humorously serious and self-revealing essay about being a critic, he admits his own vulnerability. Describing his experience of coming to New York to see whether he wanted to write for *Artforum,* published in New York, he wrote: "Archie Bunker, driving the JFK-Midtown Carey, dines immediately on my feelings of inferiority before all New Yorkers. *They know more than I do;* deference seems called for at all times. The cold authority of the East is established at once, by the way the driver takes my six bucks."[9] After a week in New York, he complains of the tediousness of "listening to somebody's opinion of *this* writer's interpretation of *that* critic's opinion of *this* artist's influence on *that* artist's early work."[10] He questions whether "MORE DISCOURSE IS BETTER—the great unexamined assumption of the art world."[11] He did decide to write for *Artforum* and eventually moved East. Before he did, however, he candidly admitted his insecurities in print: "I'm white, WASP, middle-class, married, with two kids and a house; I exercise reasonably, don't drink a lot, smoke mostly other people's dope, and am reasonably industrious (it's taken three days to *type* this). But, back here, I feel beaten down, slow, uncaring, New York brings out the spiteful recluse in me. I want coffee in the morning, basketball games on TV, the yard clean and raked, my daughter bounced on my knee, a can of beer before dinner. Chickenshit? I wonder if I've *ever* had a real art idea."[12]

Patricia Phillips acknowledges the difficulty she has in doing criticism: "This is a challenging time to write about art. There are so many ambient conditions that affect and influence it. Art is often so short-lived, so conditional, that viewing it is like coming to terms with a sensation, a memory or fast-flying thought. In the here-today-gone-tomorrow world of contemporaneous ideas, the critic frequently writes about an object or installation that has disappeared— extinguished like an ordinary event or a single day. Less frequently, the critic writes about art as speculation waiting for realization. The relationship between critic and subject has changed in this century. The writer does not stalk the object; subject and critic circle each other, ever-moving."[13]

A. D. Coleman, one of the first and most enduring critics to take recent photography seriously, began writing photography criticism precisely because he felt he didn't understand photographs or the effect they were having on our society. He was neither a photographer nor a photography historian. At the time he began writing about photographs, he was a drama critic for *The Village Voice.* He approached photography as someone wanting to know more about it rather than as an expert. He "came to feel there might be some value to threshing out, in public and in print, some understandings of the medium's role in our lives."[14] His was an outsider's rather than a practitioner's point of view.

Gilbert-Rolfe worries about being wrong, and even worse, influentially wrong, in his criticism: "It may be the case that your interpretation of the work is entirely wrong but conceivably so influential as to color the way in which the work is seen even by succeeding generations, so that you may in fact both be the one to recognize the importance of the work and the person responsible for consigning it to infinite misreading."[15]

Although critics express general enthusiasm about their profession, criticism is not always a satisfying endeavor for critics, and sometimes it can be quite lonely. Linda Burnham, who primarily writes about performance art, says that "anyone who calls him/herself a critic can look back over a very checkered career, propelled by very little encouragement from anyone."[16] Plagens, reflecting on his career as a critic and as an artist, expresses some doubt and resentment about his critical efforts: "At best, I'm seeing through the game-playing, and it's tedious; at worst, I'm just tired of being a handmaiden to other people's work (let *those* fuckers write something about my stuff for a change)."[17]

DIFFICULT CRITICISM

A common complaint about critical writing is that some or much of it is too difficult to read and too hard to understand. This complaint may also be deserved. Malcolm says about Krauss's critical writing, for example, that it has "a hard-edged, dense opacity; it gives no quarter, it is utterly indifferent to the reader's contemptible little cries for help."[18] Writing about one of his flights to New York from Los Angeles, Plagens says: "Tried to read three issues of *Artforum* on the plane coming in, got through one part of one article before my head hurt."[19]

Gilbert-Rolfe defends the difficulty of criticism based on the difficulty of art: "Art and its criticism are difficult whether one likes it or not."[20] He acknowledges that there is a general feeling that criticism should not be difficult, and that some people think art "really isn't difficult at all, but is made difficult by critics in the same way that ordinary people, with good reason, often suspect that the law itself is straightforward but is made difficult by lawyers." He does not agree. He sees art as purposely challenging and difficult. For support, he quotes George Steiner, who argues that "whatever enriches the adult imagination, whatever complicates consciousness and thus corrodes the cliches of daily reflex, is a high moral act. Art is privileged, indeed obliged, to perform this act; it is the live current which splinters and regroups the frozen units of conventional feeling."[21] The painter and conceptual artist Pat Steir also cherishes the difficulty and mystery of art: "The most intriguing art is art that you can't understand. It's this element, like the ungraspable thing that flies away, that attracts me, especially to new things."[22] Like Steiner, Steir sees moral implications in viewing challenging art: "I always think when you see something you can't understand, it reminds you of life itself, because you can't understand life. That's why there are moments when beauty is dead and painting is dead. When you're moved by something you can't understand, it reminds you of your mortality."

Nonetheless, some critics are calling for greater clarity in critical writing. Steven Durland, in an editorial in *High Performance,* a West Coast magazine devoted to performance art, very adamantly, and with some sarcasm, calls for clear communication by critics, especially those writing criticism that is theoretical: "If you theorists out there really care about the things you are theorizing about, then *tell it. WORD*. Most people are trying to develop theories on how to pay the rent. They don't have time to figure out what someone is talking about when it requires more than a ten-year-old paperback dictionary. They don't hate theorists, they just don't have time. If you're the one with some answers about how to make things work, and you can tell it, you'll be more famous than Madonna. You won't even *need* tenure. And people will love you for it. Trust me."[23]

In the same editorial, however, he expresses frustration as an editor in gauging exactly what kind of writing his readers want. "In the last *High Performance* reader's survey, we got approximately equal numbers of comments accusing us of being either 'too theoretical' or 'too lacking in theory.' Over 90 percent of those respondents claim to have a college degree and nearly 60 percent claim to have a graduate degree."[24]

As inspiration for her writing, Lucy Lippard says that she keeps a postcard over her desk that shows a little black girl holding an open book and grinning broadly. The caption on the card reads: "Forge simple words that even the children can understand."[25] Although some art and its criticism may be difficult, critics should nevertheless strive to make complex issues as clear as possible and without sacrificing the complexity of art or its criticism.

CRITICS AND ARTISTS

The relationship between critic and artist is certainly complex, often ambivalent. Bob Shay, a sculptor who usually works in clay, expressed his ambivalence about criticism this way: "Criticism lends credibility, so artists want their shows reviewed. I as an artist take the opposite view. I tend to be real skeptical anyway and I don't give a damn about reviews. I make art because I really get off on making art. I just love being in my studio making the stuff. It would certainly be nice if my work were to be reviewed in some major periodical, and reviewed favorably. But I don't expect it and I can't imagine ever being disappointed if it weren't reviewed. That's secondary or tertiary to why I make it. Criticism is more economic than anything else. It's like rock n' roll art. It's about that hype and be-bop and image and all that stuff. I don't think it has much to do with the real sanctity of making art in one's studio and of the merit of that art, the significance of that art."[26]

Despite these ambivalent but primarily negative feelings toward criticism, Shay also acknowledges that sometimes criticism can be useful to him: "Criticism can be helpful if it helps me understand, to gain insights into my own work. I work intuitively. At some point I need to come back to the work and ferret out what's going on. Good criticism can help me do that. To pick out threads of continuity from one series to the next, from one piece to the next that maybe I didn't understand. Someone can give me insights, maybe new meanings of the work that I never, at least on a conscious level, intended."[27]

Asked about the usefulness of criticism to him, Pheoris West, an African-American painter, responded: "If there's an aspect of what I was trying to get across in my work, or an insight into something that was going on in my work that I didn't necessarily, consciously put in the work, but has an appropriateness, then I get something out of it."[28]

Tim Miller, a gay performance artist, expresses what he as an artist wants of a critic: "**I want** the critic to ask me what the fuck I am doing if they don't get it."[29]

Miller goes on: "**I want** the little brat within me to listen and be open to intelligent negative criticism and not batten down the intuitive hatches when someone suggests I am not the second coming."

"**I want** us to be able to see creative work beyond the usual Cartesian linear food-chain rat race of GOOD or BAD. This bores the shit out of me."

"**I want** a thousand African-American, Latino, Queer and so on publications to flourish so that we encourage writers and criticism coming from our own communities because we can't wait for other folks to do it for us."

"**I want** critics and artists and audiences to get into juicy dialogue with each other and swap baseball cards and preconceptions so that eventually we can form a more perfect union."

Do artists pay attention to criticism? Georg Heimdal, a painter, says, "Most of my time talking about art with other studio artists is through art criticism. We talk about articles we've read. We talk about issues that are on the table. We hardly ever sit down and just talk about each other's work. We don't talk about other artists' work directly as much as we talk about art criticism about those issues, and how our work or this person's work fits into those issues."[30]

Susan Dallas-Swann, a sculptor working with light, says, "I read art criticism. I'll read almost anything that I see or that's presented to me. I am an avid reader. I enjoy most of it and I try to accept a broad spectrum of critical work. A critic can change someone's life and change society. It's a very powerful role if they accept it as a powerful role. It can be a negative or positive role, but it's powerful."[31]

Artist Richard Roth has similar attitudes about criticism: "I read everything, for very selfish reasons, as an artist. I'll look at any picture and read anything. I think maybe there's something for me. Criticism definitely is something I read in that way and I'm always hoping. If there's work I really like that I'm too lazy to evaluate maybe this person will just say it. Like, 'Ah yes, that's right, that's why I like it.' I look at it for material. I read it to get informed and to get ideas. On a lot of levels, it works for me. I like to read it. I want to know what's going on. The art world is a big conversation and everyone wants to be part of the conversation."[32]

Kay Willens, an installation artist—that is, an artist who makes site-specific sculptural environments—says, "The way in which criticism benefits artists is that it's possible to be fairly isolated and to not be in a community that is sup-

portive and to be working with ideas that are not in vogue or that are not understood on a general level. And often being able to read a certain kind of criticism
can be supportive in the sense that there are people out there dealing with certain kinds of ideas that are similar."[33]

The artist Robert Moskowitz, however, expresses a general distrust of reasoning about art: "I'm very happy to like a work of art without going through
the process of finding out why. In fact, I would try *not* to intellectualize why.
We might come up with some reasons as to why we like something, but I'm not
sure those are the *real* reasons. They're just ideas, and superficial ones at best."[34]
He goes on to say that "painting and sculpture are visual experiences, words are
something else. I'm not interested in explaining how I feel about something. It's
a gut instinct and it's nonverbal." Perhaps many artists feel this way, but not all.
Claes Oldenburg is interested in intellectually exploring his reactions: "Whatever
attaches you to a work that you can't understand is only because you don't have
enough information about yourself, or the work."[35]

Although most of these artists are at least tolerant of criticism, if not positively disposed to it, other artists express much stronger reservations. Tony Labat
offers several thoughts of artists about criticism in "Two Hundred Words or So
I've Heard Artists Say about Critics and Criticism":[36]

"I don't read that stuff anyway."
"It looks like he just read the press release and took everything out of it."
"This is a good piece, good writer. I wish he would write about my work."
"He forgot to mention my name."
"This only reflects the writer."
"He didn't get it."
"It was just descriptive."
"He doesn't take a stance."
"So fucking opinionated."
"His sexual preference really shows."
"Campy shit."
"I wish we had critics for critics."
"What the hell is he talking about?"
"I just like to see my name in print."
"All those big words and says nothing."
"That was a good piece, of course he liked my stuff."

The artists Labat quotes raise several issues, but most of the issues center
on them and the critic, their work and its criticism. Their remarks, understand-
ably, are self-centered and self-interested. There is need for a caution here, however, and a distinction. The caution is that your art professors are likely exhibiting
artists who have strong negative opinions about critics and criticism because of
how their work has or hasn't been attended to by these critics. It is good to be
aware of one's own and others' biases. Also, criticism as practiced in the art studio is usually for the purpose of teaching better art making. Professional critics,

in their writing, are not concerned with such things—art professors certainly are. Perhaps a fundamental problem between artists and critics is a difference in conception about for whom criticism should be written.

[handwritten margin note: The Point]

CRITICS AND AUDIENCES

The audience for professional published criticism is *not* the artist who made the work that is being criticized. The critic's audience is a much larger public. Terry Gross does art criticism from Philadelphia on National Public Radio, often in interview format; Plagens writes for *Newsweek;* and Robert Hughes for *Time*. For any of these critics to use such large forums to reach an individual artist would be a misuse of the forums—a letter or phone call to the artist would suffice.

Critics write for readers of books, magazines, and newspapers. They slant how they write depending on who they are writing for because they are concerned with reaching their audiences. Lucy Lippard, for example, is very concerned about communicating to a wider range of people and would like to reach beyond the limits of the art world. She says, "As a middle-class, college educated propagandist, I rack my brain for ways to communicate with working-class women. I've had fantasies about peddling socialist feminist art comics on Lower East Side street corners, even making it into the supermarkets."[37]

Patrice Koelsch, a critic who, like Lippard, is also dedicated to increasing multicultural awareness in the art world, thinks what we most need in democratic communities are "living demonstrations of authentic critical inquiry."[38] Because of recent attacks on art made controversial by politicians, such as the photographs made by Robert Mapplethorpe and Andres Serrano, she thinks it especially important to demonstrate to ordinary citizens the process of thinking critically. Koelsch wants critics to enlarge the scope of their communities and audiences by writing op-ed pieces for people who do not read the art press. She exhorts critics "to practice more honest, more informed, more engaged (and engaging) criticism." To reach wider audiences, she believes, criticism has to change: "It has traditionally been a voice of authority: purportedly omniscient, objective, and capable of discerning universal truths and values." Criticism as it has been practiced "invites the reader to observe the rational processes of the properly educated, appropriately situated, implicitly privileged writer," and this is alienating to the reader and counterproductive in effecting change. She cautions her fellow critics when they write about culturally diverse art to "be aware of our own tendencies to interpret the meaning and to ascribe value to it as it satisfies our own expectations of what that work should be."

[handwritten margin notes: importance of communicating to the mass public; traditionally (pub. often doesn't identify w/ ours); be aware of own biases]

Audiences are many and varied. Some readers are artistically sophisticated, others interested but less informed. Effective critics take the knowledge of their audiences into account. As a critic publishing in a daily newspaper, Roberta Smith sees herself "constantly talking to readers in a kind of immediate way. You can say one thing one week, and another thing another week. You don't have to say everything at once. You don't have to be right all the time."[39] Smith writes frequently for the *New York Times* and she sees what she does on a lot of levels: "It's a revelation of myself, me thinking out loud about how to look at an object, and hopefully giving other people ideas about how to look at an object, but I also hope that I get people to go out and look at art—and think about it."

About his critical writing, Robert Rosenblum says, "What you're really trying to do is to educate yourself, and educate the audience that's going to read about how you're going to educate yourself."[40] He adds that "you like language, and you like things to see, and you try to put them together in a way that teaches what you're looking at, and you hope that this will be communicated to an audience." He assumes the position of being an educator of the interested public. He doesn't write daily or regularly for a newspaper and sees more freedom of choice in what he does as a free-lance critic. He thinks Smith would have to cover everything in New York and take stances, whereas he sees himself fortunate in being able to write only about what he is enthusiastic about.

THE DIVERSITY OF CRITICS

Critics and their backgrounds are varied. Of critics already mentioned in this chapter, some are artists, one is a poet, some have degrees in art history. Arthur Danto, author of books on art theory and art critic for *The Nation* since 1984, is a professor of philosophy. Wendy Beckett, author of *Contemporary Women Artists*,[41] is a Catholic nun living in a cloistered convent in England. She writes criticism for *Art Monthly* and *Artscribe* and Catholic newspapers in England. Literary figures such as Henry James, George Bernard Shaw, John Updike, and John Ashberry have written regularly on art. David Halpern has edited a book, *Writers on Art,* that includes Jean-Paul Sartre writing on Tintoretto, Aldous Huxley on El Greco, Joyce Carol Oates on Winslow Homer, D. H. Lawrence on Cezanne, Gertrude Stein on Matisse, Norman Mailer on Picasso, and Hemingway on Miró.[42] The poet Charles Simic has written prose about the sculptures of Joseph Cornell.[43] Ann Beattie, author of the novels *Falling in Love* and *Love Always,* wrote a critically interpretive book on the paintings of Alex Katz.[44] Her editor, Anne Yarowsky, thought up the project. She had a Katz print in her bedroom and saw similarities between the work of the artist and the author; she called the two and both agreed to do the project.[45]

Today there are many critics with many voices. Rosenblum, for one, thinks this is very healthy because "the power of any one person isn't all that effective."[46] He says that "back in the '50s you could count them on the fingers of one hand. Now there are armies of critics all over, so that no single voice has much authority. Everybody wants to get into the act, and does."

In the 1950s there were also fewer journals devoted to art criticism. Today there are many. There are regional journals, such as *New Art Examiner* out of Chicago, *Artweek* on the West Coast, *Art Paper* in Minneapolis, *Dialogue* and

Columbus Art published in Columbus, Ohio; national journals such as *Artnews, Arts Magazine, Art in America, Artforum, Parachute;* and international journals including *Flash Art, The International Review of African American Art,* and *Art International.* There are academic journals such as *Art Journal,* published by the College Art Association, and *Exposure: The Journal of the Society for Photographic Education.* There are journals devoted to specific art forms, such as *High Performance* for performance art, *Craft Horizons* for crafts, and *Afterimage* for film, photography, and video.

Many academic journals publish criticism of art and reviews of books about art. Art criticism is included regularly in daily newspapers in big and small cities, and in magazines with national circulations such as *Saturday Review, Vanity Fair, Connoisseur,* as well as *Time* and *Newsweek.* The *Newsweek* issue of October 21, 1991, had four different articles on the arts: one on The Museum of Modern Art's traveling exhibition of photographs, "Pleasures and Terrors of Domestic Comfort"; another about Christo's "The Umbrellas: Joint Project for Japan and the U.S.A."; one on Richard Meier's proposed architecture for the Gettys' new headquarters in Los Angeles; and film reviews of John Sayles's film *City of Hope* and Jodie Foster's *Little Man Tate.*[47]

Critical publications are of many and varied ideologies, interlocking sets of beliefs and assumptions about the world, art, and art criticism. Some political and aesthetic ideologies are obvious: The *New Criterion* positions itself to the political right, for example, and *October* positions itself to the political left. One would likely write for one or the other, not both; and the editors of one would likely reject writers from the other. The ideological persuasions of some publications are more difficult to determine because they are embedded within the pages—informal and not clearly articulated. Informed readers and writers of criticism are aware of the political contexts in which criticism appears.[48]

Such a diversity and plenitude of critical writings is healthy. Critics give us much to think about concerning art in society. There is such diversity because critics are people with different backgrounds, beliefs, and attitudes about art. Throughout this book, a wide range of voices is quoted so readers may find some with which they agree and some with which they disagree. Reading criticism and reacting to it, and viewing art and reacting to it, can provide self-knowledge as well as knowledge about art. Eventually, through reflecting on art and its criticism, readers should develop their own critical voices and join the conversation.

SOME RECENT CRITICS

Following are brief sketches of four representative critics who have been and continue to be important influences in the development of current art writing. They vary in beliefs about art, its criticism, and the role of the critic in the world of art and politics.

Clement Greenberg

In the *New York Times,* critic Deborah Solomon opened a story on Clement Greenberg with this statement: "No American art critic has been more influential than Clement Greenberg."[49] Greenberg, whom Solomon calls "the high priest of formalism," is perhaps best known for promoting, in the 1940s, then unknown artists such as Robert Motherwell, Helen Frankenthaler, Morris Louis, and others. He is most famous for discovering Jackson Pollock: "Together they symbolize the romance of an era in which critics and artists believed that American painting could finally outshine the art of Paris, and they were right."

Greenberg vigorously championed Abstract Expressionism and created a new language for following generations of art critics. His aesthetic mission was set within a political agenda. He wanted to bring about social progress through revolutionary change and he looked to the artistic avant-garde to lead such a revolution. For him, the early Abstract Expressionists were revolutionary in their courage to internally draw upon their individual consciousness.[50]

Solomon calls Greenberg the Moses of the art world, who handed down the laws of painting. The laws were formalist; that is, to Greenberg, painting should be stripped of illusion, subject matter, artists' feelings, storytelling, or anything else that distracts from the *form* of a painting. Solomon also calls him the art world's Ann Landers because he "advised, counseled and coaxed innumerable artists." He befriended them, talked with them, gave them advice on how to paint.[51]

Besides the Abstract Expressionists, Greenberg promoted, in the 1960s, the dry, problem-solving art of Morris Louis, Kenneth Noland, Jules Olitski, and Larry Poons called "field" painting. He calls Olitski "the greatest living painter."[52]

Greenberg drew from the age of four, with no reinforcement from his parents. He graduated from Syracuse University in 1930 with a degree in literature, moved to New York City during the Depression, taught himself Latin and German, and translated books for a living. He studied art for four months at the Art Students League in New York—"I got more training even in the little time I was there than most art historians ever get."[53] In 1937, he wrote essays on culture during his idle hours as a customs agent. The essays were published in the *Partisan Review,* a journal popular among the intellectuals of New York. He also wrote for *The Nation.* About his learning to write art criticism, he says, "I educated myself in public, but you do art criticism on your own. It's not from school. I had brash confidence in my taste." He infuriated many with his blunt rejections of artists. He once received an angry letter from Alfred Stieglitz, Georgia O'Keeffe's husband, after he wrote this about her work in *The Nation* in 1946: "Her art has very little inherent value. The greatest part of her work adds up to little more than tinted photography."[54]

Greenberg's criticism is controversial. Many critics today respect his contributions but now reject his strict formalism. Because his formalist conception of art is so narrow and forceful, he is often challenged. Tom Wolfe ridiculed him with sarcastic humor in *The Painted Word*.[55] Rosalind Krauss and T. J. Clark "resent the critic for presenting art as a seamless, self-contained bubble floating high above the world of politics."[56] Some of his practices are also questionable. He paid studio visits to artists and freely offered them advice on how to paint. This practice seems beyond the boundaries of professional criticism and raises questions about critical distance and objectivity. (Of his advice to him, however, painter Kenneth Noland says: "I would take suggestions from Clem very seriously, more seriously than from anyone else."[57]) He also accepted gifts of art from those artists about whom he wrote. Such acceptance of gifts from artists by critics raises ethical issues. Greenberg left himself open to accusations of manipulating the art market for personal economic gain.

In 1947, as executor of David Smith's estate, Greenberg stripped paint from several unfinished Smith sculptures, commenting, "They looked better."[58] After Morris Louis died in 1962, Greenberg completed a few Louis paintings by deciding where to cut off the stripes. When asked about the limits of a critic's relationship to an artist, he responded: "What you can't do is write in praise of a girlfriend." (He dated Helen Frankenthaler in the 50s.[59]) Such proximity to and lack of boundaries between a critic and artists, their work, and the art market strain critical credibility and are rightly viewed much more suspectly today than in Greenberg's day.

Of his critical work, Greenberg says: "You don't choose your response to art. It's given to you. You have your nerve, your *chutzpah,* and then you work hard on seeing how to tell the difference between good and bad. That's all I know."[60] His opinions flow freely: Of Julian Schnabel he says, "He's not devoid of gifts, but he's minor," and later, "Roy Lichtenstein is a minor painter. The pictures look minor. When they're good they're minor, when they're bad, they're bad, that's all. Schnabel can paint but his pictures are awful. David Salle is—God, he's bad."[61]

Now in his later years, he is working on a book, *Home-Made Esthetics,* and he lectures, judges exhibitions, and answers correspondence. His collected writings have recently been published: *Clement Greenberg: The Collected Essays and Criticism.*

Lawrence Alloway

Lawrence Alloway[62] is probably best known for his pioneering writing about Pop art—he invented the term in the late 1950s—and his early and continual critical analysis and approval of the work of such artists as Roy Lichtenstein, Robert Rauschenberg, James Rosenquist, Andy Warhol, Claes Oldenburg, Jim Dine, and Jasper Johns.

Alloway was born in London in 1926 and died in 1989. He held no university degrees. At the age of 17, however, he began attending evening art history classes at the University of London and then began writing art reviews for

Art News and Review. His main interest became American art, but he continued to write about British art for *Art News and Review* and then, in the 1950s, for *Art International.* He visited the United States in 1961 and became a curator of the Solomon R. Guggenheim Museum during 1962–66. At the Guggenheim, his exhibitions included William Baziotes's Memorial Exhibition, Barnett Newman's "Stations of the Cross," an exhibition of hard-edged, color-field paintings he called "Systemic Painting," and the work of Jean Dubuffet. He accepted a teaching position at the State University of New York at Stony Brook in 1968, where he taught a course in twentieth-century art as a professor of art history until 1981. He was a contributing editor of *Artforum* from 1971 to 1976 and also wrote art criticism on a regular basis for *The Nation* from 1968 to 1981.

Alloway's several books include *American Pop Art, Topics in American Art Since 1945,* and *Roy Lichtenstein,* and he is represented in Donald Kuspit's prestigious series of anthologies of critics' writings with *Network: Art and the Complex Present.* Some particularly important articles by Alloway are "The Expanding and Disappearing Work of Art,"[63] "The Uses and Limits of Art Criticism,"[64] "Women's Art in the Seventies,"[65] and "Women's Art and the Failure of Art Criticism."[66]

Unlike Clement Greenberg, who tried to separate and elevate art from daily life, Alloway sought connections between art and society: "I never thought that art could be isolated from the rest of culture."[67] Alloway appreciated the diversity of art and rejected Greenberg's insistence on abstraction in art as restrictive. He also objected to art criticism that was isolated from larger cultural considerations. He stressed the inclusion of underrepresented art for critical attention, especially works by African-American, Puerto Rican, and women artists, insisting that art criticism consider all types of art.

When interpreting art, Alloway was interested in "the interaction of the artist's intention and the spectator's interpretation."[68] He considered the social origin of the artist, the artist's ideological sources, and the conceptual development apparent in the artist's work. He also drew upon statements about the work by other artists and critics and freely used the artist's own statements when interpreting his or her work. However, he believed "the function of the audience is to determine the meaning of the work when it is out of the artist's hands." Alloway believed that "it goes against all one's experience of art to presume that exhaustive interpretation is possible," and he stressed that flexibility of interpretation "is preferable to dogmatic avowals of singular meaning and absolute standards." When he was judging art, Alloway's primary criterion was the art's communicative impact. He championed much of women's art, for example, because it addressed "the social experience of women."

Arlene Raven

Arlene Raven titled a collection of her critical writings *Crossing Over: Feminism and Art of Social Concern.*[69] The book is another in the series by master art critics edited by Donald Kuspit. Raven crossed over from art history to write about the social and aesthetic avant-garde: "Crossing over is the journey into new territory of hundreds of American artists inspired by feminism and the possibility of social change."[70] Kuspit admires Raven's "tone of anguished intensity" concerning women's issues expressed through art.

Raven says of her work: "I have discussed the social issues of our day, from U.S. foreign policy to aging, with the art which seeks to address them."[71] She seeks out art "in the service of a cause greater than its own aesthetic objectness," and art that wants "to affect, inspire, and educate to action as well as to please." Artists she has chosen to write about include Leslie Labowitz, Betye Saar, Miriam Schapiro, Annie Sprinkle, Faith Wilding, Harmony Hammond, Judy Chicago, Mary Daly, Mary Beth Edelson, Cheri Gaulke, and Suzanne Lacy. The topics she writes about include violence in art, pornography, women's roles in the home, bulimia, rape, ritual and the occult in women's performance art, the healing power of art, and housework. She uses popular culture in her writing, referring, for example, to Archie Bunker in the TV show "All in the Family" when writing about women's art of the 1970s. She has also written about Lily Tomlin. She freely plays with writing style, sometimes using her own voice, and sometimes the voices of many other people, collaged together in different typefaces in the same article. She is published in *Arts, Women's Review of Books, Village Voice, New Art Examiner,* and *High Performance.*

Raven holds both an M.F.A. and a Ph.D. In the early 1970s, as an art historian, she worked with Judy Chicago and Miriam Schapiro for the Feminist Art Program at California Institute of the Arts. With Chicago and Sheila de Bretteville, she created an independent school for women in the arts, the Feminist Studio Workshop, and The Woman's Building, a public center for women's culture. She also founded and edited *Chrysalis,* a magazine of women's culture. She returned to New York in 1983: "My purpose today is to bring my perspective about the work and thought of artists committed to personal freedom and social justice to an art audience and the general reader, and thus to participate in creating change."[72]

In his preface to her anthology, Kuspit says that "the assumption of art's healing power is implicit in the best feminist art, which seeks to heal women wounded psychically—and sometimes physically—by partriarchal society."[73] Raven was the victim of a rape. The attack took place one week before she visited Los Angeles in 1972 to help in the preparation of *Ablutions,* a performance piece under the direction of Judy Chicago. Part of the piece was an audiotape of women telling their experiences of rape. "I participated in a process of feminist art which is based on uncovering, speaking, expressing, making public the experience of women."[74] Thirteen years later she accepted an offer to write the catalog for RAPE, an exhibition at The Ohio State University in Columbus, on the subject of rape by twenty women artists. In a revealing essay, she admits her personal anxieties about the project: "I don't want to board the plane to Columbus. I'll say I'm sick. . . . From one conversation to another I remained raw and opened to their 'stories' and my own brutal experience thirteen years ago, the pivot which hinged my understanding of my life until then and motivated every action since. . . . I never have been able to read more than a few sentences about rape. I leave the theatre or turn off the television at the hint of a rape scene. . . . Healing. Never healed."[75]

Lucy Lippard

Lucy Lippard's latest book (she has written many) is *Mixed Blessings*.[76] It was a seven-year project that began in Central America, took her to the Caribbean and then to all of Latin America, and finally ended up in North America. The book is exclusively about artists of color, hundreds from around the United States, most of whom are not well known and all of whom are socially opposed to the status quo. About Lippard's book, Meyer Raphael Rubinstein predicts that "this prolegomenon to the art of a future American culture may possibly turn out to be the most important book by an American art critic since the appearance of Clement Greenberg's *Art and Culture*."[77]

Not all critics, however, are as pleased as Rubinstein with Lippard's writing. Hilton Kramer has dismissed her criticism as "straightout political propaganda."[78] This is probably one of the few points on which Kramer and Lippard agree, however. Lippard embraces the label *propagandist*. In "Some Propaganda for Propaganda," she writes, "The goal of feminist propaganda is to spread the word and provide the organizational structures through which all women can resist the patriarchal propaganda that denigrates and controls us even when we *know* what we are doing."[79] She argues that people in power want to keep a distinction between propaganda and art: "There are very effective pressures in the artworld to keep the two separate, to make artists see political concern and aesthetic quality as mutually exclusive and basically incompatible; to make us see our commitment to social change as a result of our own human weaknesses, our own lack of talent and success."[80] In her article "Headlines, Heartlines, Hardlines: Advocacy Criticism as Activism," she openly admits that she is leftist, feminist, and working for social change. She explicitly and expressly seeks out and promotes "the unheard voices, the unseen images, or the unconsidered people."[81] *Mixed Blessings* is the embodiment of her critical beliefs.

Lippard sees herself in partnership with socially oppositional artists, whose work, too, is often dismissed by the term *propaganda*. She wants to reclaim *propaganda* as a positive term and equates it with *education*. She believes that critical neutrality is a myth, that all critics are partisan, and that her approach is merely more honest than those of critics who claim to be removed from special interests.

CRITICISM: A DEFINITION

Despite all these differing views of criticism by critics, defining criticism is easier than defining art. A definition will eventually be stipulated here based on what critics do and say they do. A. D. Coleman defines criticism as "the intersecting of images with words," adding that "I merely look closely at and into all sort of photographic images and attempt to pinpoint in words what they provoke me to feel and think and understand."[82] Donald Kuspit thinks of criticism similarly. He wants to know why "we respond to this artist's image of a Madonna and child rather than that artist's image? Why do we like a certain texture and not another texture?"[83] He goes on to say that "it's part of the critic's task, perhaps his most difficult task, to try to articulate the effects that the work of art induces in us, these very complicated subjective states."

Roberta Smith says that sometimes her criticism is "just like pointing at things. . . . One of the best parts of it is that occasionally, maybe more than occasionally, you get to write about things that haven't been written about yet, new paintings by new artists you know, or new work by artists who aren't known."[84]

Alloway defined the art critic's function as "the description, interpretation, and evaluation of new art."[85] He stressed the new: "The subject of art criticism is new art or at least recent art. It is usually the first written response." He understood art criticism to be short-term art history and objective information available at the moment. It is "the closeness in time of the critical text and the making of the work of art which gives art criticism its special flavor." He distinguished between the roles of historians and critics: "Though critics enjoy the art of the past, their publications on it are less likely to be decisive than those of art historians." Alloway particularly stressed the importance of description, wanting to maintain a balance between describing and the act of evaluation. For him the critic's function is "description and open-mindedness rather than premature evaluation and narrow specialization," and he wanted to stay away from saying "good and bad."[86]

Robert Pincus-Witten, past editor of *Artforum* and currently writing for *Flash Art,* agrees with the necessity of dealing with the new: "I see the critical task as being essentially that of pointing to the new . . . the real issue at hand is not new modes of criticism but what happened to painting and sculpture during the last few years."[87] He thinks it essential to empathize with the artist: "The recognition of the new must coexist with an intense empathy with the artist—so much so as to oblige the critic to adopt the artist's experience as a personal burden, a commonweal, a common cause if necessary. The critic imaginatively must be the artist."[88] His chosen mode of expression is chronicling, journaling— "recording what one is thinking or feeling."[89]

Critics differ on the importance of judging art. As we have seen, Alloway and others minimize judgment. Greenberg asserts that "the first obligation of an art critic is to deliver value judgments."[90] He is quite insistent on the point: "You

can't get around without value judgments. People who don't make value judg- *yes*
ments are dullards. Having an opinion is central to being interesting—unless
you're a child." Roberta Smith concurs, if less adamantly: "You have to write
about what you think. Opinion is more important, or equally as important, as
description."[91] She adds that "you also define yourself as a critic in terms of what
you don't like."

Joanna Frueh speaks eloquently for the need for intuition in criticism: "Art *intuition*
criticism, like other disciplines that privilege the intellect, is generally deprived
of the spontaneous knowing of intuition—of knowledge derived from the senses,
and experience as well as the mind. Nerves connect throughout the body, con-
duct sensations, bits of knowledge to the brain. Blood pumping to and from the
heart flows everywhere inside us. Knowing is being alive, wholly, not just intellectually. It is a recognition of human being, the intelligence of the body. The
intellectual may feel enslaved in matter. If only she could escape from the body.
But the mind will not fly unless we embrace the body as a path to freedom."[92]
She asserts the value of and need for feminist thinking in art criticism: "System *Feminist is*
and hierarchy. They withhold (information). Everything in its place. Discuss an *not trad.*
artist's work chronologically. Picasso was more influential than Braque. 'Straight' *masculine*
thinking. Feminist thinking is the curves, bends, angles, and irregularities of *approach -*
thought, departures from prescribed patterns of art historical logic. To be *wider ranging*
'straight' is to be upright-erect-phallic-virtuous-heterosexual, but feminists turn *+ more*
away from the straight and narrow. Deviants without their heads on straight. *sympathetic*
Logocentrism produces enclosure, tight arguments. It sews up the fabric(ations)
of discourse. Feminists with loose tongues embroider, patch new and worn pieces
together, re-fabricate."[93]

Arthur Danto agrees with the French poet Baudelaire, father of modern art
criticism, that criticism should be "partial, passionate, political."[94] Danto rails
against the no-nos of orthodox modernist art criticism: "*Don't* talk about subject *IMP*
matter or the artist's life and times; *don't* use impressionistic language or describe *to understand*
how a work makes you feel; *do* give an exhaustive account of the work's phys- *position - he is*
ical details; *do* pass judgment on its esthetic quality and historical importance." *not the authority*
He likes to talk about subject matter and he thinks it's time for art to be about *a strong voice in*
something besides itself. *wooden crit*

Critics sometimes predict future directions in art. In a review of a recent *predictions*
exhibition of the Surrealist André Breton, Peter Plagens foresees the future:
"Already there are signs of neosurrealism creeping into the art world. . . . So far,
the new style has been a little timid. But don't be surprised if, with a little boost
from the end-of-the-century Zeitgeist, surrealism makes a serious comeback."[95] *BoRIS ?*

From these samplings of what critics say about what they do, it is apparent that criticism is many things to many critics. They have different conceptions
of what they are about and place different emphases on what criticism should
be. But we can draw some generalizations: Criticism is usually written. It is for
an audience. It is not usually for the artist. It comes in many forms, from daily

newspapers to scholarly books. Critics are enthusiastic about art. They describe and interpret art. They differ on the importance of making judgments. The intuitive response is important to some. Many admit that they are in a constant state of learning when they write criticism. Criticism is concerned about recent art, for the most part. Critics tend to be passionate about art and they attempt to be persuasive about their views of art.

Others besides critics offer conceptions of criticism. Edmund Feldman, an historian and art educator who has written much about criticism, calls it "informed talk about art."[96] Marcia Eaton, an aesthetician, says that criticism "invites people to pay attention to special things."[97] Critics "*point* to things that can be perceived and at the same time *direct* our perception," and when criticism is good, "we go on to see for ourselves; we continue on our own."

Criticism should result in "enlightened cherishing."[98] This is a compound concept of Harry Broudy's, a philosopher of education who advocates education about art. "Enlightened cherishing" acknowledges thought and feeling without dichotomizing the two.

Morris Weitz, the late aesthetician best known for his "open concept of art" in which he maintains that art cannot be defined because it is an ever-changing phenomenon, does define criticism as "a form of studied discourse about works of art. It is a use of language designed to facilitate and enrich the understanding of art."[99] Weitz's definition is embraced in this book, but is supplemented with more current theorists, who stress more broadly that critics also produce meaning about culture in general. Criticism is language about art that is thoughtful and thought-out, for the purpose of increasing understanding and appreciation of art and its role in society. Weitz conducted extensive research on what critics say they do, and what they actually do. He concluded that critics do one or more of the four activities of describing art, interpreting art, judging it, and theorizing about art. This book is built around these activities, with chapters on each. The four activities are specific enough to provide structure and not too limiting to be exclusive of any critical practice. They also remind us that criticism is considerably more than passing judgments on works of art. Weitz goes so far as to claim that judgment is neither a necessary nor sufficient part of criticism; that is, one can write criticism without passing judgment, and if one only passes judgment, that mere judgment is less than criticism.

This book presents judgment as an important part of criticism, but not the most important. That distinction lies with interpretation. Usually a thorough interpretation, which necessarily includes description, will imply a judgment. A judgment without benefit of interpretation is irresponsive to a work of art and probably irresponsible. Recall Clement Greenberg's one-line dismissals of artists quoted earlier. As they were stated and quoted, his comments are conclusions, not arguments. Although such one-line dismissals or one-line pronouncements of greatness are frequently made in casual conversations about art, and in Greenberg's case, are from an interview, such pronouncements, made by prominent critics, artists, or professors, are the worst kind of criticism—unless they are developed into fuller arguments. Andy Grundberg, former photography critic for the *New York Times,* puts the point well: "Criticism's task is to make arguments, not pronouncements."[100]

CRITICIZING CRITICISM (AND CRITICS)

As we have already seen, critics do not always agree with each other. Sometimes they disagree quite harshly. John Coplans, founding editor of *Artforum,* recalls: "When I was editor of *Artforum,* I had half a dozen editors on my board. They were always quarrelling with each other. They all hated each other. They were strong people, all academically very well trained, all extremely knowledgeable, the most experienced writers and critics in America."[101] His editors were the prominent and influential critics Lawrence Alloway, Max Kozloff, Rosalind Krauss, Annette Michelson, and Robert Pincus-Witten. Rosalind Krauss also recalls those days: She remembers having "stupid arguments" with Lawrence Alloway, that Max Kozloff "was always very busy being superior—I could never understand why."[102] Referring to current times, Krauss lambasts critic Tom McEvilley of *Artforum* as "a very stupid writer. I think he's pretentious and awful. . . . I have never been able to finish a piece by McEvilley. He seems to be another Donald Kuspit. He's a slightly better writer than Donald Kuspit. But his lessons on Plato and things like that—they drive me crazy. I think, God! And I just can't stand it."[103] Coplans, however, calls McEvilley "first rate, absolutely first rate."[104] About Hilton Kramer, who was formerly an art critic for the *New York Times,* Lawson says, "Kramer and the *Times* were a formidable combination. There, on a regular basis, he could press the authority of his opinions on those who were unable or unwilling to think for themselves; there his forceful mediocrity found its most congenial home."[105]

The preceding comments are mostly critics criticizing critics. Some, of course, are *ad hominem* and logically fallacious because they are directed at the person rather than at the individual critic's writings. When they act more responsibly, critics criticize criticism, rather than the persons writing criticism. Often such criticism is positive. In his general preface to the anthologies of art critics (including Dennis Adrian, Dore Ashton, Nicolas Calas, Joseph Masheck, Peter Plagens, Arlene Raven, and Robert Pincus-Witten), Donald Kuspit calls them "master art critics" because they provide sophisticated treatments of complex art. He praises their independence in their points of view and their self-consciousness about their art criticism. He admires their passion, their reason, and their lack of dogmatism. "They sting us into consciousness."

In a book review of Arthur Danto's latest book Marina Vaizey, art critic for the *Sunday Times of London,* praises him for being able to make the reader and the essayist "feel, see and, above all, think" and to describe "the sheer captivating sensuality of a particular work."[106] Her criteria for good criticism include literary merit, judgments made in a setting that is more than local, and insights that have a relevant vitality that goes beyond the short time span implied by publication in a periodical of current comment.

The aesthetician Marcia Eaton praises the literary criticism of H. C. Goddard because she finds him to be a "superb pointer" and teacher who shows us how to contemplate and scrutinize art in ways that will produce delight.[107] He does not have to distort the text in order to get us to see things hidden in it. He does not try to force his views. He expresses humility and readiness for exchange of insights. He is a good inviter.

Good CRITERIA

Thus, Kuspit and Eaton offer criteria for good criticism: sophisticated treatment of art, critical independence, self-consciousness of the critical process, passionate reasoning, lack of dogmatism, delightful insights without distortion of the work of art, humility. Kay Larson, critic for *New York* magazine, adds fairness to the artist as a criterion.[108] Mark Stevens tries to avoid "nastiness" when criticizing art and regrets the times he has been sarcastic in print.[109] He thinks critics should be "honest in their judgment, clear in their writing, straightforward in their argument, and unpretentious in their manner." For him, good criticism is like good conversation—"direct, fresh, personal, incomplete."

THE CONCLUSION

Criticism itself, then, can and should be criticized. Indeed, most critics consider what they write as incomplete; that is, what they write is not the final word, especially when it is about new work. Instead, they feel they are contributing to an ongoing conversation about new art. Their comments are not unleashed speculations; they are carefully considered points of view—but they are views always open to revision.

THE VALUE OF CRITICISM

the need! 1

"The total burden of aesthetic communication is not wholly on the artist."[110] When Harry Broudy wrote this in 1951, he was addressing viewers rather than professional critics, but the thought serves us well here. Critics do not believe the cliché that "art speaks for itself." They willfully and enthusiastically accept the burden of artistic communication with the artist. They work for viewers of art and those members of society who want to think critically about the times and conditions in which we live. Critics, like artists, produce meanings, but they use the pages of magazines rather than swatches of canvas. Critics, like artists, have aesthetic and ethical values that they promote through their writing. When critics do their work well, they increase for their readers understanding and appreciation of the art they write about, the political and intellectual milieu in which it is made, and its possible effects on the world.

meaning 2

values 3

understanding 4

The artist Chuck Close said: "Once you get rid of the normal baggage you carry in looking at art, things happen: you find yourself liking what you hated a while ago."[111] Critics help audiences do this. Marcia Siegel, author of several books of dance criticism, says that the process of writing criticism helps *her*

help change opinion

appreciate the artwork more: "Very often it turns out that as I write about something, it gets better. It's not that I'm so enthusiastic that I make it better, but that in writing, because the words are an instrument of thinking, I can often get deeper into a choreographer's thoughts or processes and see more logic, more reason."[112] The process of doing criticism is beneficial to the one who does it. The purpose of this book is to encourage the reader to engage in the criticism of art.

"A Picture is worth a thousand words"

how many ways can you interpret this?

2
DESCRIBING ART

Although a popular misconception about art criticism is that it is primarily judgmental and negative in tone, in actuality, most of the words written by critics are descriptive and interpretive rather than judgmental, and positive in tone. Critics seek to provide readers with information about artworks, and describing these artworks, many of which will not be seen by their readers, is one of their major activities. _Describing_ is a kind of verbal pointing a critic does so that features of a work of art will be noticed and appreciated. It is also a data-gathering process. Based on his or her descriptions, the critic will form interpretations and judgments. If the critic's description is inaccurate, certainly any following interpretation or judgment is suspect.

With careful observation, descriptive information can be gathered from within the work—"internal information." For teaching purposes, internal descriptive information is sometimes grouped under three topics: subject matter, medium, and form. These are defined with examples in the following sections.

Critics also provide descriptive information about aspects not visible in the work—that is, contextual information such as facts about the artist or the times in which the art was made. This is "external information" and examples of this are given as well.

Critics rarely describe artworks without also interpreting and evaluating them, and at the end of the chapter the overlaps among these activities are examined. The chapter begins, however, by discussing separately the three areas of description, defining relevant terms and concepts with the help of brief examples. Then it examines in greater detail the descriptive activities of critics through their writings about several contemporary artists working in different media.

subject matter
medium
form
interpretation
evaluation
external info.

22

SUBJECT MATTER

Subject matter refers to the persons, objects, places, and events in a work of art. In the following bit of critical writing, Dana Shottenkirk provides a succinct overview of Nancy Spero's works of art: "Spero represents the historical nightmare that constitutes women's relationship to culture. Her representations of victims of medieval torture, Nazi sadism, and sexual abuse are hand-printed and collaged onto empty white backgrounds next to pornographic images, prehistoric female running figures, and defiantly vulgar women; it's the story of power struggles played out on the bodies of women."[1]

There is a lot of information in Shottenkirk's two sentences. The first sentence is an interpretation rather than a description. It is an interpretive generalization about all of Spero's work. The second sentence is more descriptive. Here, Shottenkirk describes Spero's subject matter as women—more specifically, women who are victims of medieval torture and Nazi sadism and sexual abuse, pornographic images, prehistoric female running figures, and defiantly vulgar women. In the first sentence, Shottenkirk can be said to be defining the artist's subject—and now we can make a distinction between *subject* and *subject matter*. According to the critic, Spero's subject (or theme or main idea or recurring topic) is women's nightmarish relationship to culture. To convey this general subject, the artist uses particular imagery, such as the prehistoric female running figure. This imagery is the subject matter of the art. To identify a theme is interpretive; to name subjects is more straightforwardly descriptive.

Some scholars make a distinction between *subject matter* and *content* rather than *subject matter* and *subject*. However, *content* is a combination of all that is in a work of art—subject matter, the handling of media, form, and intent. When an artwork has no recognizable subject matter, the form itself is the subject. *Content*, however, needs to be interpreted and may include, for example, the artist's expression of individuality.

Besides identifying the subject and naming the subject matter of Spero's art, Shottenkirk goes on to characterize the artist's treatment of her subject matter: "Spero adopts the role of loud-mouthed raconteur, telling this tale of horror that others would like to ignore." The critic also describes Spero's media, hand-printing, and collage, and mentions the formal characteristic of empty white backgrounds. Shottenkirk concludes with a further interpretation of what the works mean: "The result is a melange of images of female victimhood, extending back into prerecorded history. The costumes change; the politics don't."

MEDIUM

Sometimes the term *medium* is used to designate a general grouping of artworks, such as the medium of painting or the medium of sculpture or video. The term is also used to identify specific materials used by an artist, such as acrylic paint or polycoated resin. _Medium_ is singular; _media_ is plural.

When writing about Magdalena Abakanowicz's choice of fibers as her medium for some of her sculptures, Wendy Beckett offers this: "When the Nazis invaded Poland, Magdalena Abakanowicz saw drunken troopers fire at her mother, leaving her mutilated. It was then that the realization came to her that the body was like a piece of fabric—that it could be torn apart with ease. Years later, as an adult artist, it has been her deliberate choice to work in fibre, the humblest of materials, fragile and yielding. The very softness was a challenge to her. She felt a terrible need to protest against the comfortable, the useful, the compliant, the soft."[2] In these sentences, Beckett provides us with external information—namely, historical facts about the Nazis invading Poland and biographical facts about the artist and the tragedy of her and her mother. Beckett then connects this contextual information with Abakanowicz's use of fiber—"the body was like a piece of fabric." Beckett further describes the medium of fiber as humble, fragile, and yielding.

In a second example, David Cateforis writes about the "sheer physical power" of Anselm Kiefer's paintings—"covering entire walls, their surfaces clotted with not only paint but also straw, sand, bits of metal, molten lead, gold leaf, copper wire, ceramic shards, photographs and scraps of paper. The magnitude and material density of Kiefer's surfaces have led more than one critic to identify him as the aesthetic heir of Jackson Pollock."[3] Here, Cateforis is mixing observations about the form of Kiefer's paintings (covering entire walls, the aesthetic heir of Jackson Pollack) and the particular materials he uses such as paint, straw, gold leaf, and so forth.

Another writer, Waldemar Januszczak, is especially effective in describing Kiefer's medium and how it affects the viewer: "Kiefer's large fields of scorched earth—his most-often-recurring image—look like slabs of blasted heath itself, danced over by devils, driven over by panzers, tortured by the weather, then screwed to the wall. They seem plowed as much as painted. Many of the furrows have straw embedded in them. Some are visibly blackened with a welding torch. Others have things attached to them—bits of old farm equipment, sheets of lead, charred fence posts, mysterious numbers."[4]

The medium of drawing seems simple and straightforward enough. However, critic Michelle Meyers shows us that this seemingly simple medium can be complex. In his _Men in the Cities_ drawings of the late 1970s and early 1980s, Robert Longo used charcoal, pencil, and ink on paper. Meyers describes the subject matter of the drawings as "men in contorted poses, frozen in a moment of either forceful play (slam dancing) or violent death."[5] She tells us that Longo derived the subjects for his drawings from fashion photographs of the 1950s, and that the models are Longo's friends. The artist projected photographs of his models onto large sheets of paper and "drew the figures, omitting details of personality and place and often replacing the body parts of one model with those of another. Working through the intermediary media of photography and advertising and the cinematic practices of photographic manipulation and editing gives Longo great control over his chaotic images." Thus, the critic informs us that Longo's medium of drawing is also based in the media of advertising, photography, and cinema.

FORM

All works of art have form, whether realistic or abstract, representational or non-representational, meticulously planned or achieved spontaneously. When critics discuss the form of a work of art, they provide information about how the artist presents subject matter (or excludes it) by means of a chosen medium. They tell of the artwork's composition, arrangement, and visual construction. "Formal elements" of a work of art may include dot, line, shape, light and value, color, texture, mass, space, and volume. How formal elements are used is often referred to as "principles of design," and these include scale, proportion, unity within variety, repetition and rhythm, balance, directional force, emphasis, and subordination.

elements

principles

When writing about Nancy Graves's *Cantileve*, 1983, a large bronze sculpture with polychrome patina, Wendy Beckett tells us of the effects of Graves's formal treatment of her materials: "The real joy of this gigantic work, over two meters high, is the miraculous marriage of lightness and weight. It seems to float, airily suspended, both supremely confident and infinitely frail."[6] Thus, the formal elements the critic wants us to notice are size, space, and mass, and the principles of design are scale (it is gigantic), directional force (it floats), and emphasis and subordination (it is supremely confident and infinitely frail).

size

space

Just as critics mix interpretations and judgments with their descriptions, they also freely mix comments on subject, medium, and form, and draw upon both internal and external information: "Miriam Schapiro, one of the leaders of the pattern-and-decoration movement that emerged in the '70s, continues to delight us with paintings and mixed media works that combine active, dynamic figures, rich brushwork, and lively patterns. Flat, hard-edge figures covered with painted or collaged patterns dance on brightly painted surfaces—usually a rich lyrical abstraction of splattered, splotched, and squiggled acrylic."[7] In these two sentences, Ruth Bass describes subject matter (dynamic figures, lively patterns), media (paint and collage), and form (a rich lyrical abstraction), relying both on internal information (all the things she notices in the paintings, such as hard-edge figures, splattered, splotched, and squiggled acrylic), and on external information (the pattern-and-decoration movement that emerged in the '70s). It is also clear, though not explicitly stated, that the critic approves of the work.

approval

subject matter

form

media

In the following pages, more extended examples of descriptive writing are provided to continue examination of the very important critical activity of describing works of art.

PAINTING: LEON GOLUB

In a summary overview of Leon Golub's art, critic David Cateforis puts the painter into historical context so readers have a sense of how his art emerged. Cateforis informs us that Golub began making explicitly political art in the 1960s to protest the United States involvement in the Vietnam war: "He painted three enormous pictures of Vietnam, striving for absolute objectivity by drawing his images of men, uniforms, and weapons from news photos and military hand-books. In the first two canvases, he pictured American soldiers firing on Vietnamese civilians. In the third, he depicted the soldiers at rest, their victims lying at their feet. With these gigantic protest paintings—the largest of them 40 feet wide—Golub established himself as one of the most ambitious and uncompromising politically engaged artists of our time."[8]

Coauthors Ed Hill and Suzanne Bloom summarize the subject of Golub's work as "inquiries into the realms of power and abuse."[9] In a feature-length article in *Artforum,* Rosetta Brooks also offers another summary view: "For the past 30 or so years Golub's art has confronted hidden episodes and unspeakable acts of horror that foment beneath the surface of our mediated reality."[10]

Like Cateforis, who noted that Golub obtains his subject matter directly from news photographs and military handbooks, critics Robert Berlind and Rosetta Brooks describe Bolub's strategy for rendering his subject matter. Berlind writes: "Golub has always made use of preexisting imagery,"[11] and Brooks writes that, because of this, "we feel as if we've seen these images before—but where, we're not sure. In a sense, this is imagery to which the media denies us access." Both critics then go on to make interpretive points about these descriptive facts. Berlind: "Indeed, the origins of his imagery in the public domain constitutes one implicit level of social critique, for we are shown that all of this already exists, not only on the fringes of our global power, but at home, within our domestic visual environment." Brooks: "In a media-controlled universe, the disturbing familiarity of Golub's images asserts our sense of history as a dynamic of universal forgetting."

Critics selectively describe all that can be described based on what they interpret to be important. That is, all kinds of facts and figures could be mentioned, especially when talking about art based in historical events; for this reason, critics are purposively selective about what they detail and what they omit.

Pamela Hammond calls a recent show of four Golub paintings a "grisly exhibition."[12] Of one of the paintings, she writes: "*The Prisoner* shows figures emerging from a sooty, crosshatch haze. Fuzzy blocks of light glare from the surface, coming at us like spotlights. One of a pair of criminals fixes his steely stare on us; a gun lengthens his right arm; a holstered hip twists towards us. The other turns his head away, grimacing ambiguously." In a different review of the same exhibition, Ben Marks describes the subject matter of another of the paintings: "*Prisoners III* is a scene of two men pulling a blue suited prisoner by his hair,

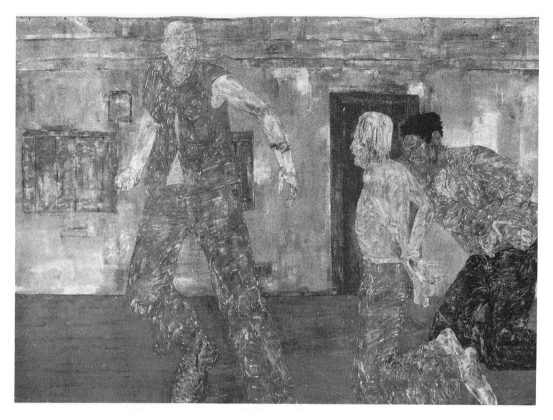

Leon Golub, *Prisioners* (I), acrylic on linen, 120" × 171", 1989. Courtesy of Josh Baer Gallery, New York City. Photograph: David Reynolds.

presumably for interrogation and torture. One man holds an Uzi and stares straight at us. His green eyes and red lips are the only other colors in this piece which is otherwise painted entirely in hues of brown, beige, charcoal and white. The other man looks forward, intent on completing this task which he neither seems to enjoy or find particularly troubling. There is a 'just doing my job' quality to the proceedings that makes the viewer nervous. The whole scene feels like the memory of a bad dream, recalled through a haze of paint and sweat as if we had just bolted upright, wrenched from our otherwise peaceful middle-of-the-night slumber."[13]

In these two quotations by Hammond and Marks are <u>examples of compelling descriptions of an artist's subject matter</u>. The critics draw us in by their use of descriptive language. When Hill and Bloom describe the sphinx in *Yellow Sphinx* (1988), they do not simply say, "<u>There's a sphinx</u>"—rather, they fashion this <u>compelling description</u> of it: "The hybrid monster rears up heraldically, its two feet supporting a massive lion's body and man's head; the beast's torso is turned away from us, while its face is seen in left profile against a large expanse of acrid yellow."

statement is not description

Several critics comment on the ambiguity of Golub's subject matter. Robert Storr writes that Golub paints "the ubiquity and humanity of the 'inhuman.'"[14] Marks observes that Golub does not allow us specificity regarding who is being depicted: "The nominal source for this particular group of paintings is the Middle East, giving the subjects an indeterminate ethnicity. Their generally non-Caucasian facial features remove any easy, stereotypical relationships of oppressor and oppressed we might want to lapse into." Brooks pays particular attention to the victims in Golub's paintings: "Frequently, the victims in a Golub painting, rather than their torturers, are 'masked,' either literally or figuratively. Their flesh is reduced to anonymous lumps of pigment. Their bodies appear as fragmented, partial, or dislocated representations, the mere pretext for a game performed on them by interrogators. It is the latter, striking their poses as they enjoy their private joke, who command our attention. The horror of *Interrogation II* (1981), for example, is generated by the smiling faces of the mercenaries turning to the onlooker, flashing their grins automatically as the camera button clicks." Hammond comments that with his use of referential ambiguity, Golub "pulls you into an open-ended narrative, forcing you to create your own version of the circumstances."

As readers already familiar with Golub's paintings or as viewers standing in front of them, we may feel that writing such descriptions of the subject matter is easy and automatic: We simply look at the paintings and describe what we see. <u>But these descriptions of the visual are inventions when they are made verbally</u>. Critics find <u>words</u> and <u>shape phrases</u> to <u>accurately and passionately tell about the work and engage the reader with it</u>. Their descriptions are discoveries that offer us insights into the work by means of carefully crafted language. Hammond writes of a criminal's "steely stare." Rather than saying he holds a

Creation verbally

gun, she writes that "a gun lengthens his right arm; a holstered hip twists toward us." In describing formal aspects of the works, Marks doesn't just list the colors, he notices and notes that the man with the Uzi has green eyes, and that his green eyes and red lips differ in color from the rest of the painting. Marks's description of the feeling of a scene being that of "a bad dream, recalled through a haze of paint and sweat" is good, inventive descriptive writing as is Brooks's description of how Golub posed the mercenaries so that they are "turning to the onlooker, flashing their grins automatically as the camera button clicks."

There seems to be general agreement among critics that Golub's works are powerful, and the critics we have quoted so far are particularly drawn to describing his subject matter. Margaret Moorman attributes the power of a series of sphinx paintings Golub made in the late 1980s to their form rather than their subject matter: "The four large paintings here are powerful, but their power derives almost entirely from their formal qualities—their size, their scraped and scumbled surfaces, their awkward but compelling compositions, their vivid color."[15] Robert Storr is puzzled by the meaning of the sphinxes and says they "ask self-addressed riddles, ones which they do not, perhaps, cannot, answer." Instead of attempting more of an interpretation than this, he offers descriptions. He particularly is impressed with Golub's use of color in these paintings: "The mutant men and beasts of his most recent work pace and gesture in a brilliant radioactive haze as if before the cameras of a high-budget film production." He adds that "the grating brilliance of Golub's tints and the extreme tactility of his usually abraded surfaces contrast sharply with the way in which the depicted forms seem to diffuse into the etiolated matrix of strokes, so that his pictures acquire a disturbing cinematic or video-screen effect." Cateforis also writes about how Golub handles paint: "He renders his figures in a harsh, acrid, illustrational mode, laying on the paint thickly, then dissolving it and scraping it down with a meat cleaver. The eroded colors and surfaces of Golub's paintings are raw, dry, and irritated, setting us on edge, increasing our discomfort."

Rosetta Brooks eloquently describes a series of Golub's paintings called "Night Scenes" (1988–89), particularly attending to their formal qualities. She writes that they "place us squarely in the realm of television imagery where the color blue dominates the canvas" and that "one searches these dark yet luminous surfaces for clues with the alert vigilance with which one concentrates on discerning the outlines of figures in the street to distinguish a mugger from a passerby. But it is the paintings themselves that are threatening; danger is suggested everywhere in that everything seems OK on the surface. These are not the sinister corners of Golub's earlier interrogation rooms. Yet the near monochromes of high-tech spectral blues create a similar atmosphere; a strange glow pervades the fragmentary scenes with the relentless evenness of an electric light bulb."

In a review of prints by Golub, Robert Berlind describes some of Golub's technique and then infers meaning based on his description of the artist's process: "The surface of the print is made by scratching and abrading the stone so that the figures emerge as much out of a negativity, a rubbing out, as by an additive process of drawing. Golub's work process becomes metaphor, and the damaged facture establishes the psychological and emotional ambience of these wraithlike personae." He adds that Golub's "perversely sweet palette plays off against the harshness of surface and emotional content."

Although these critics are all positive in their descriptions of how Golub formally presents his subjects in the media of paint and ink, other critics express reservations and disapproval. Joshua Decter, for example, expresses his reservations this way: "The career of Leon Golub has been characterized by a problematic tension between the commitment to a tradition of Abstract Expressionist painting and an engagement with certain 'radical' or 'left-wing' politics organized within the cultural sphere."[16] He goes on to say that "an awkward tension was produced between the monumentality of the painting (which referred explicitly to the scale and design of Clyfford Still and others) and the threatening images of violent acts about to commence or recently enacted." Decter concludes by saying that he is disappointed that "the content of Golub's paintings are being eradicated and diffused by a seeming dedication to the 'beautifying' requirements of the marketplace." Thus, Decter agrees with the other critics on how Golub's paintings look, but he disagrees when he judges the effects of the paintings. Here we have a clear agreement about description and a disagreement about interpretation and judgment.

SCULPTURE: DEBORAH BUTTERFIELD

Following are several descriptions, some quite eloquent, of sculptures by Deborah Butterfield (see color plate 2). The critics writing about her works seem to enjoy writing about it. They are particularly impressed with the way she handles minimal materials—sticks and mud, discarded metal—to evoke a strong presence of horses. Edward Thorp, for example, writes that she is a "virtuoso" in the way she handles steel because of the remarkable sense of volume and detail she creates.[17] He says that she is totally in control of her subject matter and materials and that she is a master in capturing the essence of her highly individual animals. He goes on to specifically describe her adeptness with scraps of metal: "Steel provides an ideal structure for these pieces, since it is skeletal at times, roundly solid at others, and often elegantly curvilinear. In her seemingly effortless manipulation of scrap metal, Butterfield is able to capture the sense of suspended movement of her subjects." Donna Brookman is also impressed with Butterfield's use of her chosen medium: "The forms have a vivid materiality and abstract beauty. All three horses are made with colorful and corroded pieces of scrap metal—old drums, pipes and fencing that remain undisguised even as they are transformed."[18]

To back up his contention that she has a commanding knowledge of her subject matter, Thorp adds the biographical information that Butterfield rides and schools her own horses: "So lifelike are her animals that they appear on the brink

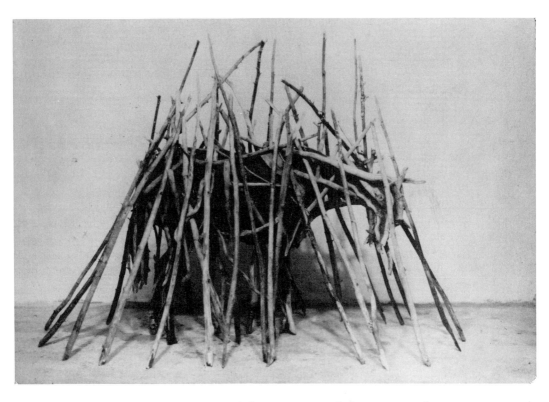

Deborah Butterfield, *Horse No. 8,* steel armatures, chicken wire, twigs, mud, dextrine, paper pulp, hog's hair, grass hap, 108" × 144", 1978. Courtesy of The Pace Gallery, NYC.

of movement, yet the twisted, crumpled, discarded metal that they are made of totally belies such fluidity." The animals communicate their individual character through "the tilt of a head, the swing of a tail, the bend of a knee."

When attending to works of art, critics draw on their own knowledge of life as well as their knowledge of art. Critic Richard Martin, like the artist, is apparently knowledgeable about horses. He writes that "in the language of horse trainers, there is an expression that a horse 'fills the eye' meaning that he or she is good to look at with fine proportions."[19] He goes on to describe the artist's sculpted horses with anatomical detail: "Butterfield realizes the essential anatomy of the horse. The crest can be elegantly maintained in a long sweep of rusted metals; withers may be reinforced by a skin of steel; a metal spur may stand up as the dock of the horse; and the juncture of two pieces of metal may serve as the hock on the horse's leg." Martin admires Butterfield's sculptures because her "examination of the horse is as passionate as the philosopher's and as engaged as the rider's." He adds: "When the line of the back is continuous and strong and the hunk of metal falls to the point of hip and an adjunct piece of metal forms the gaskin on two upper legs, there is no doubt of the presence of the horse."

Critics writing about Butterfield's works seem to delight in describing their form. Martin, for example, provides us with this description: "Another standing horse pokes its head forward and draws its neck down in an aerial and ethereal elegance generated by loose structure whereas the barrel of the horse and its hindquarters are densely described in an impacted lattice of twisted metals even including parts of a child's tricycle incorporated below the loins." Of a recent show of Butterfield's horses in Chicago, Kathryn Hixson writes: "The familiar Butterfield abstractions of the equine are compelling presences, looming larger than life, defined by delicately open fragmented shells of linear abstraction."[20]

Butterfield's work also inspires critics to examine and write about their feelings in viewing it. Hixson attends to the form of the sculptures and then moves into the emotions the sculpted horses evoke: "Adeptly controlling her formal elements, Butterfield constructs lace-like structures—crisscrossing twigs and branches, sometimes incorporating crumpled strips of metal—that become astute representations of emotionally expressive postures of this domesticated animal—as demure partner, vanquished other, and unself-conscious being." Martin also writes of the emotion in the sculptures, specifically attending here to Butterfield's reclining rather than standing horses: "In the reclining horses, Butterfield creates both sympathy and eroticism. The awkward distribution of weight, the knowledge of a delicate equilibrium required to lift the recumbent horse to an upright position, and the implication of birth, nurture, and death give these horses a particular poignancy." He adds that the supine horses are "seductive in the sense that we assuredly want to cuddle with them, but they are comforting in their generation of the blissful repose that is the horse's tranquil equivalent of real life." Of one piece, Brookman writes: "The hollow torso of this horse, with no visible supporting structure, emphasizes its vulnerable, weak quality" and she adds that

Butterfield "vividly conveys the spirit of the horse, with all of its connotations of power, grace, and sexuality, yet simultaneously makes her creatures appear elusive and threatened." Thorp says that Butterfield's horses exude an aura of pastoral calm but that the weathered and beaten metal of which they are made also suggests their mortality.

Comparing and contrasting works of art is a common and useful critical strategy. Two critics compare and contrast Butterfield's horses with other depictions of horses throughout the history of art. In his review, Martin mentions the painted horses of Géricault, Bonheur, and Stubbs; the horses in the Broadway production of *Equus* and the Hollywood films *Black Beauty* and *My Friend Flicka;* as well as the Trojan Horse. Marcia Tucker, in an interview with the artist, has Butterfield herself reflect on how her horses differ from those of other artists: "My work started out being political in a very subtle way: almost all the horse sculpture I had seen had to do with giant war horses, invariably stallions, carrying generals off to kill people. Instead, I wanted to make a sculpture of a mare expecting a baby. . . . So in my own quiet way, I was making art that was against war—about the issues of procreation and nurturing rather than destruction."[21]

GLASS: DALE CHIHULY

This is a clinically accurate description of one of Chihuly's artworks: *"Davy's Gray Sea Form Set with Black Wrap Lips.* American, designed and made by Dale Chihuly with Kate Elliott and other glassblowers, probably at Pilchuck Center, Seattle, 1985. Glass, clear greyish tinted, with coloured glass inclusions; an eight part assemblage consisting of one large 'container' in the shape of a wavy-edged shell with six smaller forms of varying dimensions and shapes nesting inside the other and a small sphere. Marks: CHIHULY 1985 incised on base of the largest. 24.7 cm. long. C.111 & A-G-1987."[22] This type of description attempts scientific objectivity. It is written anonymously, conveying the impression that it is objective and without bias. It is not, however, critical writing; it is a catalog entry for an archive. It is not the type of descriptive writing found in art criticism. Descriptive writing of this type would be deadly to read—it is not an example of engaging critical description.

Andrea DiNoto, writing for *Connoisseur* magazine, offers more typically lively descriptive information about Dale Chihuly and other artists who have recently taken up the medium of glass: "The work is virtually brand new—no piece is more than twenty years old—and the concept is revolutionary: glass as an art medium, not for elegant factory-made tableware or accessories, but for sculpture and even 'painting' that is designed and executed by studio artists."[23] Her descriptions overlap with the catalog information, but she is aware of herself as a writer and of her audience. Readers of *Connoisseur* include potential investors, and DiNoto, with an appeal to authority, informs them that curators of the Metropolitan Museum of Art and the Smithsonian "admire not only the technical virtuosity of these young, mostly American artists but also the stunning variety of form and color that glass allows in its alchemical partnership with light." She describes the range of capabilities of glass from "blown glass sculptures that exploit the sensual quality of the material to cold-worked prismatic forms that express its optical perfection. Between these two poles are whimsical assemblages, massive cast pieces, flat panels." She also states that Dale Chihuly "is generally considered the most charismatic of the glass artists working today, and one of the most creative."

DiNoto then indirectly introduces a question of value: Is this new glass work good? Behind this question lurks a larger one: Is it art or (merely) craft? "Distinguishing between the good, bad, and ugly is not always easy, because glass objects tend to have an immediate superficial appeal." She cites criteria offered by Paul Gardner, a curator at the Smithsonian: rarity, technical excellence, and beauty. Gardner suggests that glass collectors take glassblowing courses, as he did, to understand the medium. He expresses his enthusiasm concerning "the idea of transparency and light and thickness and permanence and quickness—It's glorious."

Robert Silberman, writing for *Art in America,* also raises questions of value, more directly than DiNoto: "With glass, only a fine line separates 'works of art' from *objets d'art*; as the work of lesser artists too often demonstrates, the opposite of functionalism is often a merely decorative formalism—what might be called the Glorified Paperweight Syndrome."[24] He asserts that "a separation remains in force among museums, galleries and collectors between *glass work* and *art work*" and goes on to say that "it still remains unclear whether even the most successful of the established artists, such as Littleton and Chihuly, should be thought of as good artists, or good (for) glass artists."

In a review of a 1981 exhibition by Chihuly in New York City, however, Gene Baro asserts that, in this exhibition, there is "no condescending distinctions between fine and decorative arts."[25] He asserts that this exhibition "must be among the most creatively inventive and technically challenging to be seen this season in New York. Thought of as plastic expression, Chihuly's forms have an organic integrity missing from most sculpture. Assessed for their variety of interacting colors and textures, they challenge the illusionism of current painting. As small objects, they achieve generosity of scale, even a certain monumentality. And they are beautifully made, with a rare refinement that speaks absolutely of the essential characteristics of the glass medium."

Clearly these critics are raising questions of value and of theory rather than description. The critics acknowledge that some glass art, especially that of Dale Chihuly, is very appealing, but ask about its value as *art*. The theoretical questions are: Is glass work art or craft? Is there a meaningful or useful distinction between what is termed *art* and what is called *craft*? These are questions of judgment and theory, which are discussed in later chapters. Nevertheless, judgment and theory do influence how one understands a thing (interpretation) and how one describes it. Conversely, how one describes something depends on how one understands it and values it. Because of these unresolved issues in the case of glass, the following critics writing about it struggle with describing, and defining, its properties as an art form.

Silberman describes the art form this way: "There is undeniably something special about glass as a medium. Its purity, fragility and hardness, combined with its ability to flow, hold color and exist in states ranging from the transparent to the opaque, make it almost fatally attractive." Calling it "almost fatally attractive" indicates his continuing skepticism. In *Artweek,* Ron Glowen describes the medium this way: "Glass is a visually seductive and glamorous material. The hot glass process—with its mesmerizing mix of fascination and danger, rigorous physical discipline and showman's flair, teamwork and timing—adds greatly to its allure. No one has exploited this more than Chihuly."[26]

Glowen also describes the history of the "studio glass movement," which, he explains, began in this country in 1962 when Harvey Littleton designed and built a small glassblowing furnace at The Toledo Art Museum in Ohio. Chihuly is a student of Littleton. Chihuly founded the Pilchuck Glass Center in 1971 in northern Washington state, and he travels and teaches extensively, producing almost half his pieces in other artists' studios. Glowen continues that Larry Bell manufactured glass cubes in Los Angeles in 1965, and that, in the 1970s, when Italo Scanga incorporated "crafted" glass into "fine art" installations, glass art was assigned dual traditional (craft) and avant-garde (art) roles. In the tone of his writing, Glowen expresses discomfort with implied distinctions between art and craft.

Because the movement is new, many of the critics writing about Chihuly describe the techniques he and others use. Linda Norden in *Arts Magazine* writes of "Chihuly's continuing commitment to the exploitation of properties unique to hot glass and the glass blowing process."[27] She describes glassblowing as "an elaborately choreographed tug-of-war between the artist (blowing, spinning, rolling, etc.) and gravity" and is impressed by the tremendous kinetic energy inherent in glass making—far from the familiar associations of glass with fragility and preciousness. She relates that Chihuly favors spontaneity but does produce watercolor sketches before blowing. She also explains that by blowing tough soda-lime glass into a mold with interior ridges, Chihuly pushes glass to new extremes of thinness. By corrugating the glass, he provides increased structural stability, and thus he can allow close inspection of his pieces, further refuting the fragility and preciousness usually associated with glass (see color plate 3).

David Bourdon writes that "obviously reveling in the elasticity of his molten medium, Chihuly emerges as a red-hot virtuoso who exalts the craft of glassblowing into an uncharted new realm of artistic significance."[28] In describing the clusters of bowls Chihuly is well known for, Bourdon describes how the artist achieves a line of color around the edges of bowls, or lip wraps: "The lip wraps are lengths of glass rod—often about the thickness of a line of extruded toothpaste—affixed to the rims of the bowls. Visually, they function like colored contour lines." Bourdon also explains that to overcome the size limits feasible with blown glass, Chihuly clusters related forms to augment the scale of his pieces.

technique   Marilyn Iinkl describes the technique Chihuly used to make a series of vessels in response to his love of Navajo blankets. She explains that he makes flat drawings out of thin glass threads pulled from Kugler color rods. They are assembled by hand and fabricated with a propane torch. Molten glass is placed on the drawing and blown into the cylinder shape. "The motifs wrap the cylinders as the blankets wrapped the Indians."[29] About these same pieces, Penelope Hunter-Stiebel writes: "The resulting heavy, nonfunctional vessels speak of the precision of textiles and the freedom of abstract painting."[30]

Chihuly produced a series of vessels he calls the Pilchuck Basket series. Norden informs us that these were inspired by Tacoma Indian baskets of Chihuly's native Northwest. She says that, with these glass pieces, it is evident *form* that Chihuly favors asymmetry and distortion as well as delicacy and spontaneity. Some of the forms are "nearly two feet in diameter; the slouching and distended bubbles were decidedly glass in their thinness and shiny translucence, but still very much baskets in their tendency toward ambers, burnt orange, straw, and slate brown coloring." Hunter-Stiebel writes that, in making these baskets, Chihuly "flirts constantly with their destruction, allowing varying degrees of collapse." She adds that "the baskets form families, nestling within each other or in near proximity as if seeking shelter in their vulnerability."

Bourdon provides some very engaging descriptive writing about Chihuly's wall-mounted clusters of blown bowls, referring to them as "flamboyant corsages"—"four or five bowl-like shapes with outward-flaring sides and crimped or crinkled rims, clustered like bunches of fantastic flowers." He writes that these glass reliefs command attention "both for the sheer gorgeousness of their undulating forms and for the spectacular manner in which they seem to spill into the room." He calls their shapes "biomorphic" and writes that their "intricate and ornate edges seem all but alive with potential movement." He informs us that the bowls are generally wider than they are deep, sometimes flattened like platters. He describes the forms as abstract but nature-based, reminiscent of spiraling forms and coiled growths in marine creatures such as sea anemones or mollusk shells: "The undulating sides, swirling lips and progressively spaced stripes suggest they may have been shaped by eddying water or gusts of wind. Though the scalloped edges are in fact stationary, their apparent fluidity hints at potential movement, like the swaying bodies of organisms responding to tidal changes."

color   Peggy Moorman is drawn to Chihuly's use of color and provides some very lively descriptive writing about it. She says that his colors are "so vital they seemed fresh from the fire."[31] She continues: "Chihuly's colors range from raw and gaudy, with an orangy yellow as bright as jewelweed, to the subtle, dusky red of a certain species of starfish that lives in the cold tidal pools of the northern Pacific coast of Washington, where the artist lives and works." She describes a particular "milky cerulean blue that glows through orange, ochre and rust" and writes of "shamelessly gorgeous colorations and his rash and fluid distortions." She continues: "Chihuly's laminated colors produce an effect like that of a seashell—he makes the interior of each piece a single smooth color, which glows from behind a speckled, variegated exterior the way a cowrie's pale inside is set off by its brindled back."

PERFORMANCE ART: LAURIE ANDERSON

The difference between describing glass objects and describing the performance art of a living person is enormous. In reviewing a performance by Laurie Anderson in 1986, John Howell in *Artforum,* describes her costumes over the years: In the early 1970s she wore "a white minimalist/hippie gown"; in the late 1970s, "punkish sci-fi suits"; and in the mid-1980s, at the time of his review, "all out glitz" in a gold lamé suit, bright green shirt, silver tie, and red shoes.[32] "This glittering concert character, like all pop personas, has changed clothing to update her assumed role, that of symbolic stand-in for the collective unconsciousness of the moment."

costumes

Howell credits Anderson with continuing (more than ten years at the time he was writing) "to refine a small vocabulary of rich ideas that seems to be capable of infinite development." He describes the performance he is writing about as a "talking electronic-blues performance" that shows "subtle changes in her trademark formula of musical monologues accompanied by elaborate mixed media visual imagery and quirky props." He also describes the lyrics as "the further adventures of her staple wide-eyed 'I,' the Anderson who sees funny things, has peculiar thoughts, dreams a lot (the word 'dream' occurs in most of her song sketches), and who comments in a *faux naif* manner on the comic absurdity of it all." Howell typifies Anderson as a lyric poet rather than a systematic analyst, and admires the variety, clarity, and sheer drama of her audiovisual pieces. He also mentions problems with the performance—namely, the starting and stopping of brief pieces—and wonders whether their meanings contain small insights or large theories.

persona

In a 1990 review of Anderson's *Empty Places,* Ann-Sargeant Wooster, writing in *High Performance,* a magazine devoted to performance art, provides some historical perspective on Laurie Anderson. Wooster writes that "she has come a long way from the time in the early '70s when she used to play the violin on street corners wearing ice skates embedded in a block of ice and the performance was over when the ice melted."[33] Wooster also declares that Anderson now "defines performance art." The critic places Anderson in the tradition of American storytelling with O'Henry, Jack Kerouac, and Bruce Springsteen. She goes on to identify a frequent theme of Anderson's as "loneliness and the alienation rendered by our modern technological world."

historical

Wooster describes the setting for Anderson's musical performance: "Anderson's singing was accompanied by abstract black and white films that

setting

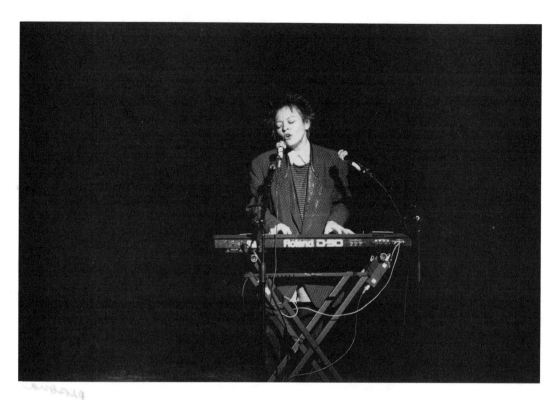

Laurie Anderson performing at the Wexner Center for the Arts, The Ohio State University, November 16, 1990. Courtesy of the Wexner Center for the Visual Arts. Photograph: Kevin Fitzsimons.

looked like scratchboard drawings. Walls of images that included footage of passing subway cars were stretched and pulled into space until they became electronic billboards mirroring the ceaseless mobility of the onlooker rather than advertising a product."

A considerable portion of Wooster's review concerns Anderson's music, and here it is as much music criticism as it is art criticism. She writes of Anderson's "elegaic mood" and the music's "quality of mourning." She describes the "lush opulence" formed by Anderson's "electronic tableaux" when she surrounds herself on stage with the accoutrements of high technology. She describes Anderson's voice in earlier performances as "gravelly" especially because of the artist's use of a "vocoder." Wooster also informs us that Anderson has been taking voice lessons, and the critic now characterizes her voice as lighter and more pleasant, similar to that of Joni Mitchell or Syd Straw. The critic thinks Anderson has replaced her former "androgynous persona" with a more feminine stage presence that corresponds more closely to her new voice. She describes Anderson's music as content-laden, in a singsong, talking manner.

Wooster expresses gratitude for audio recordings: "As the beauty of live performance soon vanishes from memory as does its flaws . . . we can think of the importance of records for performance artists of all kinds. Anderson's songs from *Empty Places* linger on in a stronger and more haunting way in the form of her favorite, democratic object, a record." The recording emerging from *Empty Places* is *Strange Angels.*

INSTALLATIONS: ANN HAMILTON

The medium for an installation created by Ann Hamilton in collaboration with Kathryn Clark in Chicago and called *Palimpsest* is cabbage, snails, wax, and notes on paper (see color plate 4). Kathryn Hixson offers this description of the piece: "The installation was a room filled with two-by-three-inch notes on yellowed newsprint—tacked in neat rows onto every inch of the wall. The texts seemed to be from diaries and letters—a litany of different voices whose manners of speech and the graphic detail of the penmanship mixed to identify vaguely the gender, class, age, education, and social position of the absent speakers."[34] The critic goes on to describe her reaction to the experience of reading the notes: "By limiting detail from each voice, and collecting a great number of voices, the viewer became aware how they were manufacturing the individuals behind the voices." She also describes her experience of being in the room: "The claustrophobia of being caught in a room with so many personalities was heightened by the treatment of the floor, which was also obsessively covered with notes that were protected by layers of smelly beeswax, perhaps referring to the wax used to seal letters, once a common practice, which personalized and privatized correspondence. The coloring of the wax—very close to the yellowed hues of the newsprint—gave the room the golden glow of a royal tomb." She informs us that the cabbages

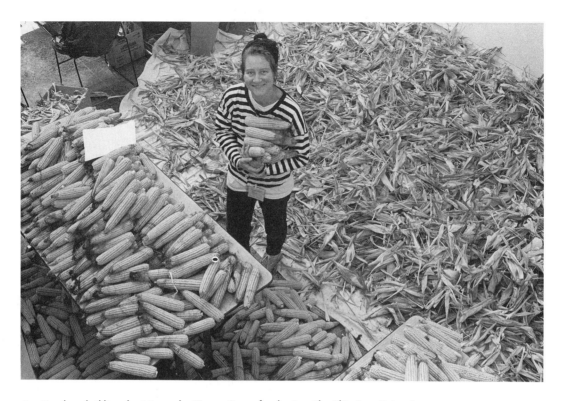

Ann Hamilton, building *dominion* at the Wexner Center for the Arts, The Ohio State University, 1990. Courtesy of the Wexner Center for the Arts. Photograph: Jo McCulty.

and the snails feeding on them were in an elegant glass vitrine. The snails left a slime trail everywhere they traveled, and Hixson associates their trails with the notes on the walls, which are like the tracings of the individuals who wrote them.

In another of her pieces, called *between taxonomy and communion,* Hamilton covered with raw wool the walls (about waist high) and the floor of a large room with a low ceiling and a single doorway. She covered the wool with slats of glass joined with flexible silicone adhesive. Kenneth Baker, writing in *Artforum,* carefully articulates his experience of moving through this installation: "Seen through the glass, the matted fleece looked something like soiled, compressed clouds. The sensation underfoot was a combination of brittleness and yielding to pressure. Every step felt as if one were treading on thin, fractured ice atop a layer of mud, though without the ooze. The uncertain footing forced visitors to alter their ways of moving, a bodily sensation that amplified the metaphorical force of the situation."[35] He interprets the metaphorical situation to be "the difficulty we have in identifying with other forms of animal life, a difficulty now known to have global ecological implications."

Hamilton's work expands notions of *medium.* In a feature-length article about Hamilton's work, David Pagel discusses several pieces, three of which are noted here for their use of diverse media.[36] In *Suitably Positioned,* a barefoot model stood in the center of an empty gallery wearing a suit made of a dense layer of toothpicks that stood upright like porcupine quills. In *reciprocal fascinations* (1985), Hamilton "enclosed forty pigeons in a narrow glass-and-metal cage that lined the perimeter of a windowless gallery. The interior space contained a seated figure whose head was covered by a sheet of billowing white silk, a standing figure who wore a suit covered with flashlights and who periodically pumped a fog horn, and a steep autopsy table whose imperceptible vibrations created frenzied wave patterns in the shallow pool of water that covered its surface." Pagel describes a third piece, *privation and excesses,* this way: "Hamilton exchanged her project's budget for 750,000 pennies, and, with a group of assistants, laid these coins on the honey-coated floor to form a shimmering copper surface that resembled the overlapping scales of a gigantic fish."

In describing Hamilton's installations, critics need to refer to specific spaces and times because Hamilton's pieces are site-specific—planned around and made for an exact location—and meant to last for a specific period of time. Sarah Rogers also points out that Hamilton's projects are "site specific not only in formal configurations but in associative references to the context of their sites."[37] The materials she uses are often from the region in which her installations are built, and the references in her pieces are often in response to local history and recent occurrences.

A SUMMARY AND CONCLUSIONS ABOUT DESCRIPTION

It should be clear by now that description is not a prelude to criticism—it is criticism. Given the rich descriptions provided by critics, we come away with a knowledge and appreciation of the art they are describing. Description, then, is language to facilitate understanding and appreciation of works of art, and so is criticism.

Lively Writing

It should also be clear by now that although descriptions can be clinically accurate and scientific sounding, as with the language quoted earlier describing a Chihuly piece—"Glass, clear greyish tinted, with coloured glass inclusions; an eight part assemblage consisting of one large 'container' in the shape of a wavy-edged shell with six smaller forms . . . —they are rarely this removed, unemotional, or so coolly intellectual. When critics describe, they often do so quite passionately. Recall the more typical descriptions of Chihuly's work: "flamboyant corsages," "clustered like bunches of fantastic flowers," "sheer gorgeousness," and "the spectacular manner in which they seem to spill into the room."

Critics' descriptions are lively. Critics write to be read, and they must capture their readers' attention and engage their readers' imaginations. Critics want to persuade their readers to see a work as they do. If they are enthused, they try to communicate their enthusiasm through their choice of descriptors and how they put them together in a sentence, a paragraph, and an article. If Golub's work frightens them, they want us to experience the chill: "The whole scene feels like the memory of a bad dream, recalled through a haze of paint and sweat as if we had just bolted upright, wrenched from our otherwise peaceful middle-of-the-night slumber."

In this chapter, the academic distinctions of subject matter, medium, and form were used. Professional critics make these categories come alive. Anselm Kiefer's paintings often use the subject matter of burnt fields. In good descriptive writing, however, they are not just burnt fields, they are "large fields of scorched earth [that] look like slabs of blasted heath itself, danced over by devils, driven over by panzers, tortured by the weather, then screwed to the wall." Deborah Butterfield's subject matter is horses, but it is also "the tilt of a head, the swing of a tail, the bend of a knee." This is insightful and engaging descriptive writing.

The medium can be oil on canvas, but it can also be wax, or—more interestingly—"smelly beeswax" or 750,000 pennies laid on a honey-coated floor that form "a shimmering copper surface that resembled the overlapping scales of a gigantic fish." Medium may also be costuming, but not just a costume, but rather "a white minimalist/hippie gown" and "punkish sci-fi suits" and "all out glitz." When writing about the performances of Laurie Anderson, art critics had to come up with terms for her music and wrote of her "elegiac mood," a "quality of mourning," and "lush opulence."

In subdividing form, the elements of dot, line, shape, light and value, color, texture, mass, space, and volume were mentioned. Again, this is an academic list, useful in teaching and in learning to notice and describe details in a work of art. However, in professional critical description, color is not merely the name of a hue, but rather it becomes "a high-tech spectral blue" or a "perversely sweet palette." A good critic does not simply describe one of Golub's canvases as dark; rather, she writes: "One searches these dark yet luminous surfaces for clues with the alert vigilance with which one concentrates on discerning the outlines of figures in the street to distinguish a mugger from a passerby." In lively critical language, texture becomes "laying on the paint thickly, then dissolving it and scraping it down with a meat cleaver. The eroded colors and surfaces of Golub's paintings are raw, dry, and irritated, setting us on edge, increasing our discomfort." And paint is not simply acrylic; it is "splattered, splotched, and squiggled acrylic."

Internal and External Sources of Information

Critics describe what they see in a work of art and also what they know about the artist or the times in which the art was made. The critics describing Chihuly's work felt a need to provide a history of the glass art movement. Critics usually know a lot about the artists whose work they are writing about and they offer it to their readers. Sometimes critics need to do research in libraries to find external information that will enable them to better write about an artist or exhibition. To prepare for an interview with Anselm Kiefer, because of the many literary references in his paintings, Walter Januszczak tells of "scampering from the librettos of Wagner to the musings of Heidegger, from Nietzsche to Jung, from the short stories of Balzac to the epistles of Eusebius of Caesarea, from Goethe to William L. Shirer, from image to image, from quote to quote, in a kind of marvelously addictive game of Nontrivial Pursuit."[38] Information about art and artists is endless, however, and the ultimate test for the critic whether to include or exclude such descriptive information is relevancy: Will this information help or hinder an understanding of the art, the flow of the article?

Truthful Descriptions

In theory, descriptions are said to be true or false, accurate or inaccurate. That is, when a critic makes a descriptive claim about a painting—points to something in it and names it—we should be able to see it and agree (or disagree) with the critic's observation. Description is said to deal with facts, and it does. However, all facts are dependent on theory, and all descriptions are interwoven with interpretation and evaluation. As we have seen, the descriptions quoted in this chapter are not independent of how the critic understands the piece of art. Critics could write descriptions in a painstaking way so as not to reveal their preferences and biases; and such an exercise in critical writing might be valuable in learning to write descriptively, and in learning to identify value-laden descriptions. Critics' descriptions, however, are rarely value-neutral because they are writing persuasively. When a critic approves or disapproves of a work of art, this approval or disapproval comes through in the critic's descriptions of the work. Interpretations are more speculative than descriptions, and judgments are more argumentative than descriptions. Interpreting and judging art are the topics of the next two chapters.

Take a short descriptive essay piece for analysis

Look at art work
what kinds of things would you mention in ?
collective list

Group assignment - print for each group
list things

3
INTERPRETING ART

Interpretation is the most important activity of criticism, and probably the most complex. This chapter is built around critics' interpretations of the work of three contemporary artists: William Wegman, an artist who makes photographs, videotapes, and paintings; Jenny Holzer, who works with language; and Elizabeth Murray, a painter. The purpose of the chapter is to help readers understand what interpreting an artwork entails, to explore different strategies of interpretation used by critics, to examine the similarities and differences of a variety of interpretations of the same work, and, ultimately and most importantly, to derive principles of interpretation that will enable readers to read interpretations more intelligently and help them formulate their own interpretations of works of art. A number of such principles are derived from the criticism samples that follow, and then they are listed and defined in the final section.

INTERPRETING THE PHOTOGRAPHS OF WILLIAM WEGMAN

The chapter begins with William Wegman because his work challenges the very value of interpreting art. Wegman's work is so accessible it seems to make attempts at interpretation unnecessary. Although the work is in virtually every important museum collection in the world, he and his videotapes and photographs have been on Johnny Carson's "Tonight Show," "Late Night with David Letterman," "Sesame Street," "Saturday Night Live," and "Tomorrow." Wegman's photographs of his dogs have been on the covers of such diverse magazines as *Avalanche, Artforum, Camera Arts,* and Sotheby's auction catalog. He and the dogs have been featured in *People Magazine*[1] and in a human interest story for Valentine's Day in the *New York Times*.[2] Some of Wegman's work is undeniably cute—*Marigolds, Petunias, Weimaraners* (1989) is a color photograph of eight adorable puppies in a flower box. Does art that is so easily enjoyed by the public *need* interpretation? Do such interpretive endeavors yield worthwhile insights? These are the questions to be answered in this section.

William Wegman paints, draws, photographs, makes videotapes, and occasionally does site-specific sculpture. Although this section concentrates on interpretations of his Polaroid photographs, it also touches on his other media. Critics writing about Wegman's work often include biographical information about him and his dogs. It is generally true that modern critics offer more contextual information about artists and how their work evolved than did critics of fifty years ago, who wanted to focus primarily, if not exclusively, on the artwork itself. Nevertheless, contemporary critics seem particularly interested in Wegman's personal life. They may sense in his work a relationship between him and his dogs that makes them want to know more about the lives of both, or his work may make them especially curious about the person creating the work. In any event, the biographical information given here is condensed from articles by Michael Gross,[3] Elaine Louie,[4] and Brooks Adams.[5]

William Wegman lives in New York City on the Lower East Side of Manhattan in a building that was formerly a synagogue. He also spends time in a home on a lake in Maine. Wegman lives with his two Weimaraners, Fay Ray and her daughter Battina. The dogs have a couch with separate dog beds on it in the bedroom and a dog run of dirt and concrete. They freely roam the space. Louie writes that Wegman plays with them frequently and that Fay, Battina, and William "simply adore each other."

Gross writes that "at 48, Wegman has survived the Vietnam-era draft, a first brush with fame, a risky dalliance with cocaine and Old Crow, and even his seemingly inescapable association with charismatic canines, to reach, at his maturity, a career peak." Wegman grew up in a working-class environment in Holyoke, Massachusetts, drawing pictures as a child. He attended Massachusetts College of Art and graduated with a BFA in 1965, later earning an MFA from the University of Illinois at Champaign-Urbana in sculpture and performance art. As a student, he was friendly with photo-conceptualist Robert Cumming and shared studio space with painter Neil Jenney. He considers his mentors to be Ed Ruscha, Bruce Nauman, and John Baldessari. Artist Robert Kushner designed costumes for Man Ray, Wegman's first dog. Ruscha is pictured with Fay Ray in *Sworded* (1987).

Wegman got his first and most famous dog, Man Ray, in 1970, as a puppy. He considered naming him "Bauhaus" but then settled on "Man Ray," the name of the famous Dadaist who made photographs. The dog, Man Ray, died of cancer in 1981 at 11 years, 8 months. About Man Ray, Louie quotes Wegman saying "I could do him as a dog, a man, a sculpture, a character, a bat, a frog, an elephant, an Airedale, a dinosaur, a poodle. I never got tired of him." Wegman spent three years without a dog after Man Ray died. In 1984, he got another Weimaraner, but it was stolen; a third died of a virus. He got Fay Ray in 1985 and named her after the actress in the original *King Kong* movie.

Of Weimaraners, Wegman says they have a lap-dog sensibility with hunting and pointing capabilities and that they are very good at holding a pose. As models, they have the added advantageous characteristic of not drooling. They like to work, and they pester Wegman when he is painting canvases rather than photographing them. Wegman goes to dog shows, and he frequents thrift shops in search of such items as fake leopard coats, mink jackets, brocade robes, and satin and lace wedding gowns.

In 1978, when Wegman was invited by the Polaroid corporation to their studio in Boston, he began making large 20" × 24" instant color photographs on Polacolor film of Man Ray. Wegman has now been using the camera for over ten years. The camera and studio cost about $1000 a day, and the prints are about $30 each and take eighty-five seconds to develop. On a typical day, he shoots about sixty frames, of which about five will be usable. He employs a camera technician, a film handler, and a lighting specialist.

Man Ray was an elderly dog when Wegman began using the Polaroid camera, so he often costumed him to hide his age and weight. Wegman says that Fay hyperventilates in the morning but that by afternoon she will do about anything. When Fay had a litter of eight puppies, Wegman kept Battina and placed the other offspring with family and friends; those dogs also model for Wegman. In 1993, he published *Cinderella,* featuring Battina as Ella and Fay in the triple role of fairy god mother, evil stepmother, and ugly stepsister.[6]

In 1982, Wegman published *Man's Best Friend,* a book dedicated to Man Ray the artist and Man Ray the dog, with a brief introduction by Laurance Wieder.[7] In 1990, he published a catalog of his touring retrospective exhibition of videotapes, photographs, drawings, and paintings. Martin Kunz, Peter Weiermair, Alain Sayag, and Peter Schjeldahl wrote essays for the catalog.[8] Such catalogs, especially of retrospective exhibitions, are generally a summary of current thinking about the work in the exhibition. They are written by critics or scholars sympathetic to the work. (It would be strange to commission someone to write a catalog essay who disapproved of the art in the catalog.) These critical writings about Wegman are played off the essays in the book and catalog because these sources are sanctioned thinking about Wegman's work.

Kunz's writing is succinct and his essay brief. In that sense, it is like Wegman's work. Of Wegman's videotapes, Kunz writes in his introduction that Wegman's "productions stood out against the early works of video art by others, which were characterized by an esthetic of consciously extended duration and artificially constructed boredom." In this brief statement, Kunz is assuming an audience knowledgeable of conceptual art of the 1970s. Although he does not provide examples to back up his claim, one example is the following: Andy

Warhol's *Sleep,* an eight-hour film of a person sleeping, shot and shown in real time. All of Wegman's videotapes are shot in real time, in black and white, with one camera, and without cuts, and all play out a single idea. They are all very short, some as brief as thirty seconds, others only as long as two minutes. They are all funny and entertaining. They are anything but the "consciously extended duration and artificially constructed boredom" of other art of the time such as Warhol's *Sleep.* Thus Kunz contrasts Wegman's art with other art, and he interprets the videotapes to be art about other art.

In his essay on Wegman's photographs, Peter Weiermair reinforces the art about art interpretation. Writing about Wegman's photographs of the early 1970s (see *Handles*), the same time period as the videotapes, Weiermair says, "Wegman created these single shots, diptychs, and series during the period when Minimal, Conceptual, and Process art, for which the photograph was an important means to record events in time and space, were flourishing. No importance was placed on style and composition, or other esthetic values of art photography. But if on the one hand Wegman came from the circle of Minimalism and Conceptual Art, on the other hand he made fun of their seriousness, their ideology of reduction, and above all, their lack of humor."[9] To reinforce his claim that Wegman is making fun of the seriousness of the art of this time, Weiermair points to Wegman's 1971 black and white photograph *To Hide His Deformity He Wore Special Clothing.* It depicts a masonite square leaning against a wall and resting on two shoes. Weiermair sees this photograph as a clear parody of the work of the distinguished sculptor Richard Serra, who often uses squares of steel for his very minimal sculptures. *Falling Glass,* a glass of milk supposedly falling to the floor and landing upright with no breakage or spillage, mocks scientific photography by Eadweard Muybridge, Etienne Marey, and Harold Edgerton, and art based on that photography, such as Marcel Duchamp's *Nude Descending a Staircase.*

Other critics concur that Wegman has a penchant for making witty comments about the art of others with his own. Craig Owens wrote that Wegman's photographs in the 1970s parodied the work of Serra and the sculpture of Robert Morris, as well as the serial and systemic art of Carl Andre, Mel Bochner, and Sol LeWitt.[10] Robert Fleck considers Wegman's videos and photographs of Man Ray "a high point of body art" and credits the 1980s' Polaroids with "one of the most surprising solutions in 'conceptual sculpture.'"[11] In a photograph of Fay Ray, Wegman pictures her with a tiny Campbell soup can turd; and this photograph, according to critic Lewis Kachur, is a comment on the mania in the marketplace for Andy Warhol's works.[12]

Ken Sofer writes in *Artnews* that "despite the dictum that if you want to be taken seriously as an artist, never do children or dogs," Wegman is "an artist serious about critiquing the conventions of serious art."[13] In a feature article on Wegman's work in *Arts Magazine,* D. A. Robbins interprets it to be conceptual art and states that Wegman's drawings have been largely ignored by critics because of "their difficult conceptual nature."[14] Kevin Costello links Wegman to Dada: "Wegman is assuredly a conceptualist—a point of view in contemporary

wit + parody

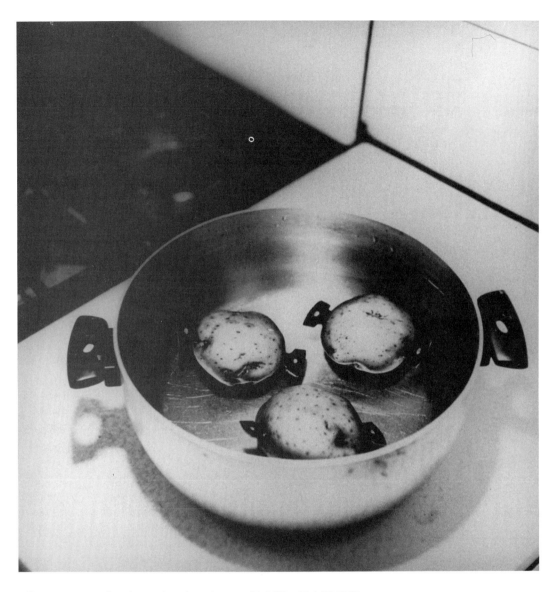

William Wegman, *Handles,* photographs, gelatin silver print, 10 3/4" x 10 1/2" 1972.
Copyright, William Wegman, courtesy of Pace/MacGill Gallery, New York City.

art where the idea, the concept underlying the visual documentation, has equal or more importance than the object, painting, or photograph itself. . . . His art presents complex redirections to the viewer, not only to the image of the dogs or paintings but also to the highbrow seriousness of much of art as history, which under the worst circumstances is presented with a preciousness which stands in the way of the truly human sensibility that art addresses and reflects."[15]

Wegman seems to agree with these interpreters. Robbins quotes Wegman about his graduate education: "I rebelled against what I was supposed to be thinking about at that time, having to read Wittgenstein and Levi-Strauss." He goes on to say that he didn't want to be a dilettante philosopher, and thought Robert Smithson, the sculptor of earthworks, was being a dilettante scientist when he wrote about art. Once he left the university environment, Wegman says, he drifted back to what was more immediate: explicitly autobiographical subject matter, simple domestic scenes, household objects, menus, grammar school, the world of men and women, cats and dogs.

Weiermair interprets Wegman's early black and white photographs as being about the medium of photography itself: "Wegman starts with the supposition that our consciousness is partly controlled by the medium of photography as a system of symbols, and that we have internalized this medium. We always assume that photographs do not lie and tend to identify photographic reality with truth. Many artists of the 1960s and 70s have examined this topic and have scrutinized the medium with the medium itself. The photograph is a shadow of reality, light makes its existence possible. In *Crow* (1970), a witty apposition of a stuffed bird with a shadow that does not belong to it, Wegman not only suggests that birds are able to recognize the shadows of their enemies, but also that the photograph itself is an illusory shadow."

Craig Owens interprets Man Ray's passive and submissive modeling to be a parody of fashion photography, with Wegman substituting the dog for the woman.[16] In the same article, written about work done up until 1983, Owens also posits that Wegman's work exhibits a "deliberate refusal of mastery." (In his catalog essay, Weiermair gives credit to Owens's interpretation.) Owens interprets this refusal of mastery to be an important theme of Wegman's works. He writes that they speak of failure more often than success and of intention thwarted rather than realized—especially the videotapes of Wegman trying unsuccessfully to impose his will on Man Ray, at the expense of the dog. Owens's is a psychoanalytic interpretation: The narcissistic ego attempts to assimilate, to appropriate, to master the other, and Wegman's work, prior to 1979, refuses such mastery over an other. Owens continues: "When we laugh at Man Ray's foiling of Wegman's designs, we are also acknowledging the possibility, indeed the necessity, of another, non-narcissistic mode of relating to the Other—one based not on the denial of difference, but upon its recognition. Thus, inscribed within the *social* space in which both Bakhtin and Freud situate laughter, Wegman's refusal of mastery is ultimately political in its implications." Here Owens is drawing upon a large interpretive framework to make sense of Wegman's tapes of Man Ray.

More recently, another critic also reads psychological content in Wegman's Polaroids. Jean-Michel Roy asks, "Where does the real power of these shots come from? What sets them above and beyond the tradition of animal art to which they are often linked? The photographs' force seems to come from the original and complex manner in which they twist the roles of master and dog—evoking a consciousness and resigned sense of the fundamental powerlessness, which appear a reflection of the human condition."[17] He argues that "posing is a subordination of the gaze of the self to another, an offering of one's self to the viewer," and that "Wegman is imposing an attitude that is at odds with their fundamental animal nature, at least in principle. He forces them with his master's authority to play human, to mimic beings imbued with consciousness and desire."

John Yau, writing five years later, also deals with Wegman's refusal of mastery, but he is referring to a refusal of aesthetic rather than psychological mastery: "In the early 70s, William Wegman was one of the first artists to gain attention for work that deliberately ignored well-established critical paradigms such as unity, mastery, and ambition. Instead of upholding the standards associated with the notion of integrity, Wegman has drawn 'throwaway' sketches, produced 'homemade' videos, and posed and photographed a Weimaraner in an assortment of goofy costumes and oddball situations."[18]

Owens writes of Wegman's ability to undermine belief, to dislodge certainty, and to discredit dogma. D. A. Robbins also asserts that Wegman's work undermines the ways one usually experiences reality. Weiermair cites the interpretations of these two critics and reinforces them: "Questions are posed. Answers are not given." As an example to reinforce this interpretation, Weiermair mentions Wegman's Polaroid diptychs, with which he creates a narrative situation and then disrupts it. The first picture presents a premise, but the second does not continue it, does not complete the thought.

Robbins writes of the mystery of the Man Ray Polaroids, and Weiermair, citing and agreeing with this interpretation, writes: "Looking through the photographs one is struck by Man Ray's muteness, his final unknowableness; Man Ray *referred* to personality. His silence placed him at the center of the camera's (and the artist's, and our own) search for meaning. Our erotic desire to know, to recognize and make contact with the charged presence of life, is at once massaged by Man Ray's nobility and thwarted by his non-human inarticulation."

Both Weiermair and Kunz credit Man Ray with being a turning point in Wegman's artistic career. Weiermair writes that "were it not for his star model, Man Ray, and recently, after a break of a few years, Fay Ray, who give his enigmatic art such a palpable and comprehensible appearance, Wegman's imagery would be accessible only to a very small public." That is, it would have probably continued to be witty work about relatively obscure art and artists and hardly the stuff to appear on commercial television. About the Polaroids, Weiermair goes on to write that "in single photographs, Wegman and Man Ray manage to condense the extended conceits of the video performance into one elegantly composed and articulate image. Diptychs and triptychs tell spare stories." Kunz credits the Polaroids of Man Ray as being a turning point in this way: "In his work with the Polaroid camera—which called for teamwork in the production of the photographs (model, lighting specialist, cameraman, artist)—he renounced the austerity of his early work. An unaccustomed opulence and a pictorial quality not exercised previously became characteristic of his photography."

In writing about the later Polaroid stills, (see color plate 5) Kunz states that Wegman "analogizes the instant camera to video playback, which allows the artist to see immediately the work he has done. But unlike the grainy video image, the resulting glossy color prints have the presence and uniqueness of paintings: paint by camera, not by hand." Weiermair claims that the most important feature of Wegman's approach in the Polaroid prints "resides in the tension between the perfection of the technical process being employed (Polaroid photography in a room) and the grotesque or humorous nature of the playlet that is being portrayed." He writes that the frozen beauty of the Polaroid prints have all the formal qualities of commercially produced pictures: "The object is seen frontally, the colors have that saturated and brilliant look that advertisers are so fond of; not one detail, not one aspect of the object that has been photographed eludes us. And it is this tension between the formal beauty of the photograph and the makeshift character of the arrangement that forms the basis of Wegman's approach."

Weiermair interprets many of the Polaroids to be playing-off advertising photography: "By appropriating the dominant language, the language of advertising, for his own purpose, he claims the right to treat serious subjects in a light-hearted way, subjects that include death, boredom, solitude, and what Michel Nuridsany has called the 'generalized derision of the world.'" Robbins offers a parallel interpretation: "The manipulator of the media is by extension the manipulator of the audience; in this way Wegman associates himself with authority, with the generators and controllers of information, in order to make transparent the mechanisms by which power manipulates us."

Several of the critics writing about Wegman's Polaroids share a theme expressed and summarized by Weiermair: "Beneath the beautiful surfaces of the Polaroids lurks still a moralist, for whom the inscrutable, 'impenetrable' animal—Man Ray and, later, Fay Ray—is the 'It' of the world, which, at best, we are able to train through our words but cannot understand." Charles Hagen interprets this same mystery as liberating: "the liberating edge of the unexplained and unexplainable that is Man Ray's personality—always a puzzle, never a question."[19] In a related interpretation, Martha Ronk interprets Wegman's Polaroids of Fay Ray to be raising the question "What is the relationship between man and dog, culture and nature, photograph and reality?"[20] In the most extreme interpretation of the work, Robbins thinks it is very radical artistically and socially, that it is angry and has "genuinely subversive aims" and that his "humor actually harbors a threat so potent that we come to provide the humor as a kind of safety valve, a candy coating on a poisonous pill."

Although all these critics offer interpretations of Wegman's work, they also acknowledge that they do not fully understand it and that it is not fully understandable. Jerry Saltz writes that "in each medium [photography, video, drawing and painting] the meaning is never preciously located or emphatically stated. Everyday objects and situations are examined and turned topsy-turvy and inside out. A snake-pit of references, jokes, and off-handed intentions lie in wait ready to ambush the unsuspecting viewer. Somehow Wegman subverts the familiar without becoming pedantic or didactic. All of this combines to produce an often inexplicable but palpable aesthetic pleasure in the work."[21] Kunz concludes his essay on Wegman with this analogy: "Like any clown, William Wegman makes us laugh and enters our hearts while never quite allowing us to penetrate his own spiritual and mental depths."

What conclusions can be drawn from these interpretive writings about the work of William Wegman? First and probably most importantly, Wegman's seemingly transparent and definitely humorous work has sustained considerable interpretation by a number of critics. The themes in his work identified by these critics are those of antimastery of one ego over another and antimastery concerning aesthetic technique in the early videotapes and black and white photographs. The critics see his later color Polaroid work as being very masterful aesthetically. They interpret the work to be mysterious and to be about the mystery of the other. They all interpret the work to be art commentary about art and photography, and interpret the Polaroids as photographs about fashion and advertising photography. Thus, even art that can be enjoyed on the "Tonight Show" can also be interpreted seriously by professional critics.

Any artwork can both generate and tolerate multiple conjectures about its meaning. Wegman's work is a good example of this principle. Wegman's art readily sustains the interest of children seeing it on "Sesame Street" and of psychoanalytic critics giving it much deeper readings. Audience members of the "Tonight Show" and David Letterman's "Late Night" enjoy Wegman's videotapes and photographs, and so do readers of *Artforum*. The meanings of Wegman's works are not merely discoverable, as in an archaeological sense; they are also generated by active, engaged, and articulate viewers.

None of these critics claim to fully understand Wegman's work. Their admissions lend support to another principle: No single interpretation will exhaust the meaning discoverable in a work of art.

All the critics enjoy the humor of Wegman's art. Saltz writes, "Having been a funny video artist and a funny photographer, William Wegman has now turned out to be a very funny painter, a fact that does not diminish the seriousness or the importance of his work one iota." Although they differ in their interpretations of the humor, they all see the work as being much more than funny, much more than one-line jokes. Jeremy Gilbert-Rolfe's statements about criticism in general are very apt here when applied to Wegman's work: "In criticism one is often being serious about things which are by definition not serious. Works, that is to say, which are seriously not serious and difficult by not being difficult."[22]

There are several interpretations here by several critics, all of them mutually reinforcing, none of them contradictory. Different interpretations are beneficial because they expand our knowledge and appreciation of art.

Owens and Robbins base their interpretations of Wegman's work on psychoanalytic theory. From them, another principle emerges: Interpretations of art are often based on a larger world view.

The following sections, on the works of Jenny Holzer and Elizabeth Murray, test and expand on the generalizations found in the interpretations of Wegman's work. Here are some immediate generalizations: Art is interpretable, even if it seems very straightforward. Art can be understood from several different points of view and with different levels of understanding, from naive to sophisticated. Interpretations further thinking about art. No single interpretation exhausts the meaning of a work of art. Several interpretations enrich the understanding of a single body of work. There are many ways to interpret art. Some of these ways involve theories from other areas, such as psychoanalytic theory.

INTERPRETING THE WORK OF JENNY HOLZER

Jenny Holzer makes language pieces. Some contain a phrase, others brief essays. She shows them in a variety of formats and media, including posters, etched bronze plaques, decals, billboards, LED electronic signboards, T-shirts, baseball caps, stickers pasted to phone booths and parking meters, embossed metal signs similar to No Parking signs, rubber stamps, the Sony JumboTRON video scoreboard in San Francisco's Candlestick Park during a baseball game, the Maiden Spectacolor Board in London's Picadilly Circus, the 800 square foot Spectacolor Board in Times Square in New York, the marquee of Caesar's Palace in Las Vegas, baggage turnstiles at the Las Vegas airport, various marquees on city streets, the outside of train cars in Hamburg (in German), the cable music video channel, MTV, as well as in galleries and museums.

At least two critics find very little to interpret in Jenny Holzer's work. Jeremy Gilbert-Rolfe dismisses her art as "arid and trivial" and goes on to say: "The pieties of Jenny Holzer, expensively produced slogans offered as works of art, while directly comparable to the fatuous pieties of Mao Tse-Tung or the Ayatollah Khomeni, completely fail to generate anything like a new thought. What they do instead is exactly what the slogans of the Maoists or of Islamic fundamentalists do, which is to pretend that difficult ideas can be reduced to simple formulations."[23] Robert Hughes holds a similar position regarding her art. He calls it "limpidly pedestrian" work that makes no demands on the viewer, and in *Time* magazine he writes: "Holzer is the modern version—rewired, subsidized, eagerly collected, but still recognizable—of those American maidens who, a century ago, passed their hours stitching improving texts as samplers: THOU GOD SEEST ME, ABC, XYZ. The main differences are that instead of using biblical texts, Holzer writes her own, and that instead of using needle and thread, she inscribes them in LEDs and marble."[24]

Gray Watson, however, writing in *Flash Art* about Holzer's electronic signs in London, says that they greet the casual passerby with a genuinely unsettling and refreshing provocation to think.[25] And Peter Plagens, Hughes's counterpart at *Newsweek,* holds Holzer in much higher esteem than Hughes. Plagens reviewed the work she showed in the 44th Venice Biennale, which he refers to as the oldest and most prestigious international art exposition. He explains that the United States chose its own representative, that a solo turn in Venice is practically an Oscar, and further that "her spectacular display of deadpan *Truisms,* blazing across rows of LED (light-emitting diode) signs, and her Roman-letter *Laments,* carved into marble floors and benches, was awarded the grand prize for the best national pavilion."[26] He finds Holzer's work to be full of poignancy because of its mix of personal confession and huge spectacle. He also thinks that "it's simply a visual knockout. The effect is like looking out from the center of the carousel on Saturday night and still being able to read all the neon signs."

Michael Brenson writing in the *New York Times* expresses ambivalence about Holzer's work and her selection as the American representative in the Biennale: "There is nothing approaching a consensus on Holzer's work. Because of its dependence upon electronics and words, it has been understood almost as specialist art, with inherent limits. In addition, the work has developed so rapidly in the last three years that only devoted followers can keep up with it."[27] He recognizes that her work was a likely choice for the Biennale because it reflects a current interest in site-specific, socially concerned art. He states that the phrases in her works "seem private and public, solitary and shared" and that there are so many voices in some that a point of view is impossible to discover. He notes that "Holzer is against power. She also wants to make room for thoughts and feelings that people keep to themselves and that art has generally excluded." Without personally committing himself to a judgment, he offers this negative caution from unnamed others: "For many people, however, her work is just too thin. There is a persistent belief that using words as visual art is intrinsically limited, and art that has to be read cannot begin to have the full, rich texture of painting or sculpture."

Although at this point the discussion is a bit ahead of itself—dealing as much with the topic of judgment as with interpretation—some important and relevant points can be made immediately based on these conflicting examples. First, there was critical consensus regarding the work of William Wegman, but there is not concerning the work of Holzer. Thus, it is clear that critics sometimes disagree. There was a variety of interpretations of Wegman's work, with some critics seeing more meaning in the work than others. The critics also used different interpretive strategies, but their conclusions were in general agreement. With interpretations of Holzer's work, however, there are clear disagreements, both about the value of the work and what it means. Gilbert-Rolfe and Hughes interpret the work to mean nothing; they see it as empty pieties that cause little reflective thought and have no merit. Precisely because Gilbert-Rolfe and Hughes interpret the work to be not worth interpreting, they judgmentally dismiss it. Brenson calls it "thin." Thus, the ability of artworks to generate interesting interpretations is a criterion of judgment for some critics. In these examples interpretations and judgments are intertwined. Plagens, however, is very positive both about the content of the work and especially about how it looks. Because there are conflicting interpretations, interesting and difficult questions about interpretive correctness arise. Namely, are all interpretations, even those by professional critics, correct even when they are contradictory? Are some interpretations better than others? How should one decide among competing interpretations? How should interpretations themselves be judged? These questions are addressed in the final section of this chapter.

The discussion continues now with interpretations of Holzer's work from the writings of other critics, beginning with some general interpretive observations; concentrating particularly on *Truisms,* her best known pieces; and including her more recent work.

In a human interest story about the artist, Candace Bridgewater writes that Holzer "combines harsh political statements, environmental and social concerns, intense personal feelings and poignant observations with elements of poetry. Her works instruct, baffle, electrify and sometimes offend her readers."[28] Grace Glueck writes that Holzer "hatches messages that range from deadpanned aphorisms to dark meditations about the human condition, embosses them on plaques, engraves them on marble and granite benches or sarcophagus lids and—with skilled technological choreography—sets them prancing in dazzles of colored light."[29] She identifies Holzer's issues as "nuclear holocaust, AIDS, the environment, feminism, the poor, the power of big business and big government." Ann Goldstein says that Holzer challenges and obfuscates verbal meaning and continues: "Her works engage the viewer by insinuation through the accessibility of language. They speak rhetorically the language of mass culture, but at the same time they 'promiscuously' confuse the authority of language as the validation of meaning" (she attributes the term *promiscuously* to Hal Foster, who will be considered soon).[30]

In a feature article on Holzer in 1988, John Howell relates what prices her pieces were then obtaining. The LED pieces were selling for between $10,000 and $25,000 depending on the number of works in an edition and the size and complexity of the boards. Some were as much as $40,000. Her granite benches were $30,000 and sarcophagi were $50,000.[31] A year later, Glueck puts the prices of the sarcophagus and some computer-animated signs at $100,000, and her T-shirts and caps between $15 and $20.

Jenny Holzer was born in Gallipolis, Ohio, reared in Lancaster, Ohio, and graduated from Ohio University with a BFA in art in 1972. (Glueck comments that while she was growing up she was "surrounded by Republicans and horse people.") She did her graduate work at The Rhode Island School of Art and Design, where she made abstract paintings influenced by those of Mark Rothko and Morris Louis. She incorporated some writing in her paintings. In 1977, as a member of the Whitney Museum's Independent Study Program, she read Marx, psychology, social and cultural theory, criticism, and feminism. It was between 1977 and 1979 that Holzer's work became exclusively verbal, when she made her *Truisms,* or "mock-clichés," as she calls them. "I started the work as a parody, the Great Ideas of the Western World in a nutshell."[32] Several of the *Truisms* follow, in alphabetical order, as Holzer always presents them.

IT'S A GIFT TO THE WORLD NOT TO HAVE BABIES
IT'S BETTER TO BE A GOOD PERSON THAN A FAMOUS PERSON
IT'S BETTER TO BE LONELY THAN TO BE WITH INFERIOR PEOPLE
IT'S BETTER TO BE NAIVE THAN JADED
IT'S BETTER TO STUDY THE LIVING FACT THAN TO ANALYZE HISTORY
IT'S CRITICAL TO HAVE AN ACTIVE FANTASY LIFE
IT'S GOOD TO GIVE EXTRA MONEY TO CHARITY
IT'S IMPORTANT TO STAY CLEAN ON ALL LEVELS
IT'S IMPOSSIBLE TO RECONCILE YOUR HEART AND HEAD
IT'S JUST AN ACCIDENT YOUR PARENTS ARE YOUR PARENTS
IT'S NOT GOOD TO HOLD TOO MANY ABSOLUTES
IT'S NOT GOOD TO OPERATE ON CREDIT
IT'S VITAL TO LIVE IN HARMONY WITH NATURE
JUST BELIEVING SOMETHING CAN MAKE IT HAPPEN
KEEP SOMETHING IN RESERVE FOR EMERGENCIES
KILLING IS UNAVOIDABLE BUT IS NOTHING TO BE PROUD OF
KNOWING YOURSELF LETS YOU UNDERSTAND OTHERS
KNOWLEDGE SHOULD BE ADVANCED AT ALL COSTS
LABOR IS A LIFE-DESTROYING ACTIVITY
LACK OF CHARISMA CAN BE FATAL
LEARN THINGS FROM THE GROUND UP
LEARN TO TRUST YOUR OWN EYES
LEISURE TIME IS A GIGANTIC SMOKE SCREEN
LETTING GO IS THE HARDEST THING TO DO
LISTEN WHEN YOUR BODY TALKS
LOOKING BACK IS THE FIRST SIGN OF AGING AND DECAY
LOVING ANIMALS IS A SUBSTITUTE ACTIVITY
LOW EXPECTATIONS ARE GOOD PROTECTION
MANUAL LABOR CAN BE REFRESHING AND WHOLESOME
MEN ARE NOT MONOGAMOUS BY NATURE
MODERATION KILLS THE SPIRIT
MONEY CREATES TASTE
MONOMANIA IS A PREREQUISITE OF SUCCESS
MORALS ARE FOR LITTLE PEOPLE
MOST PEOPLE ARE NOT FIT TO RULE THEMSELVES
MOSTLY YOU SHOULD MIND YOUR OWN BUSINESS
MOTHERS SHOULDN'T MAKE TOO MANY SACRIFICES [33]

In an exhibition catalog, Diane Waldman informs us that Holzer set the *Truisms* first in Futura Bold Italic and then in Times Roman Bold type.[34] When Holzer first made the *Truisms,* she put forty to sixty on a page, alphabetically, with black letters on white paper. The *Truisms* are statements fashioned by Holzer but presented anonymously, posted on buildings in SoHo in New York and later in other parts of Manhattan. Waldman quotes the artist as saying that with her *Truisms* she tries to represent all points of view, contradictory meanings, and feelings. She says she is identifying and commenting on these contradictions and extreme situations in society in the most neutral voice and in a laconic but sincere style she can create.

Ann Goldstein describes the *Truisms* this way: "Comprised of alphabetically ordered one-line statements, these logical, often disquieting, proclamations are presented in uppercase italics that project the authority of reason. The messages absorb and emulate a variety of viewpoints, both masculine and feminine, across the political spectrum." Glueck typifies the *Truisms* as "pithy to platitudinous" and notes that they variously embody roles of "the feminist militant, the callous Yuppie, the sage buckeye, and psychobabbler." About the *Truisms,* Plagens writes that "her straight-faced declarations range from naive anarchism ("Any surplus is immoral") to the visceral discoveries of motherhood ("I am indifferent to myself but not to my child").

Hal Foster has offered a more complete interpretation of the *Truisms* than the other critics. In a feature article that appeared in *Art in America* in 1982, early in Holzer's career, Foster too sees the artist's work as "the babble of social discourse," but he takes his interpretation of her work considerably further.[35] In the article, he compares the work of Holzer with that of Barbara Kruger, an artist using similar strategies but with language and photographs. Foster bases his interpretation of Kruger's and Holzer's work on the semiotic theories of Roland Barthes, the late French scholar who devoted his career to the study of sign systems and how they function in society. Barthes is particularly impressed with the power of language. For Barthes, and for Foster's interpretation, language is legislation; to utter a discourse is not to communicate, it is to subjugate; language is quite simply controlling.

Foster notes that the *Truisms* seem to offer information, but they are mostly opinions, beliefs, and biases—conflicted and cogent by turns, they intend everything and nothing, and they result in "verbal anarchy in the streets." He makes the further points that Holzer's images are as likely to derive from the media as from art history; its context is as likely to be the street wall as an exhibition space. According to Foster, Holzer is a manipulator of signs more than a maker of art objects, and her pieces turn the viewers into active readers of messages more than contemplators of the aesthetic. He says that few of us are able to accept the status of art as a social sign entangled with other such signs and that this entangling is the very operation of Holzer's art. He thinks of her antecedents as conceptual artists Joseph Kosuth, Lawrence Weiner, Douglas Huebler, John Baldessari, and site-specific artists Daniel Buren, Michael Asher, Dan Graham.

Very importantly, he sees her work with language to be critical rather than accepting. She treats languages simultaneously "as targets and as weapons." Foster relates that others also see her work as a weapon, and that an installation of *Truisms* at a Marine Midland Bank in Lower Manhattan was canceled after one week because bank officials disagreed with the credit truism, "It's not good to operate on credit." Foster argues that in her work we see not only how language subjects us but also how we may disarm it. He understands her *Truisms* to place in contradiction ideological structures that are usually kept apart; they present truths in conflict and imply that under each truth lies a contradiction. In the *Truisms,* discourses of all sorts collide. Proverbs clash against political slogans. Holzer places her reader in the midst of open ideological warfare, but oddly, Foster argues, the result is a feeling of release rather than entrapment. That is, he argues, because she exposes coercive languages that are usually hidden, and when they are exposed, they look ridiculous. Thus, the *Truisms* rob language of its power to compel and offer their viewers freedom rather than coercion.

Whereas the other critics consider Holzer's *Truisms* a morass of conflicting statements, Foster does not. If the *Truisms* were only to show that all truths are arbitrary, subjective, and equal even when they contradict each other, we would be rather helpless and our world rather hopeless. But Foster interprets the *Truisms* more optimistically. He sees them as a way out of the abyss that language seems to create because the *Truisms* express a larger, simple truth—namely, that "truth is created through contradiction. Only through contradiction can one construct a self that is not entirely subjected." To Foster, the *Truisms* suggest dialectical reasoning—truth, countertruth, new truth—and thus, for him, the *Truisms* do not merely state a problem, they also provide a solution.

Holzer followed her *Truisms* with a series of *Inflammatory Essays* written at the same time as the *Truisms* between 1979 and 1982. The essays are more assaultive than the *Truisms*. Foster says that they heat up and expand the *Truisms*. Here is one *Inflammatory Essay:*

DON'T TALK DOWN TO ME. DON'T BE
POLITE TO ME, DON'T TRY TO MAKE ME
FEEL NICE. DON'T RELAX. I'LL CUT THE
SMILE OFF YOUR FACE. YOU THINK I DON'T
KNOW WHAT'S GOING ON. YOU THINK I'M
AFRAID TO REACT. THE JOKE'S ON YOU. I'M
BIDING MY TIME, LOOKING FOR THE SPOT.
YOU THINK NO ONE CAN REACH YOU, NO
ONE CAN HAVE WHAT YOU HAVE. I'VE BEEN
PLANNING WHILE YOU'RE PLAYING. I'VE
BEEN SAVING WHILE YOU'RE SPENDING.
THE GAME IS ALMOST OVER SO IT'S TIME
YOU ACKNOWLEDGE ME. DO YOU WANT TO
FALL NOT EVER KNOWING WHO TOOK YOU?

Goldstein refers to these essays as "a series of incendiary paragraphs—proclamations of righteousness, the tactics of terrorism, power of change, leadership, revolution, hatred, fear, freedom." She informs us that Holzer produced these paragraphs as posters or texts in publications. In them, she addressed recognizable, common issues, and "their authoritative, aggressive, violent tone and poetry unnerve the viewer/reader." Waldman tells us that the *Inflammatory Essays* are set in Times Roman Bold. Each essay is one hundred words long, divided into twenty lines in the same square size. Each essay is printed on a different color. Waldman, like Goldstein, sees them as more political than the *Truisms*. They exhort the viewer to action. Foster interprets the essays to be more concerned with the force of language than with its truth. He continues with his semiotic reading of them. For him, they show that some voices insinuate, others demand. The essays show how language, truth, force, and power can pervert each other.

In his article, Foster interprets one more of Holzer's early pieces, *The Living Series,* for which the artist made embossed metal signs (like No Parking signs) and cast bronze plaques. One says this: "The mouth is interesting because it is one of those places where the dry outside moves toward the slippery inside." Foster claims that with these pieces Holzer distorts the official-ese that is really our social discourse of efficacy and etiquette. He enjoys how Holzer beguiles officialdom by using the plaque, which is the form of administrative truth: It commemorates a place or celebrates a man, and thereby exalts a piece of property as the very presence of history. He interprets Holzer's signs and plaques as foiling such markings. Rather than present a public place, they may pose a subversive private one, or rather than announce "George Washington Slept Here," they may offer this: "It takes a while before you can step over inert bodies and go ahead with what you were wanting to do."

Waldman sees 1982 as a breakthrough year for Holzer because at this time she began reaching larger audiences through her use of electronic signboards—"matrices of computer activated light-emitting-diode lamps that display texts and graphics in a variety of colors and presentation styles." The artist first used *Truisms* on LED signs, then created *The Survival Series* between 1983 and 1985 for the signs. Waldman thinks of the signs as "eminently suited to the device of repetition which Holzer often uses with her swift, accessible consumerist language to persuade the viewer effectively." Glueck quotes Holzer as saying that with *The Survival Series* she "switched from being everyone to being myself." This series was not limited to electronic signs. She pasted the following silver offset lithographed sticker, 2 1/2" × 3", made in 1983, on a garbage can lid in New York City: "When there is no safe place to sleep you're tired from walking all day and exhausted from the night because it's twice as dangerous then."

She reintroduced part of *The Survival Series* in 1991 as a limited edition set of pencils embossed with these single phrases:[36]

**THE BEGINNING OF THE WAR WILL BE SECRET
WHAT URGE WILL SAVE YOU NOW THAT SEX WON'T?
PROTECT ME FROM WHAT I WANT
THE FUTURE IS STUPID
MEN DON'T PROTECT YOU ANYMORE
YOU ARE TRAPPED ON THIS EARTH SO YOU WILL EXPLODE**

In 1986, Holzer introduced *Under a Rock.* Of these pieces, Waldman writes: "In *Under a Rock* a commentator is watching horrific events and describing them as they happen, still in a relatively objective tone." This is one of them: "Blood goes in the tube because you want to fuck. Pumping does not murder but feels like it. You lose your worrying mind. You want to die and kill and wake like silk to do it again." Holzer etched texts such as this one into stone benches and sarcophagi and also put them on electronic signboards. Waldman credits the juxtaposition of stone and electronics with creating "a somber mood of contemplation with an intense and jarring physical presence." Waldman thinks that with these pieces Holzer is continuing her advocacy of social and political issues but that her expression is more individual and pensive. Another critic, Holland Cotter, offered this interpretation of *Under a Rock:* "Written in a pungent, often poeticized and syntactically episodic prose (that occasionally simulates the idiomatic peculiarities of bad translation), they speak in an accusatory direct address that is sometimes obscene, sometimes high-flown, always angry."[37] He understands *Under a Rock* to be speaking about the effects on people of "escalating militarism and the cult of machismo which underpins this escalation." Cotter expresses concern that the text just quoted might be read as an excitement to sexual violence rather than as a critique of it.

In an outdoor installation in New York City, Holzer combined *Truisms* and *Under a Rock,* etching texts onto stone benches, one set in black granite, and the other in white marble. She used a Government Style typeface, developed by the War Department in the 1930s, that is still used by the Veteran's Administration on all its headstones and markers. Waldman says *Benches* is "quietly authoritative and understated, yet has a compelling power."

Holzer followed *Under a Rock* with *Laments,* which she first showed in 1987. Of these, Waldman writes: "The Laments series expresses Holzer's social and political concerns in more explicit terms than those of her earlier works; here her message is more complex, and she speaks now of broader, more universal themes. The language of the individual signs and sarcophagi retains its formidable clarity and directness but achieves a texture and nuance, an elegiac quality that is new to the work." This is one of the *Laments:*

**I WANT TO LIVE IN
A SILVER WRAPPER.**

I WILL SEE
WHOOPING ROCKS FLY.
I WILL ICE ON MY BLACK SIDE
AND STEAM ON MY OTHER
WHEN I FLOAT BY SUNS.
I WANT TO LICK FOOD
FROM THE CEILING.
I AM AFRAID TO STAY
ON THE EARTH.
FATHER HAS CARRIED ME
THIS FAR ONLY TO HAVE ME
BURN AT THE EDGE OF SPACE.
FACTS STAY IN YOUR MIND
UNTIL THEY RUIN IT.
THE TRUTH IS PEOPLE ARE
PUSHED AROUND BY TWO
MEN WHO MOVE ALL THE
BODIES ON EARTH INTO
PATTERNS THAT PLEASE
THEM. THE PATTERNS SPELL
OH NO NO NO
BUT IT DOES NO GOOD
TO WRITE SYMBOLS.
YOU HAVE TO DO THE
RIGHT ACTS WITH YOUR
BODY. I SEE SPACE AND IT
LOOKS LIKE NOTHING AND
I WANT IT AROUND ME.

Glueck interprets the *Laments* etched into the sarcophagi to be in the voices of the tomb's fictive occupants, and she writes that they resonate like those in Edgar Lee Masters's *Spoon River Anthology* and Thornton Wilder's *Our Town,* in which the dead speak from their graveyards, creating a sense of human dialogue. Waldman observes that for the first time in *Laments,* Holzer uses the personal pronoun "I," thus abandoning the role of narrator and objective observer.

In one installation, Holzer placed vertical LED signs in one room and sarcophagi in sizes ranging from infant to adult in an adjacent room. Each carried an inscription that is reiterated in the other room, and Waldman writes "a sense of noise and speed emanate from the flashing signs, while silence shrouds the room in which the sarcophagi are located: the emotional disruption created by the contrast could not be more extreme."

Because Holzer was chosen as the American representative to the prestigious Venice Biennale, several critics examine in what way her work is "American." Brenson sees her as "An Ohio-born artist rising from the mean streets of New York." He also interprets her art to be "democratic work" in that it is "a repository for the voices of ordinary men and women around the country. Many opinions, feelings, and ideas are invited into her work, and they are allowed to settle there without fear of exclusion or judgment. Her work fits America's view of itself as a melting pot in which everything and everyone eventually gains a place." He also states that she is "decidedly unpretentious." Bridgewater refers to Holzer's "terse Midwesternisms," and Glueck sees her as American in her "ease with technology, her nonelitist approach, her impatience with tradition and her wish to reach multitudes." Waldman states that Holzer, like other American artists in prominence in the 1980s, is a product of the TV age and advertising and billboards, who, like Duchamp and Warhol, borrows freely from mass culture, addresses originality and the value of the artist's hand in making art, contrasting the impersonal common objects, billboards and signs, with a message that is personal and sincere.

So, what can be immediately concluded from these interpretive writings about the work of Jenny Holzer? This section began with quotes from critics who dismissed the work, claiming that it did not have enough substance to merit interpretation. Other critics, most notably Foster and Waldman, however, found much to interpret in the work. Thus, there is the immediate problem of conflicting, indeed contradicting, interpretations of the same body of work by credible, professional critics. Based on the wealth of thought that Foster and the other critics derived from Holzer's work, it seems that Gilbert-Rolfe and Hughes were premature in their dismissive judgments. Unfortunately, readers are unable to learn much about their negative views of Holzer because these critics refuse to treat her work seriously and are content to dismiss it. If they took the time to develop more elaborate arguments as to why the work is empty, they would provide their readers with more to think about, and ultimately readers might even agree with their positions.

Critics can and do disagree with each other, even when interpreting the same body of work. They might agree with each other's descriptions of the work, but vary greatly in their interpretations and judgments of it. This leaves the reader of criticism with the problem of negotiating these differences. Interpretations are not so much right or wrong as they are enlightening, insightful, useful, or, contrarily, unenlightening, misguided, incomprehensible, or perhaps unaccountable to the facts. Critics who without elaboration dismiss Holzer's work do not add to the knowledge of and insight into her work, and in this sense, other critics' interpretations are better. When critics dismiss work without discussing it or their reasons for dismissing it, they may well have ideological or political reasons—they may be saying this kind of work is not worth my (or your) time. Such curtly dismissive criticism, however, is simply unenlightening.

Many of the critics included biographical information, stressing Holzer's midwestern influences; many also examined the way in which her work is or isn't American. Art does not arise in a vacuum. It is influenced to a greater or lesser degree by the artist's cultural milieu. Whether to include such information depends on its relevancy: If the information extends and deepens an interpretation, it is beneficial and should be included.

The critics are also attentive to how Holzer's work has changed, and they document the changes and attempt to make sense of them. They are very aware of and eager to relate to their readers the specific history of any work. This is another form of contextual, historical information that critics consider important in deciphering meaning in art.

The critics of Wegman's and Holzer's work stress which artists seem to have influenced them. Critics consider all art to be influenced by other art, and they attempt to make this clear to their readers.

INTERPRETING THE PAINTINGS OF ELIZABETH MURRAY

Deborah Solomon recently wrote a feature article on Elizabeth Murray for the *New York Times Magazine*.[38] In it, the critic provides a good overview of Murray's career. Her article provides a basis for establishing interpretive themes and strategies and a basis of comparisons to other critics' writings. In preparing for her feature, Solomon may have read some or all of the other critics cited here. She bases her story on studio visits with the artist and provides the additional point of view of the artist.

Solomon relates that Murray lives in a loft in lower Manhattan and that her studio is long, bright, and in the front of her living space. "Brushes in all sizes and crumpled tubes of oil paint are heaped on wooden carts, and the air is thick with their greasy scent. A miniature easel, complete with a picture by one of the artist's children, stands in a corner." Solomon may mention the snapshot of the artist's child early in her article because she eventually interprets Murray's paintings to be, in significant part, about home life. Throughout the article she provides other biographical information about the artist. Murray is "modest and unassuming," soft spoken, wears no makeup, and has frizzy gray hair. She was born in Chicago in 1940 into an Irish-Catholic family. She earned a BA from the Art Institute of Chicago and attended graduate school at Mills College, in Oakland, California. Solomon comments that Murray's life with her second husband and two young daughters seems pleasantly normal. She has a son in college. She does not approve of a rich life style.

Solomon also tells us early in her article that the artist has postcard reproductions of favorite paintings near her table, including several of Cézanne's. The critic eventually introduces art historical references as a second important interpretive theme of Murray's paintings.

Solomon writes a lively descriptive and interpretive summary of the artist's work: "A Murray painting is easy to recognize. More often than not, it consists of a big canvas loaded up with forms and colors that bounce off one another in an anarchic, ebullient way." Although the paintings seem abstract, "they are full of references to human figures, rooms and conversations. Narratives quickly present themselves. The pictures can suggest squabbling children, for instance, or a woman sitting alone at a table, feeling edgy. But usually their meanings aren't so literal and their protagonists aren't people but personable shapes and objects: Cracked cups, chubby paint brushes and overturned tables (with legs that can vehemently kick) are among the artist's favorite motifs" and "vibrant, eccentrically shaped canvases in which giant coffee cups and flying tables put a homey spin on vanguard art." Solomon also writes that "one of the hallmarks of a Murray painting is that it looks clunky and even awkward, yet is layered with subtle psychological meanings." She interprets Murray's essential theme to be interiors through which she gets at "life's frayed, dangling ends."

Solomon explains Murray's process of creating her elaborately three-dimensional canvases. The artist makes a pencil sketch and then fashions a clay model of the shaped canvas she wants, and assistants build the stretcher out of plywood, and stretch the canvas over it. Murray says that she paints not knowing what will go onto the shapes of the canvas. The critic quotes the artist saying "I want my paintings to be like wild things that just burst out of the zoo." It usually takes about two months for Murray to complete a painting, and she usually goes through a period of hating the painting before she resolves it and is then excited about it.

In addition to the mention of Cézanne reproductions in the artist's studio, the critic writes that Murray's "work recapitulates great moments in 20th-century art. Cubism's splintered planes, Fauvism's jazzy colors, Surrealism's droopy biomorphic shapes, the heroic scale of Abstract Expressionism—it's all there in a Murray painting." The critic also posits what is not there in the painting: "Unlike most other art stars of the 1980s, Murray isn't interested in art that cleverly comments on its own limitations. Her work isn't ironic. It doesn't turn art history into a joke. It's not about gender politics. And it doesn't try to demonstrate that painting is being swallowed up by the media. Rather, it uses an admittedly post-modern apparatus—the shaped and sculpted canvas—to posit an old-fashioned (and even corny) belief in the pleasure of paint." Solomon argues further that Murray does not "appropriate" and mock the past; rather, she shows how the past can still speak to us today.

Solomon also claims that feminists see Murray's paintings as a reworking of abstract painting from a female perspective, and that the "high and low crowd" sees salutes to Dagwood and Dick Tracy. Solomon concludes that Murray's paintings are both abstract and representational, and that in their abstractness they appeal to Modernists who desire to separate art from life, and in their representational aspects, they appeal to Postmodernists who see a direct tie between art and life.

Solomon relies heavily on art theory to develop her interpretation of

Murray's work. The critic understands the history of 20th-century theory, mainly Modernism and Postmodernism, and explains how Murray uniquely negotiates between the two. Her reference to the high and low crowd refers to those debating the merits or lack of merit in making a distinction between fine art and popular art. Such discussion was raised by an exhibition organized by the Museum of Modern Art, "High and Low: Modern Art and Popular Culture." Generally, Modernists maintain a strong dichotomy between fine art and kitsch; Postmodernists find such a distinction elitist and reject it. Regardless, theory and interpretation are clearly linked in general, and here theory is specifically related to interpretations of Murray's paintings. The role of theory in criticism, and Modernism and Postmodernism, is explored more fully in Chapter 5.

Other critics pick up, reinforce, and expand on Solomon's interpretive arguments. None refute or contradict those arguments. All the critics writing about Murray seem challenged to find inventive language with which to describe and encapsulate the spirit of her work. The following summary statements from different critics are examples of good, lively, interpretive writing about art.

Robert Hughes writes that "for her, art is about dreaming and free association, the goofy insecurity of objects that sidle through the looking glass of a tactile sensibility and peek out, transformed, on the other side."[39] Jude Schwendenwien in the *New Art Examiner* writes about Murray's "cakey paint" and states that "the topsy-turvy arrangement of biomorphic-shaped canvases suggests jigsaw puzzle pieces waiting to be reunited."[40] Robert Storr writes about Murray's "saturated hues, jutting and twisting elements of relief, and a general imagistic tumult of swollen shapes, household objects and writhing limbs typify the direct, at times almost overwhelming address of her work."[41] He also writes about the dark palette she employs and her anxious touch, and the increasingly complex skeleton and tense musculature of her shaped canvases. He continues: "At once gut-turning and thrilling, her images vibrate optically with the stresses she has learned to place upon her canvases. . . . Dimpling and splitting at the seams like over inflated Mae Wests, jackknifing across the wall like collapsing lawn chairs, and separating into thick strands like pizza dough." Storr also writes of arcing bars and bulbous shapes, a washing-machine tumble of elements, her rowdy and cartoony vocabulary, a picture's silly-putty surface, and concludes that Murray is unafraid of making a mess, and that when using paint she takes "fervent interest in all the elemental states, from liquid to solid, that this miraculous muck can assume."

Ken Johnson, writing in *Arts Magazine* about a 1987 show of Murray's paintings, offers this summary paragraph: "The new paintings look like huge slabs of clay. The waxy rich painterly surfaces suggest not the delicate thinness of paint on canvas, but, rather, the visible part of a fleshy solidity. You feel as though you could dig your fingers inches deep into the paint and pull out heavy handfuls of it."[42] He also writes of two kinds of shapes, amorphous and rectangular, which are "stretched like Silly Putty by a pair of giant hands . . . the normally static rectangle seems to be buffeted by a languid breeze, drooping like a wet sheet on a clothesline, corners flapping this way and that." He terms the paintings "hyperactive" and compares them to a clinically manic person acting out uncontrollable impulses. Whether the paintings are angry, gloomy, or gleeful, Murray shows her excitement with the process without bringing the paintings to "finicky completion."

In addition to these general interpretive remarks, Johnson offers some specific interpretations of a few individual paintings. These are quoted here because they are clear examples of sexual interpretations. Johnson interprets a 1987 painting (see color plate 6) to be "dream symbolism of sexual intercourse": "Consider *My Manhattan,* the central image of which represents an encounter between a monumental teacup full of orange liquid and a hugely swollen, weirdly flexible spoon. The cup, seen from overhead, is precisely outlined but cubistically skewed, its structure jauntily raked, its mouth a vast circle filled with the hot drink. The spoon's structure, by contrast, is at once turgid and unnaturally fluid. Along the picture's top edge looms its bulbous handle which narrows to a serpentine tube winding in a clockwise spiral around the picture's right edge to enter the cup from below. It ends, not as the broad concavity of a normal spoon, but rather, as a sort of knob with a canvas-penetrating hole in it. From the point where the spoon splashes the liquid, giant orange droplets shoot out of the cup." In a following paragraph, he offers this further evidence for his interpretation: "the rippling contour of the picture's edge, the three dimensional table limbs attached onto each side like embracing arms and legs, the splay-legged table collapsing under the weight of the cup, and the pervasive, mistily harmonious blue ambience around the hot center. It all adds up to an allegory of perceptual dissolution in sexual ecstasy." In *Chaotic Lip* (1987) he sees a reference to menstruation, in *Pompeii* (1987) "a phallically over inflated spoon volcanically ejaculates a massive, seminal drop."

Nancy Grimes, writing in *Art News,* is also exuberant in her critical expression about Murray's paintings and also sees some sexual implications in the work, although not as many as Johnson. She writes that Murray has allowed painting "to get wet again, to roll around in pigment, humor, narrative, and sex."[43] She then adds a paragraph about one painting to amplify her point: "*Beginner's* three forms—loopy line, kidney-shaped biomorph, and rectangular ground—bud, break, and multiply into a profusion of eccentric, garishly colored shapes that trigger chain reactions of associations. The line relaxes into meandering ribbons of steam, crackles across forms like bolts of lightning, puckers into ropes of intestine, and, in the latest works, ties itself into a hangman's noose. The embryonic blob swells, shrinks, and branches into palettes, stomachs, question marks, paintbrushes, penises, cups, hands, dirigibles, clouds, dogs. The rectangle tips, becoming a diamond; explodes into stars and zigzags; ends gently, assuming the form of an open book; and fractures into the planes of architectural spaces and furniture."

Like Solomon, other critics also give interpretive emphasis to the importance of Murray's deliberate inclusion of the domestic into her semi-abstract paintings. Janet Kutner writes in *Artnews:* "Murray continues to base her imagery on ordinary still-life, household and studio items such as cups and saucers, tables and chairs, paintbrushes and palettes; on punctuation marks such as commas and exclamation points; and on variations of cartoon characters including Tweety Bird, Popeye and Gumby."[44] She also observes that Murray's "signature shapes, whether household objects or punctuation marks, refuse to give up their identity no matter how greatly she distorts them."

Gregory Galligan, in *Arts Magazine,* is very explicit in his interpretation of the "domestic presence" in Murray's paintings and gives it his primary interpretive attention in his review of her work.[45] He specifically mentions Murray's recurring use of the table "which rears up like a horse on its two hind legs. This is a ghastly, near ghostly presence, which Murray would return to time and again over the following years." He asks of this "demonic presence," with its four legs twisting grotesquely toward the spectator, if they are "striving to stamp upon one's limbs, or to wrap around one's torso in a suffocating squeeze?" He asks of another comic and cartoonlike reference, "What could be the meaning of an outburst of crimson tears, which are discharged from a metallic-colored tube the dumb shape of a car muffler?"

Galligan interprets Murray's paintings to provide "equivocal truths about daily life; in one sense such truths are mundane and harmless, and in another they are extraordinary and unpredictably aggressive." For him, her sculptural images of stout coffee cups, plump paint brushes, floating kitchen chairs, twisted dining tables with legs like rubber are symbols both familiar and fantastic. "They are symbols of everyday domestic routine and yet near-sacred idols of some secret, spiritual meditation. Like an autistic child who seems to commune with the most mundane kitchen utensils, Murray celebrates the domestic world with a spasmic, attractive sense of humor."

Interpretations of her work are not limited to discussions of the domestic and psychological implications of the ordinary; they also discuss Murray's bold experimentation with form based on the artist's solid knowledge of art history. Grimes, for instance, praises Murray's ability "to fuse monumental scale and manic formal invention with a chatty intimacy and rigorous attention to tradition." Similarly, Johnson writes that Murray's paintings "are a collision between the worlds of Bosch and Disney," and, most importantly, he interpretively asserts that "a formalist reading will get only half of what Murray's art is about." That is, Johnson is arguing, if one attended only to all the formalist inventions that Murray has achieved, one would have half an understanding of her work.

Also like Solomon, other critics find Murray's knowledge of and references to art history important. In her article, Solomon noted Cubism, Fauvism, Surrealism and Abstract Expressionism. In his review, Johnson interprets Murray's paintings with the help of references to Picasso, Kandinsky, Miró, Gorky, de Kooning, Kline, anti-Minimalism, Jennifer Bartlett, Susan Rothenberg,

Nicholas Africano, Joel Shapiro, and the schools of New Image or Bad Painting. Storr writes that "with Matisse, Murray shares an exquisite sensitivity to the erotics of color; with Davis, a robust instinct for the sheer materiality of paint. For the former, pleasure was totally available to the eye; for the latter it was all pulse and pressure." Galligan interprets Murray's work to be referring to the past while it simultaneously points out directions for future developments in art. He states that "with a keen sense of art history, Murray integrates the past with pure, unbridled innovation." He also credits her with "a synthesis of a cartoon like funkiness, and expressionistic angst, and an almost Cubist ordering of her impressions." Grimes writes that Murray has learned the formalist lessons of the 1960s and has incorporated them with the desire for autobiographical work of the 1980s.

Just as the critics interpret her work to be not only about domestic issues—although they make it clear that her work importantly refers to real life—so do they also interpret her work to be about other art, but not exclusively. They think it significant that her art refers both to life and to the history of art. Storr expresses the idea this way: "Consistent with this emotional urgency and sensory immediacy, her formal intuitions always resonate with existential as opposed to merely art-historical significance, and like all psychic experiences they deepen with duration." That is, if her art were merely full of art historical references, and not about real-life situations, it would be much less than it actually is. Some art of the past—modernist art, for example—was primarily about itself and other art and purposely divorced from daily living. Some art is exclusively or primarily about social life and demonstrates little reference to or knowledge of the history of art. According to these critics, though, Murray's is referential both to life and to art.

Some of Murray's paintings raise interesting interpretive issues about an artist's intent and the meaning of a work. In 1983, Murray painted *More Than You Know,* a 9' × 9' 3"–shaped canvas (see color plate 7). Solomon tells us the work is clunky and awkward, yet it is layered with subtle psychological meanings. She tells us that the painting is made of ten overlapping canvases, and that at first it seems haphazard but then a story quickly emerges: "The painting depicts an interior—a sitting room perhaps—that appears to be furnished with a green table and a red Windsor chair. A patch of blue suggests a window filled with sky. It all looks perfectly serene until you notice the note on the table, a scrap of paper inscribed with an urgent red message. And then you see the bean shape next to it, an undisguised reference to the gaunt, howling face in Edvard Munch's masterpiece, *The Scream.* The table, it seems, is really a human figure, its arms flung up in despair. What is going on here?" Solomon asks the artist and Murray responds that the painting is about her dying mother and is based on a memory of when she visited her mother in a hospice—"She looked very thin and it was horrible." Murray says that the Munch face is supposed to be her mother's face and also her footprint. The table is supposed to be her mother's body, flying out of the room. Interestingly, there is much the critic can determine without this additional information from the painter. The painting looks clunky, yet it is layered with psychological meaning. It refers to Edvard Munch's *The Scream*. There is a story in the painting. It is of an interior with a green table and a red chair, and the room has a window. The table has a scrap of paper on it. The table looks like a human figure, with its arms flung up in despair. How did Solomon the critic do before she heard the story from Murray the artist? She came pretty close to the artist's view of the painting.

Murray made two other paintings, *Deeper than D* (1983) and *Can You Hear Me?* (1984) in which she referred to her dying mother. Two other critics write about these paintings, also without knowing Murray's intended reference to her dying mother. About the second painting, Storr writes: "*Can You Hear Me?*, whose title amplifies a perfectly ordinary query into an edgy plea, features a small ghostly head from which emanate a pair of swelling armlike shapes painted a chill blue tinged with acid yellow, and a single inflated exclamation-point form painted red and acid green. The face is a direct reference to the contorted visage of the figure in Edvard Munch's *The Scream,* while the monstrous blue extensions are something we have not seen before; or rather something we have never seen in a form at once so abstract and so visceral." Thus, he too seems to come close to the artist's stated intent and private references, although he is not aware of the specific reference.

Galligan writes about both *Can You Hear Me?* and *Deeper than D,* as well as about *More Than You Know.* He found that they referred to the artist's mother only after reading the exhibition catalog. He discusses the seriousness of her paintings and writes that one begins to sense their seriousness in *Deeper than D*: "Here the form of a blue kitchen chair, its legs splayed wide, is suspended in a seemingly airtight room. Everything is viewed from a high aerial perspective. Even if we did not know as we do now (thanks to the catalog notes), that the painting is a meditation on the subject of her dying mother, we might have suspected that this was a rather spiritual symbol by virtue of the intense light that pours in through a slight window, penetrating the chair like a strong, celestial beam." He too infers the sense of the painting without knowing the specific intent of the artist. Thus, although an artist's intent, when known, might be interesting and may be relevant to the interpretation of an artwork, it is not necessary to the interpretation.

Finally, regarding interpreting Murray's paintings, critics also write about what Murray *doesn't* do in relation to art history and to her fellow artists. Solomon interprets what Murray's work is *not* about—namely, it is not ironic (but direct), it is not about its own limitations (as is much Postmodern art), and it is not about gender politics. Hughes writes that "Murray is not a 'feminist artist' in any ideological sense, but her work, like that of Louise Bourgeois or Lee Krasner, gives a powerful sense of womanly experience: Forms enfold one another, signaling an ambient sense of protection and sexual comfort—an imagery of nurture, plainly felt and directly expressed, whose totem is the Kleinian breast rather than the Freudian phallus." Storr agrees with Hughes on this point, but says it differently: "Indeed, while Murray is neither doing 'woman's work' nor making avowedly 'feminist' art, the situations presented and emotions evinced by her pictures reflect a decidedly female perspective." A point that should be made here concerns relevancy. Murray's paintings are *not* about many things, but how they are or are not about feminism is relevant for the critics to consider because of the social context of the period during which the paintings were made. Feminism was a force in the world and the art world in the 1980s, Murray was painting in the 1980s, and she is a woman dealing with subjects in the home. Whether her work is feminist or feminine is a relevant and interesting topic for critics and readers to consider interpretively.

When drawing conclusions about the interpretations of Wegman's work, the discussion claimed that all art is influenced by other art and that some art is about other art. These themes are particularly true of interpretations of Murray's work.

The critics cited have generally agreed in their interpretations of Murray's work, but have different emphases. Johnson, for example, employed a sexually interpretive strategy to decipher Murray's paintings. He offered a sexual interpretation and then provided explicit evidence, based on what he had noticed and pointed out in the paintings. Johnson's is a clear example of an interpretive argument. Interpretations are arguments based on evidence that may be drawn from within and without the artwork itself.

Although others did not also use this interpretive strategy, Johnson's argument is nevertheless reasonable. These differences among critics support another generalization—namely, different interpretations of the same work can broaden and deepen understanding of the work.

In the next section, several principles of interpretation are presented that derive from the various interpretations of the work of Wegman, Holzer, and Murray, and from a few other examples.

PRINCIPLES OF INTERPRETATION

1. **Artworks have "aboutness" and demand interpretation.** This is the fundamental principle on which this chapter depends. It is very basic and readily accepted by critics and aestheticians, but it is sometimes disputed by artists, an occasional art professor, and, more frequently, by art students who hold that "art speaks for itself," or "you can't talk about art." All the examples of interpretations in this chapter disprove the latter position. Even art that seems readily understandable, such as Wegman's, can and does sustain interesting interpretations that would not readily emerge from merely viewing the work. That art is always *about* something is also a principle around which whole books have been written—Nelson Goodman's *Languages of Art*[46] and Arthur Danto's *Transfiguration of the Commonplace*,[47] for example. Very briefly, this principle holds that a work of art is an expressive object made by a person, and that, unlike a tree or a rock, for example, it is always about something. Thus, unlike trees or rocks, artworks call for interpretations.

2. **Interpretations are persuasive arguments.** This principle might better be

written as two separate ones: Interpretations are arguments and critics attempt to be persuasive. Because critics attempt to be persuasive, their interpretations rarely jump out as logical arguments with premises leading to a conclusion. One clear example of an interpretive argument is Ken Johnson's argument concerning what he sees as the sexual content of Murray's paintings. He argues that *My Manhattan* is a painting full of symbols referring to sexual intercourse. His evidence is a list of persuasive descriptions of aspects of the painting. He notes a cup and a hugely swollen, weirdly flexible spoon. He writes that the spoon is turgid and unnaturally fluid. The spoon's handle is serpentine and winds around the canvas's edge and enters the cup from below. The spoon's handle does not end like a normal spoon with a broad end, but rather it turns into a knob with a hole in it. The knob penetrates an actual hole in the shaped canvas. At the point where the spoon splashes the liquid in the cup, giant droplets shoot out from the cup.

If Johnson's interpretation were put into a logical argument, his descriptions of the painting would be his premises leading to his conclusion that the painting is about sexual intercourse. Criticism, however, is persuasive rhetoric. That is, the critic would like the readers to see a work of art the way the critic sees it. And there is more than one way to be persuasive about an interpretation. One could put forth a formally logical argument, with premises and a conclusion—a syllogism, for instance. Critics, however, are much more likely to be persuasive by putting their evidence in the form of lively writing, using colorful terms in carefully wrought phrases, to engage the reader with the critic's perception and understanding so that eventually the reader will be likely to think, "Yes, I see what you mean. Yes, I agree with the way you see it." Several well-written summary paragraphs quoted about Murray's paintings are good examples of such persuasive critical writing. Critics do rely on evidence in their interpretations, evidence from observations made about the artwork, or from information about the world and the artist. But they present their interpretations not as logical arguments, but as persuasive literary essays. Interpretations can and should, then, be analyzed as arguments to see if they are persuasive because of both the evidence they present and the language in which they are written.

3.   **Some interpretations are better than others.** This principle defends against the often heard objection, "That's just your interpretation," by which is usually meant that no one interpretation is better than any other, and further, that no interpretation is more certain than any other. On the contrary, all interpretations are not equal. Some interpretations are better argued, better grounded with evidence, and therefore more reasonable, more certain, and more acceptable than others. Some interpretations are not very good at all because they are too subjective, too narrow, don't account sufficiently for what is in the artwork, are irrelevant to the artwork, don't account for the context in which the artwork was made, or simply don't make sense.

4   **Good interpretations of art tell more about the artwork than they tell about the critic.** Good interpretations clearly pertain to the work of art. Critics come to a work of art with a history, knowledge, beliefs, and biases that do, should, and must affect how they see a work of art. All interpretations reveal something about the critic. But critics should show the reader that her or his interpretation applies to what we all can perceive in and about the art object. This principle guards against interpretations that are too subjective—that is, that tell us more about the critic than about the art.

None of the interpretations quoted in this chapter are too subjective. However, it is easy to imagine an interpretation that tells us more about the interpreter than the artwork. Naive viewers of art sometimes offer subjective information about artworks. For example, if shown Wegman's photographs of dogs, young children might tell about their pets at home and how they once dressed up their pets. These remarks would inform us about the children and their pets and not about Wegman's photographs of Man Ray and Fay Ray. Their remarks would be true, might be insightful, and probably would be amusing, but they would not be directly informative about Wegman's work.

If we cannot relate the critic's interpretation to the work of art, the interpretation may be too subjective. If it is, it will not be enlightening about the object, will not be valuable as an interpretation of the artwork, and hence should not be considered a good interpretation.

5   **Feelings are guides to interpretations.** Amid this discussion about reasons and evidence and convincing, persuasive arguments and the desirability of objectivity over subjectivity in interpreting art, we may lose sight of the fact that feelings are important to understanding art. A person's ability to respond to a work of art is emotional as well as intellectual, from the gut and heart as well as from the head. The dichotomous distinction between thought and feeling is false; on the contrary, thought and feeling are irrevocably intertwined.

If a critic has a gut feeling or strong emotional response, it is important that he or she articulate this in language so the readers can share the critic's feelings. It is also important that the critic relate the feeling to what is in the artwork. A feeling that is not referred back to the artwork may be or may be seen to be irrelevant. The connection between the gut feeling and what in the artwork evoked it is crucial. Without an expressed correspondence between feelings and the artwork, the critic is in danger of being irrelevantly subjective.

6.   **There can be different, competing, and contradictory interpretations of the same artwork.** This principle acknowledges that an artwork may generate very many good and different interpretations. Interpretations may also compete with each other, encouraging the reader to choose between them, especially if they are contradictory.

This principle also encourages a diversity of interpretations from a number of viewers and from a number of points of view. It values an artwork as a rich repository of expression that allows for a rich variety of response. Amid the many interpretations of the art of Wegman, Holzer, and Murray, one critic has noted something that another has overlooked or has not mentioned. One critic has presented an interpretation that contributes to another critic's previous interpretation. These enrich our understanding of a work of art. They also enrich our appreciation of the responding human mind.

Despite this appreciation of diversity, it may not be logically possible for one to hold all interpretations about the artwork if those interpretations are mutually exclusive or contradictory. We ran into such a situation with interpretations of Holzer's work. Some critics said there was nothing to interpret; others found much to interpret. We could not logically hold both positions simultaneously. We could, however, sympathetically understand contradictory interpretations if we understood the beliefs of the critic, or in ordinary language, understood where the critic was coming from.

7. **Interpretations are often based on a world view.** We all move through the world with a more or less articulated set of assumptions about existence, and it is through these that we interpret everything, including works of art. Some critics have a more finely articulated and consistent world view, based on a study of philosophy or psychology, for example, than others. They may operate on the basis of psychoanalytic theory or offer neo-Marxian critiques of all works of art they encounter. This chapter includes a psychoanalytic interpretation of Wegman's work, a semiotic interpretation of Holzer's work, and a sexual interpretation of Murray's paintings. Sometimes critics make their basic assumptions explicit; more often, however, they leave them implicit. Once the critic's world view is identified, by either the critic or the reader, we need to make a choice. We can accept the world view and the interpretation that it influences, or reject both the world view and the interpretation; we can accept the world view but disagree with how it is applied to the artwork, or reject the general world view but accept the specific interpretation it yields.

8 **Interpretations are not so much absolutely right, but more or less reasonable, convincing, enlightening, and informative.** This principle holds that there is no one true interpretation of an artwork and that good interpretations are not so much "right" as they are compelling, original, insightful, and so forth.

9 **Interpretations can be judged by coherence, correspondence, and inclusiveness.** A good interpretation should be a coherent statement in itself and should correspond to the artwork. Coherence is an autonomous and internal criterion. We can judge whether an interpretation is coherent without seeing the artwork. Either the argument makes sense or it doesn't. Correspondence is an external criterion that asks whether the interpretation fits the artwork. A coherent interpretation may not sufficiently correspond to the work being interpreted. For instance, regarding Wegman's humorous videotapes and Polaroids of dogs, Robbins interprets them as angry and argues that Wegman employs humor that masks the artist's genuinely subversive aims. This interpretation is coherent, but does it correspond to the pictures? Are you, the reader, convinced that Wegman is a very angry radical who wants to subvert society? This principle also protects against interpretations that tend toward unleashed speculation by asking them to adhere to what is actually in the artwork.

The demand for inclusiveness ensures that everything in a specific work is attended to, or that everything in a body of work is accounted for. If an interpretation omits mention of an aspect of an artwork, that interpretation is suspect. If an interpretation *could* have accounted for that aspect, it is not as flawed as if the interpretation *could not* have done so. The critics in this chapter and throughout the book usually discuss several of an artist's works, not just one. When interpreting Wegman's work, for example, they deal with his early video-tapes as well as his later Polaroid photographs; they try to account for both and for the changes that have taken place in his art making. It is risky to arrive at a confident interpretation of one piece of art without knowing something of an artist's other works.

10   **An artwork is not necessarily about what the artist wanted it to be about.** Minor White, the photographer and photography teacher, once commented that photographers frequently photograph better than they know. He was cautioning about paying too much attention to what photographers said about their own work. Because of his experience in leading many photography workshops, he felt that photographers' works were often much different from what the photographers thought them to be—and better than they knew them to be. Thus, he minimized the importance of the artists' interpretations of their own work.

We can probably all agree that the meaning of an artwork should not be limited to the artist's intent. Its meaning might be much broader than even the artist knows. The critics of some of Murray's paintings were quite able to derive relevant meaning from the paintings even though they were unaware she was referring to her dying mother. They correctly saw the paintings as more generally about dying and loss. It is reasonable that these paintings not be limited to the artist's specific reference.

Some artists do not work with specific, conscious intentions to express particular and definite ideas. Some are quite comfortable having no specific intent while they are working. About making her paintings, Susan Rothenberg, for example, says: "The results are a way of discovering what I know and what I don't, what I didn't know I knew, and what I want to learn—which are things that seem close to unpaintable, which is why I love painting, which is not quite like the donkey and the carrot, but close."[48]

An artist's interpretation of his or her own work of art (if the artist has one and expresses it) is only one interpretation among many, and it is not necessarily more accurate or more acceptable just because it is the artist's. Some artists are quite articulate and speak and write insightfully about their work, others do not. Still others choose not to discuss the meaning of their work, not wanting their art to be limited by their own views of it.

This important principle actively places the responsibility of interpretation squarely on the shoulders of the viewer, not on the artist.

11.   **A critic ought not be the spokesperson for the artist.** This is to say that the critic should do much more than transcribe what artists say about their work. It demands that critics criticize.

12   **Interpretations ought to present the work in its best rather than its weakest light.** This principle is in the spirit of fair play, generosity of spirit, and respect for intellectual rigor. A critic's dismissal of an artist's work is a contrary example of this principle.

13   **The objects of interpretations are artworks, not artists.** In casual conversation about art, it is artists who are often interpreted and judged rather than the work they make. In criticism, however, it should be the objects that are interpreted (and judged), not the persons who made the objects. This principle does not exclude biographical information. Over and over again, the critics quoted here have mentioned the lives of the artists. This biographical information, however, is ultimately meant to provide insight into the work. Whether Elizabeth Murray wears makeup and has graying hair may be interesting to the reader wanting to know about her, but facts about her training, for example, are more relevant to understanding her work.

Biographical information reminds us that art does not emerge apart from a social environment. The critics of Holzer's work, for example, discussed her midwestern upbringing and how it is reflected in her artwork. In a few sentences in *Artnews,* critic Curtia James provides a good example of how biographical information can be interpretively informative regarding a sculptural installation by Beverly Buchanan: "Buchanan's *Shack South: Inside and Out* was a full-size shack patched together out of cedar, pine, tine, and cardboard. Buchanan is from Athens, Georgia. As a child she traveled with her father, a professor of agriculture who documented the lives of black farmers. She saw many shacks like this and perceived how each inhabitant put his or her own stamp, or imprint, on the dwelling, an imprint that identified the individual in the community. Buchanan's loving ability to capture that individual imprint made *Shack South* an image of humble nobility."[49]

There is a caution, however, concerning what might be called biographical determinism. Artists should not be limited to their pasts, nor should one argue that if someone is of this race or that gender or this historical background, then their art must be about such and such.

14   **All art is in part about the world in which it emerged.** Donald Kuspit reinforced this principle when he discussed his study of psychoanalysis and its effect on his criticism: "I began to feel that the artist is not exempt from life. There is no way out from seeing art as a reflection or meditation or a comment on life. I became interested in the process, including the artist's life. I became interested in how art reflected the artist's life as well as how it reflected life issues, or existential issues with which we are all involved."[50] Another critic, Pamela Hammond, reminds critics of the importance of this principle, especially when interpreting the art of artists from a different culture. When she writes about the sculpture of ten Japanese artists showing in America, she informs us that traditional Japanese art does not recognize "sculpture" in and of itself. When interpreting the massive, shaped timbers of Chuichi Fujii, she informs us that Japanese

tradition teaches that material possesses a life force equivalent to that of a human, and that "the dualistic Judeo-Christian view that nature defers to man opposes the belief of Eastern cultures rooted in the harmonious coexistence of man and nature, life and death, good and evil."[51] The critic's knowledge of traditional Japanese aesthetics informs her interpretation and our understanding of the work.

All art is in part about other art. The critics quoted in this chapter noted over and over again the artists who influenced Wegman, Holzer, and Murray; they also discussed whose art the works of these artists could be commenting on. Art does not emerge within a vacuum. Artists generally are aware of the work of other artists, and often they are especially aware of the work of certain artists. Even naive artists, or artists who have not been trained in university art departments or academies of art, are aware of and influenced by the visual representations in their societies. This principle asserts that all art can be interpreted, at least in part, by how it is influenced by other art, and further that, in many cases, some art is specifically about other art.

Wegman's art, for example, has been interpreted by several critics as being funny in response to other art being serious. Holzer's art has been characterized as being different from much other art because it is much more concerned with the political world than the art world. Murray's work was interpreted as being about both the history of art and the trials of daily living. Art can be about life, about art, and about both. An important guide to interpreting any artwork is to see how it relates to and directly or indirectly comments on other art.

No single interpretation is exhaustive of the meaning of an artwork. This chapter has provided numerous examples of this principle: the many interpretations of the same works of art. Each interpretation provides subtle nuances or bold alternatives for understanding. According to this principle, one comprehensive but exhaustive interpretation is not a goal of interpretation.

The meanings of an artwork may be different from its significance to the viewer. Any artwork may be more personally significant to one viewer than to another because of connections that viewer makes with the work. Finding personal significance or meaning for one's life in a work of art is one of the many benefits of contemplating art. This principle cautions, however, against assuming that personal interpretations are, in fact, communal.

Interpretation is ultimately a communal endeavor, and the community is ultimately self-corrective. This is an optimistic view of the artworld and scholarship that holds that critics and historians and other serious interpreters will eventually correct less-than-adequate interpretations and eventually come up with better interpretations. This happens in the short run and the long run. Essays in exhibition catalogs of contemporary art can be seen as compilations by scholarly critics of the best thinking about an artist's work to that point. An exhibition catalog of an historical retrospective of a deceased artist is a compilation of the best thinking about that artist's work to that point. Such an historical interpretation would give more plausible interpretations and reject less informative ones.

In the short run, interpretations might be very nearsighted. This principle asserts that eventually, however, these narrow interpretations will be broadened. Feminist revisionist accounts of historical art made by women are a case in point. Scholars for years and for centuries have ignored the art of many women, and it is only now, through work begun by feminist historians, that the historical record is being repaired. This is a good example of the scholarly community correcting its own mistakes, however belatedly. Chapter 4 expands on this notion with the example of Frida Kahlo, whose work is now being given more serious consideration than when she was living and making the work.

Good interpretations invite us to see for ourselves and to continue on our own.[52] This principle follows the previous one as psychological motivation for getting involved with meaning in art. It might also serve as a goal for interpreters: Be friendly to readers by drawing them in and engaging them in conversation, rather than halting discussion with dogmatic pronouncements.

4
JUDGING ART

This chapter examines the critical activities involved in judging works of art. It proceeds similarly to Chapter 3, on interpreting art, because the two sets of activities are very much alike although their results are different. Making interpretations and judgments are both acts of making decisions, providing reasons and evidence for those decisions, and formulating arguments for one's conclusions. When critics interpret works of art, they seek to determine what the works are about. When critics judge works of art, they seek to determine how good the work is or isn't and why and by what criteria. Judgments of art, like interpretations, are not so much right or wrong as they are convincing or unconvincing.

In this chapter, the art of Frida Kahlo, Martin Puryear, and Romare Bearden is examined in light of how critics have judged it. Any number of artists and their critics could have been chosen, and the selection of these three artists is somewhat arbitrary. They were chosen because they make interesting art, and because they represent a diversity of ages, races, ethnicities, and genders. They are three artists of color, two African-American men and a Mexican woman. Puryear is professionally young; Kahlo has been long deceased but her work is enjoying renewed interest; and Bearden recently passed away, and his work is in retrospective exhibition. Two of the artists work in two dimensions, and the third in three dimensions. Consistent with previous chapters, this one examines judgments from many critics, not all of whom agree with each other. The chapter then discusses criteria for judging art and related concerns.

JUDGING FRIDA KAHLO'S PAINTINGS

Peter Plagens

27 May 1991   54-55

In "Frida on Our Minds" in *Newsweek,* Peter Plagens[1] provides an overview of who the artist is, what she accomplished, and how she is being received today. As is typical of Plagens's writing, his review is entertaining, skeptical, at times sarcastic, and occasionally iconoclastic. This section begins by analyzing his review and then comparing it to Hayden Herrera's writings on Kahlo. Herrera has written a biography and several articles about Kahlo and has curated an exhibition of Kahlo's work. Herrera provides a good contrast to Plagens because she is unyielding in her devotion to Kahlo. Next, the views of other critics are examined, and finally some conclusions are reached about critics' judgments of Kahlo's art.

The subheading of Plagens's review is: "With a record sale at Christie's and a biography that keeps selling, the late Mexican painter ranks with the greats. Do we need a movie with Madonna?" The review is two pages long, consists of eight paragraphs, and is accompanied by a black and white photograph of Frida Kahlo and Diego Rivera captioned "Rivera and Kahlo in 1939, in a moment of calm between the pain and other lovers." Two color reproductions of Kahlo's paintings accompany the review, *Two Nudes in a Forest* and *Self-Portrait*. The former depicts two nude females in a landscape; one woman holds the other in her lap and caresses her hair. The latter painting is captioned "The $1.65 million Self-Portrait." Anyone browsing through the weekly newsmagazine and scanning these two pages has already gotten a lot of information from these journalistic teases: The artist is important, she is deceased, she is Mexican, her work is selling for record amounts, her recently published biography is very popular, Madonna wants to play her part in a movie, she and Rivera were troubled lovers.

In the first paragraph of the review, Plagens establishes the undeniable economic value of Kahlo's paintings. He remarks that the record prices in auctions for her paintings are particularly impressive because they were obtained during a recession that was felt especially in the art market. In addition, the record $1.65 million sale price was for a painting by a Latin American artist. The self-portrait will be shown in Mexico, where her work was declared "national patrimony," which means that it cannot permanently leave the country.

In his second paragraph, Plagens details the popularity of the artist herself: There is a PBS television documentary, a Mexican feature film of her life, and the possibility of a Hollywood film with Robert De Niro and Madonna. Madonna visited a high school boyfriend of Kahlo to find out more about her. Plagens quotes Madonna as saying that Kahlo "is my obsession and my inspiration." Plagens relates that Hayden Herrera's 1983 biography of the artist has sold about 100,000 copies and sarcastically calls it "the reigning sisterhood-solidarity gift of choice." In this paragraph, Plagens uses sarcasm again when he refers to the interest in Kahlo as "a highbrow version of the Elvis phenomenon," and he coins the summary term "Fridamania" to characterize her current popularity.

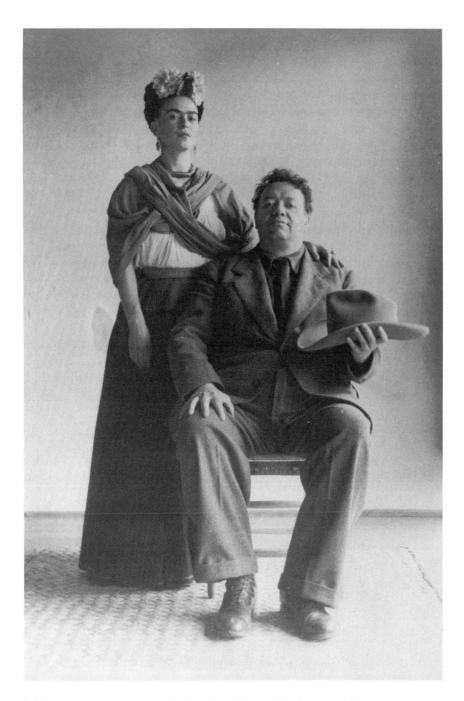

Nicholas Murray, *Diego Rivera and Wife Frida Kahlo,* ca 1930s. Courtesy of George Eastman House.

Plagens's third paragraph is a jumble of thoughts and information. In the lead sentence, he states that good art is often bought for bad reasons, such as status or investment, and that bad art is often bought with the good intention of enjoying the way it looks. He doesn't follow these observations with implications or conclusions about Kahlo's work but asserts that judging Kahlo's art is particularly difficult because of the "saga" of her life. Her life story "strikes about every emotionally correct nerve in the contemporary art world." These are: She was a "faux-naïf surrealist who specialized in confessional self-portraits"; her father was German Jewish, her mother Mexican; as an adult she lived in the shadow of Diego Rivera, the famous muralist. Plagens recounts that Rivera was "gross (300 pounds)" and abused Kahlo emotionally, even seducing her younger sister. He writes that Kahlo was bisexual and "retaliated" with affairs of her own, including some with Rivera's female lovers and one with Leon Trotsky.

The fourth paragraph has the subhead "Brief career." In it, Plagens details the "grisly accident" Kahlo suffered when she was a teenager. He relates that a streetcar hit a bus she was riding, and a handrail entered her abdomen and exited through her vagina. She was semicrippled, endured many operations, had several unsuccessful pregnancies, was in constant pain for which she took drugs and drank alcohol, and, according to Plagens, was possibly an alcoholic. She was politically conscious, changing the date of her birthday so that it would coincide with the start of the 1910 Mexican revolution, and she had a hammer and sickle flag draped over her casket. Plagens writes that, unlike Georgia O'Keeffe or Louise Nevelson "(who may have been one of Rivera's apprentice-lovers)," Kahlo did not make it into the coffee table books while she was still alive. But today "she is as close to a martyr as ever turns up on Park Avenue."

In the fifth paragraph, about halfway through the review, Plagens returns to the question that is the major and organizing theme of the review: "But are the paintings *that* good?" As if to protect himself before giving his own less-than-enthusiastic judgments he first quotes an "83-year-old feminist" in the art world who declines to refer to Kahlo as a "genius" or to her paintings as "masterpieces." Plagens writes that "in general, Kahlo's paintings were better than Rivera's," but here he is referring to Rivera's easel paintings, not his murals, for which Rivera is most revered. For Plagens, "the best Kahlos exude a spiritual intensity inextricably bound to genuine visual invention and technical adroitness." Then comes the "but": According to Plagens, most of the audience's "infatuation" with Kahlo comes from the stories in her pictures—that is, *not* from the "spiritual intensity" or "genuine visual invention, and technical adroitness." The best ones "have a shock-simpatico feel that make you suspect the presence of a psychologist coaching her to draw all the terrible things that the world and Diego did to her." He calls her "a feminist equivalent to Van Gogh," which seems a great compliment until he goes on to say that Van Gogh's tragic life caused his paintings to be "overvalued too."

In the next paragraph, Plagens offers his explanation as to why we are in the midst of what he calls "Frida fever": Today's art world is more interested in artists than their art; Kahlo is a dramatic woman who wore native Mexican costumes; this is a time of revisionist history, during which, according to a male art historian whom Plagens quotes, "almost any woman who ever touched a brush is being systematically studied"; and much art by contemporary women is "as awash in argumentative autobiography as Kahlo's ever was." He also quotes Herrera's biography of Kahlo and the biographer's assertion that Kahlo did not engage in Surrealism to escape life as did the European surrealists; rather, she came to terms with reality through her art. Plagens sarcastically states that this is the "culturally correct" thing for her to have done.

His final two paragraphs are subheaded "Too passionate." In the first of them, he admonishes Kahlo for her political activism—she painted a portrait of Stalin, in her diary she expressed solidarity with the Soviets, she and her husband were members of the Communist party, and they invited Trotsky to Mexico as part of a plot for his assassination. Herrera denies the last claim. Plagens also blames her "fans" for overlooking these things—"Hey, we're talking heroine worship here." He quotes a female curator, who derides current interest in Kahlo by comparing it to "Warhol mania."

Finally, Plagens raises more concerns about what he calls "Fridaphilia" by claiming, without further explanation, that Mexicans are less enthusiastic about her popularity than Americans because they fear that the art of an essentially inwardly directed Mexican artist is being hyped by Americans. He concludes that "the line between exhibitionism and exhibition is razor thin these days," and, "for better or worse, Frida Kahlo is the woman of the hour."

Hayden Herrera *N Y T   28 Oct 1990   1, 41*

In an article appearing on the first page of the <u>arts section</u> in a Sunday edition of the *New York Times,* Hayden Herrera gives her answers as to "Why Frida Kahlo Speaks to the 90's."[2] Her article appeared about eight months earlier than Plagens's review in *Newsweek,* and is about three times longer. It may well be that Plagens read Herrera's article when preparing his own because the two articles share many of the same facts Plagens refers to Herrera's biography of Kahlo, and a major part of his review addresses why the artist is resonant with the times. <u>Plagens's is a skeptical view</u>; Herrera's is <u>completely positive</u>. In her opening paragraph, she writes: Frida Kahlo "has captivated everyone from scholars writing dissertations to Chicano muralists, fashion designers, feminists, artists and homosexuals. According to *Sassy,* a magazine for teenage girls, she is one of 20 women of this century that American girls most admire." Herrera tells us that Kahlo is the subject of books, films, theater pieces, and dance performances, and that revisionist historians and Postmodernists have gotten her into university curricula. Whereas Plagens derides Kahlo's popular acclaim, Herrera boasts that Kahlo is an "international cult figure" and that Kahlo buttons are available, as well as posters, postcards, T-shirts, comic books, jewelry, and even a Kahlo mask and a framed self-portrait into which a silver sacred heart has been inserted.

Herrera explains that Kahlo had only two one-person exhibitions in her lifetime; she lists where her work is currently being shown internationally and tells of its success at auctions. She mentions three different Hollywood projects underway, the most spectacular involving Madonna, who wants to play Kahlo. She relates that Madonna has bought two of Kahlo's paintings, one of which is *My Birth,* a bloody depiction of childbirth. Herrera praises this particular picture, which she says must have been shocking in its time and in its place of origin: "As a marginalized voice—a woman, an invalid, a Mexican and the wife of one of the most famous painters in the world—Kahlo had the freedom to break rules."

Herrera interprets Kahlo's chief subject to be her pain—pain from the accident and thirty-five surgical operations; pain at not being able to bear children; and pain from her turbulent marriage of twenty-five years to Rivera, "who deceived her often—even with her favorite sister" and who divorced her once for a year. Herrera praises Kahlo's use of her pain as her content: "All women, indeed, anyone who has experienced loss or rejection in love, can empathize with the misery Frida expressed in her self-portraits with broken hearts." And further, "Kahlo's autobiography in paint is exemplary . . . For people preoccupied with psychological health, fearful of AIDS and appalled by drug abuse, the gritty strength with which she endured her illness is salutary. Although her paintings record specific moments in her life, all who look at them feel that Frida is speaking directly to them." So, although Plagens is disapproving of the "shock-simpatico feel" of Kahlo's paintings, Herrera praises her for showing her self-discovery and self-disclosure, and for sharing the private facets of her living. Herrera argues that Kahlo's portraits "go beyond petty self-absorption. . . . When she displays her wounds we immediately know that those wounds stand for all human suffering. She is thus a kind of secular saint. People look at her image and find strength." In his review, Plagens derides Kahlo as a "martyr"; in hers, Herrera praises Kahlo as a "saint."

Herrera values Kahlo for overcoming the limitations of her culture: "Although she lived in a conservative, male-dominated culture and in the heyday of muralism when a woman making small, highly personal easel paintings could not win much respect, she valued her idiosyncratic talent." She continues: "Frida never competed with nor deferred to Rivera. . . . She was fiercely independent as an artist, and her paintings could not be more different from his."

Herrera makes the further point that when Kahlo painted women, she presented them much differently from the way in which male artists paint women: "When Kahlo painted herself, she did not see a passive repository of a man's gaze; she saw an active perceiver, the female painter scrutinizing her own being, and that included her sexual being." In support of Kahlo's feminism, Herrera quotes the painter Miriam Schapiro: "Frida is a real feminist artist in the sense that during a period of history when the accepted modes of truth were truth seen through men's eyes, she gave us truth seen through the eyes of woman. She painted the kinds of agonies women in particular suffer, and she had the capacity both to be feminine and to function with an iron will that we associate with masculinity." Herrera also admires as liberating Kahlo's unconventional approach to sexuality, arguing that she did not hide her bisexuality—she quotes Kahlo as saying that she delighted in Diego's marvelous breasts—and that she ignored the repressive forces of Mexico's Roman Catholic conservatism, and "swore like a mariachi." Herrera likes that Kahlo wore men's clothing and that in her paintings she emphasized her mustache.

Herrera also credits Kahlo with being ahead of her times by embracing with pride her Mexican heritage and for denouncing racism. She relates a story about Kahlo and Henry Ford, a known anti-Semite. During a formal dinner to which she was invited, Kahlo turned to him and said, "Mr. Ford, are you Jewish?" Thus, although Plagens derides what he calls Kahlo's "cultural correctness," Herrera argues that Kahlo and her work were positive forces in repressed and repressive societies of the past and of today.

Plagens and Herrera agree on many facts concerning Kahlo and her life, but they disagree on the value of these facts. He praises some of Kahlo's paintings for their spiritual intensity and form, and faults others for relying too heavily on psychological narratives. Herrera sees the biographical narratives of the paintings as essential to the work and expressly values the artist for being so unabashedly revealing about her life and her pain. Plagens seems to hold to the assumption that an artist's biography ought not to influence one's aesthetic judgment of the artist's work; yet, inconsistently with this view, he faults the artist for her politics. Herrera does not allow for a separation of Kahlo's biography from Kahlo's paintings.

Both Plagens and Herrera credit Kahlo with being ahead of her time and in sync with ours, but Plagens suspects contemporary art world thinking of being "emotionally and culturally correct" for its "reigning-sisterhood-solidarity," overvalued art, supposed excesses of feminist revisionism, and women's art "awash in argumentative autobiography."

Herrera is pleased with the popularity Kahlo has achieved some thirty years after her death, but Plagens faults Kahlo's audience for its uncritical heroine worship. He also faults the art market for economically overvaluing her work. Herrera implies that the prices are deserved and that, because of Kahlo's life and how she expressed it in her paintings, her work speaks to contemporary viewers of all kinds, especially women, persons with AIDS, and others on the margins of society, and that these people find it salutary. Plagens asserts that just because people like it doesn't mean that it is good.

In his arguments, Plagens employs inventive and effectively sarcastic terms and phrases such as "Fridamania," "feminist equivalent of Van Gogh," "Frida fever," and "Fridaphilia." He gives examples of her popularity, such as the proposed movie starring Madonna, and provides statistics concerning what he considers to be the economic inflation of her art. He quotes supporters of his views, especially women—one whom he identifies as an "83-year-old feminist"—as being knowledgeable and authoritative. Herrera uses the same facts of Kahlo's popularity as evidence of support of her status of greatness. Herrera, too, quotes others in defense of the artist. Herrera offers reasons why people identify with the work and why they admire it. Plagens implies people who like it are being duped.

Other Critics and Kahlo

Joyce Kozloff, writing in 1978, in *Art in America,* seems to agree with some of Plagens's assessments: "This is not an even body of work. Kahlo's early paintings are charming, but the allegorical symbolism can be simplistic. The late works, mostly still-lifes painted while she was very ill, reveal a slackening of touch and concentration. But the work of the middle period is exquisitely crafted, intense and concise in imagery."[3] Unlike Plagens and like Herrera, though, Kozloff embraces Kahlo's use of her suffering and her feminism: "Her suffering can be seen as a metaphor for the oppression of women, and she is exemplary in having dealt openly with taboo female subject matter at a time and place where there was no precedent."

Kay Larson wonders why it took so long for Kahlo to be recognized. She answers that question with "her race, her sex, her subjects, and her proximity to Rivera" and complains that "if an artist of Kahlo's stature remained invisible for so long, how many others might there be?" Larson praises Kahlo for copying "no particular style, not Rivera's, not folk art, not Mexican peasant art, and certainly not Surrealism."[4]

Michael Newman reviewed Kahlo's work by comparing it with the photography of Tina Modotti, with which it was shown in a New York City gallery.[5] Both artists are Mexican and political and, like Kahlo, Modotti was also intimately involved with a prominent male artist—in Modotti's case, Edward Weston. Newman also praises Kahlo for her break with the artistic tradition of her times: "Both artists were women, both of them were influenced by radical tendencies in Mexico and both were politically active; each developed her esthetic influence under the shadow of a well-known male artist with whom she had an emotional relationship; and both challenged the dominant traditions of high art from a marginal position."

In addition, Newman compares Kahlo's and Cindy Sherman's self-portraits. He argues that both women assume roles, but Sherman's portraits are mass-media stereotypes—passive, masochistic images for the male gaze. Kahlo's portraits suggest an autoeroticism, perhaps linked to her bisexuality—portrayals of herself for herself. In this, he argues, Kahlo significantly alters how the female body is presented within the Western tradition of representation. That is, Kahlo is a woman making images of herself for herself, not for a man, not for an oppressive male gaze.

Kozloff writes about the emotional force of Kahlo's paintings: "Even though I was already familiar with Kahlo's work I again felt a shock in confronting it. The extreme smallness of the paintings was disconcerting, somehow contradicting their power and expressiveness, setting up an uneasy dialogue between fierceness and vulnerability." Jeff Spurrier notes the contrasting emotions he felt when passing from Rivera's paintings to Kahlo's at the Dolores Olmedo collection of Mexican art, saying that it was "like going from Charles Dickens to Emily Dickinson, grand to specific, the popular to the personal. Moving from Rivera's jazzy black-dancer series to Kahlo's *The Broken Column* (see color plate 8) is like stepping out of a warm tropical rain into a bone-chilling blizzard of pain."[6]

Many critics identify personally with Kahlo's paintings. Georgina Valverde, for instance, offers a detailed description of *The Broken Column:* "We see a suffering Frida commanding the picture plane. She delicately holds a white drape, which gives her an air of martyrdom. Her body cracks open below the chin to reveal a crumbling Ionic column in place of the spine. Sharp nails of different sizes pierce her flesh, penetrating just enough to stay in place but having no other apparent purpose than to exacerbate the torture. . . . Her tears stream down freely, but her expression is unmoved. She seems to be saying, 'I am this decaying body. My suffering is as infinite as the horizon line. But I am something more, something enduring and strong.' "[7] Valverde's conclusion about this painting and all of Kahlo's work is: "When I see a Frida Kahlo painting I am reminded that to be alive comprises many experiences, all of which, whether sweet or bitter, tender or harsh, joyful or sad, have their worth."

Of particular interest regarding judgments of Kahlo's work is the intermingling of biographical facts with these judgments. Even a permanent exhibition of her work mixes the two: Her birthplace and home in Coyoacán, on the southeastern edge of Mexico City, is now the museum for her paintings. Few critics fail to give biographical information when writing about her paintings. They find her life fascinating. Meyer Raphael Rubinstein, for example, in an article in *Arts Magazine,* quotes a Kahlo letter about being in Paris with its art crowd: "You have no idea the kinds of bitches these people are. They make me vomit. . . . They sit for hours on the 'cafes' warming their precious behinds, and talk without stopping about 'culture' 'art' 'revolution' and so on and so forth thinking themselves gods of the world . . . *shit* and only *shit* is what they are."[8]

Angela Carter writes lovingly of how "Frida Kahlo loved to paint her face. She painted it constantly, from the first moment she began seriously to paint when she was sixteen up till the time of her death some thirty years later. Again and again, her face, with the beautiful bones, the hairy upper lip, and batwing eyebrows that meet in the middle."[9] Carter also interprets Kahlo's hair as a metaphor in her life. "If wild, flowing hair is associated with sensuality and abandon, then note how the hair of Frida Kahlo, the most sensual of painters, hangs in disorder down her back only when she depicts herself in great pain, or as a child." Carter relates that Kahlo cut off her hair after she divorced Rivera for a year in 1940, then grew it back, and plaited it. Carter, like Herrera, argues that Kahlo's paintings emerged directly and irrevocably from her life: "Her work as a painter came out of that accident; she painted in order to pass the time during the lengthy period of recovery nobody ever really expected. . . . The accident and its physical consequences not only made her start to paint, they gave her something to paint about. Her pain." Carter, like Herrera, praises Kahlo for her choice of self as subject matter, for overcoming pain through art, for her suffering, for revealing herself, for being a woman.

Serge Fauchereau, however, calls such biographical information "extrapictorial."[10] He writes that "most of her strengths are extrapictorial; her work moves us, intrigues us, but we don't look to it for the formal qualities that one discovers in a Tamayo or even a Mérida." He writes that "her friends, lovers, infirmities, abortions, and obsessions are part of the subject of practically all her paintings" and that "ordinarily, all this would not necessarily relate to the artist's work, yet in the case of Kahlo one cannot overlook it, since her art is openly autobiographical."

Most of the critics quoted here who value Kahlo's work do not seem to have intellectual difficulty in meshing Kahlo's art and biography, but Plagens, and probably others, are uneasy with such a merge. These latter would rather keep biographical information from interfering with aesthetic judgment. This was certainly the old position held by Formalists, who wanted the viewer to concentrate solely on the work itself, particularly its formal properties, and not be distracted by factors they considered extraaesthetic and therefore irrelevant to art. Recent critics, however, tend to ignore or disdain the separation of biography and social context from critical judgments. (This specific issue is examined more carefully in Chapter 5, on theory.) In summary, then, critics such as Plagens and Herrera may agree on facts but disagree on the value of those facts. Plagens and Herrera have similar descriptions and interpretations of Kahlo's work, but they disagree about its worth—perhaps because they hold different criteria. Plagens, for example, favors formal invention over emotionally gripping narratives in paint. That critics disagree about the same art is healthy if it causes viewers and readers to think through the issues and draw their own conclusions. Different judgments offer us different lenses through which we may view art.

JUDGING MARTIN PURYEAR'S SCULPTURES

There is general agreement that Martin Puryear makes wonderful sculptures (see color plate 9). Neal Menzies writes "Were this the Middle Ages, he might be called the Master of the Forms Which Evoke Feelings."[11] Ann Lee Morgan writes that "like the best art of the twentieth century, his is a vibrant meditation on what art can be."[12] In *Art in America,* Nancy Princenthal calls him "one of the leading contemporary interpreters of form."[13] Carole Calo, in *Arts Magazine,* claims that he is "one of the most exciting and influential sculptors working today."[14] What reasons do these critics give for their judgments?

[handwritten margin notes:] Same as decision making in crit thinking - must understand the perceptual lenses through which we see the world -

When are we coming from? must know + analyze self before we can analyze so judge a situation or an artwork

Menzies rates Puryear's sculptures so highly because they present "a variety of emotional states that range from light-heartedly playful to dangerously sinister and serious." Morgan backs her praise with her observations that Puryear "recharges forms and meanings from the past with sophistication and elegance, investing each synthesis with his own civilized and passionate sensibility—an introspective self-sufficiency entwined with a romantic attraction to the unknowable, to feeling, and to nature." Calo admires Puryear's work because he "is an independent talent who values his own individuality and refuses to conform to what is considered 'in' and marketable. His increasing national recognition attests to the ability of talent, skill, integrity, and vision to override fashion."

Calo, very eloquently and with impassioned writing, sums up her thoughts about the appeal of his work this way: "Martin Puryear's evocative objects appeal to our frazzled spirits. In sculptures that resolve dichotomies, yet present paradoxes, there is a tension that insistently reminds us of the complexity of being. As Puryear reintegrates human experience, nature, and a primal life force, we become aware of the impoverishment of our modern lives. A universal consciousness that extends beyond chronological, geographic or socioeconomic boundaries is expressed in objects which fuse art historical awareness, primitive allusions, and technical sophistication. With quiet conviction Martin Puryear reconciles the disparate fragments of modern existence with the timeless texture of being, instilling in us a longing for a sense of connectedness and wholeness."

These evaluations of Puryear's work are clearly favorable and enthusiastic, yet they are somewhat vague. If one reads these judgments without visual memories or reproductions of Puryear's work, one would probably not be able to imagine what his works look like. This is partially so because his work is so different from that of other sculptors, and critics writing about him acknowledge this directly or allude to it, as in the preceding quotations. Several critics point out that although Puryear has been working and teaching in Chicago since 1978, his work is quite different from and bears no resemblance to the "Chicago style" of a school of artists working in that city during the same years. His work shows "what art can be," not what it has been. He is "independent" and he refuses to conform to what is considered 'in.' Princenthal states that his work has "surprising variety," which affirms that it is difficult to write accurate generalizations about it. One of the problems of writing about any new and different work is that the critic has to invent ways to write about it.

Sculpture (and performance art) is perhaps difficult to present in writing because reproductions of sculpture are even less adequate than reproductions of paintings or photographs, for instance. In most reproductions of the latter, we lose size and scale, and usually color is distorted; in reproductions of sculpture, however, we also lose the all-important third dimension.

The critics' judgments of Puryear's sculpture might also be vague because critics see it as powerful but mysterious. They hesitate to, or can't, pin it down in language. Rather, they write inventively about "forms which evoke feelings," about how the sculptures evoke "a variety of emotional states," and of Puryear's

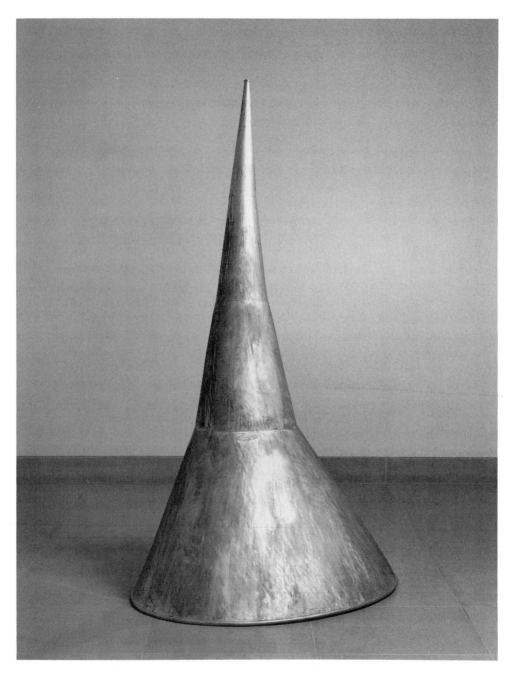

Martin Puryear, *Noblesse O,* red cedar, aluminum paint, 97" × 58" × 46", 1987. Courtesy McKee Gallery, NYC. Collection of Dallas Museum of Art Central Acquisitions Fund and a gift of the 500, Inc. Photograph: Robert Mates.

"romantic attraction to the unknowable, to feeling and to nature." Calo writes of Puryear's "richly allusive forms" and about how the artist "reconciles the disparate fragments of modern existence." These phrases are good examples of how to write meaningfully about mysterious art without overdetermining it or suffocating it with writing that is too specific.

Each of the critics who writes about his work describes and interprets it as well as evaluates it. In an *Artforum* review of a Puryear show, Colin Westerbeck is complimentary of the work but is primarily descriptive and interpretive. He draws an interesting inference about some of Puryear's hutlike pieces from observations about the artist's personality: "From his reticence in interviews and his obvious shyness on public occasions, it is clear that Puryear is a very private person. Several pieces looked as if they were attempts to build a refuge for himself, a hiding place, an interior space large enough for only one man."[15]

Most critics writing about Puryear's work mention one or more of his three major sources of inspiration: other art, other cultures, and nature. They relate his work to the Minimalist sculpture of the past but quickly point out how Puryear's work is different from Minimalism. Morgan states that Puryear rejects Minimalism's disavowal of the expressive self. Calo states that Puryear's sculptures are influenced by an awareness of Minimalism, but that, unlike Minimalism, they are "imbued with interiority," and that, unlike Minimalism, "there is an underlying sense of the human gesture in his work." Princenthal relates his work to that of sculptors Arp, Brancusi, Noguchi, and Bourgeois, but she too talks about how his work is different from that of artists who may have influenced him: "Puryear's accomplishment is to keep such sources in constant, allusive play with other, non-Western references, all the while asserting his own highly idiosyncratic sense of sculptural form."

One non-Western reference Princenthal is referring to is African. She and other critics writing about Puryear usually tell the reader that the artist is an African-American, and that he worked in the Peace Corps from 1964 to 1966 in Sierra Leone, Africa. She also writes of his first-hand experiences with tribal art, and credits these for the "eerie, almost shamanistic sense of presence that emanates from" his work. Princenthal notes that he did a series of installations dedicated to Jim Beckwourth, an African-American frontiersman, and an installation inspired by the yurt, the domed and portable shelter used by nomadic Mongols. Others speak more generally about his references to ritual function. Judith Russi Kirshner, for instance, writes in *Artforum* that "his objects, which connote ritual function but of course have none, communicate through the very intensity of their making."[16] Calo writes of his "raw primal objects," "primitive allusions," and his interest in "communal or tribal ritual and patterns of behavior."

Critics also point out Puryear's surprising unification of African and Scandinavian cultural influences. The artist has long had an interest in woodcraft and has studied woodworking techniques, both in furniture making and in shipbuilding, from craftsmen in Africa and northern Europe, as well as America. Ann

Morgan relates his work to both culture and nature: "He recharges forms and meanings from the past with sophistication and elegance, investing each synthesis with his own civilized and passionate sensibility—an introspective self-sufficiency entwined with a romantic attraction to the unknowable, to feeling, and to nature." Princenthal reviewed a show of Puryear's that featured what she calls "a subtly expressed aquatic theme," with works hinting of birds' necks and a duck's foot. She also calls him "one of the leading interpreters of organic form." Judith Kirshner doesn't see representations of nature but rather references to it in Puryear's sculpture: "Without representing nature his work sometimes evokes the sense of awe usually associated with nature." Calo writes that "one perceives a sense of wholeness, of a primal connection to all living things."

Calo mixes her interpretation of Puryear's work with praise for it. She identifies his themes as "change, mobility, survival, captivity, and communal or tribal ritual and patterns of behavior." For her, his forms are "highly evocative and distinctive." She attributes the formal and emotional tension in his work to his fusing of opposites into meaningful wholes: raw primal objects and sophisticated craftsmanship; an ever-present dialogue between open and closed, linear and massive forms; his simultaneous investigation of interiority and exteriority; a reconciliation of such diverse materials as wire mesh, tar, oak, steel, and wire. Princenthal also observes Puryear's unification of seeming opposites: "A tension runs through Puryear's work between the insinuatingly graceful and the unabashedly awkward." Menzies writes that Puryear evokes "a variety of emotional states that range from light-heartedly playful to dangerously sinister and serious."

Praise for Puryear's craftsmanship is constant. Kirshner praises the craft of Puryear's work because "the pleasure of making was evident in it." Calo writes that Puryear prefers organic materials and insists on fashioning his pieces by hand and that there is "an underlying sense of the human gesture in his work." Calo offers an interesting twist to the traditional criterion of having art that is well crafted. She writes that Puryear's sculptures are well crafted, but that he rejects "an obsessive, fussy attention to detail in favor of a fluid, problem-solving process." She argues that his restraint in using his "excellent technique and craft" is integral to his work and results in a "powerful rawness." When Morgan praises his craft, she too approves of its "fastidious avoidance of excess." Thus, these two critics applaud the careful crafting of objects but see too much finesse with craft as a flaw rather than as something meritorious.

In general, these critics praise Puryear's work for its inventiveness with materials; its successful mixture of bizarre forms; its workmanship, which exhibits great skill but stops short of fastidiousness; and for the evocative presence his pieces have. Importantly and significantly, they praise Puryear's sense of form but also enjoy the works' references to life and to other cultures. Thus, for them, Puryear's art works on formal grounds, but its content is not limited to art about art, as is much Formalism.

Kahlo's art is very specific and Puryear's is vague. Those who like Puryear's work are likely to be comfortable with ambiguity. Different art evokes different reactions and calls into play different criteria.

JUDGING ROMARE BEARDEN'S COLLAGES

This section on Romare Bearden begins with a lovely passage written by Joanne Gabbin, a scholar of African-American literature and an author, about a woman lying on a bed in a collage, *Patchwork Quilt,* made by Romare Bearden in 1970 (see color plate 10). "She represents continuity. Her figure dominates the collage with bold darkness. Shades of black, brown, tan, and red suggest her diverse heritage and her beauty. She is Africa, rooted in the fertile soil of Egypt and Ethiopia, her feet replicating those that graced the burial vaults of the great pyramids. Her torso is stiff and shapely like that of a Ghanaian fertility doll. She is Antilles with her breast ripe to suckle generations of slaves who would endure ocean passage, slavery, and repressive conditions. She is the intense, blues-tinged elegance of America, bowed yet unbent. Her face resembles an African mask in its angularity, softened only by the rose bandanna that circles her head. She is in the past and the present."[17]

Gabbin's remarks are very descriptive and interpretive, yet it is clear by her choice of descriptors that she greatly admires the collage. In fact, this quotation is taken from a two-page "Appreciation" essay of Bearden in a book of art history. It is a tribute to him by a fellow African-American written after his death. Bearden died at age 75 on March 12, 1988. In her brief essay, Gabbin provides much biographical data about the artist. She informs her readers that Bearden was born in 1914 and that he grew up in Harlem during the Harlem Renaissance. She writes that jazz musicians Duke Ellington, Fats Waller, Earl Hines, Count Basie, Ella Fitzgerald, and Cab Calloway influenced the spontaneity and rhythms in the collages Bearden made of remembered performances by these renowned musicians. She also informs us that because of childhood sojourns to Charlotte, North Carolina, and his connections with the people of surrounding Mecklenburg County, he is rooted in southern Black culture. She praises Bearden's "spirited originality" and relates that he studied with George Grosz, that he knew Constantin Brancusi and Georges Braque, and that he also studied at the Sorbonne in Paris, where he explored French Impressionism. She writes that he knew traditional Chinese painting; seventeenth-century Dutch genre painting, from which he learned about representing interior space; and African tribal sculpture; as well as Cubism, Surrealism, and the Social Realism of Diego Rivera.

In another tribute to Bearden published shortly after his death, Michael Brenson, in the *New York Times,* wrote about Bearden that "in his hands, water, paste, paper become instruments of an orchestra, threads in a novel."[18] He also writes that "Bearden was a grand intimist, an improviser who knew all the rules, a virtuoso collagist for whom cutting, tearing, daubing and pasting was both an

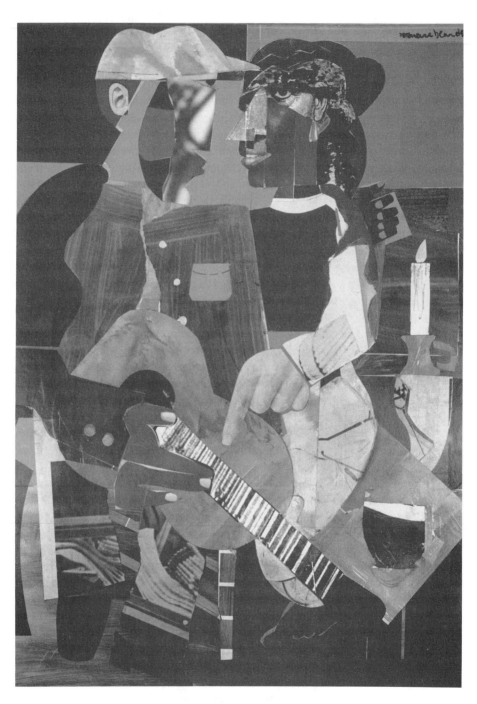

Romare Bearden, *Serenade,* collage and paint on panel, 45 3/4″ x 32 1/2″ 1969. Courtesy of the Estate of Romare Bearden.

interior journey and a narrative adventure. His work is spontaneous and hieratic, rigorous and sensual." However, Brenson faults some of Bearden's work, especially his larger pieces, in size as well as theme—"When he set out to make epic statements, the results could be anecdotal." But he goes on to say that Bearden was a master when he worked on a smaller scale and with personal experience: "No postwar artist poured more epic feeling into intimate content and scale." He adds that "the collages have a voluptuous immediacy." Brenson also praises the consistent growth and unified development of Bearden's work at a time in American art when a rapid change of styles was being rewarded: "His art grew freer, wiser, more poignant in a way that is rare in postwar American art, where the demand for newness and change has pressured artists into defining personal evolution as continually re-creating themselves from scratch." Brenson writes that Bearden's culture always remained important to his work, even at a time when the art world was hostile to narrative, to "memory and place, and preferring art that challenges conventions." Brenson likes the fact that Bearden went against the art world by keeping his work intensely personal. He writes that Bearden chose to depict New York City jazz clubs and family gatherings in the rural South—"the artist as bard whose duty is to give voice to members of the human comedy who cannot always speak for themselves." About women, whom Bearden frequently depicted, Brenson writes: "Women are sources of reverence and wonder throughout Bearden's work."

Brenson gives some biographical information about Bearden not mentioned by Gabbin. He was born in the rural South. He played baseball. He wrote songs and studied jazz, literature, and art. He began making collages when he was 50. He was involved in the civil rights movement and the Black artists movement. He was in sympathy with American Indians because of childhood experiences on a Cherokee reservation in Mecklenburg County, North Carolina. Brenson claims that Bearden remained an outsider in the art world even though his art was well recognized, and that in the 1960s his collages on social themes and Black history began to reach a wide audience.

Peter Plagens reviewed a large retrospective show of 140 of Bearden's works that traveled to Chicago, Los Angeles, Atlanta, Pittsburgh, and Washington D.C. Plagens praises his work: Bearden "found not only a perfect match of subject (urban life in Harlem and memories of its rural Southern roots) and medium (collage). He also discovered a working method with which he could distill sentiment into real beauty. In Bearden's best work, the color sense is every bit as fine tuned as Josef Albers's (and a lot less lablike) and the composition is as tight as that of Stuart Davis, whom Bearden admired."[19] He goes on to write that Bearden used "ingeniously incongruous figure fragments" and "blazing reds and subtle grays" with "surgeon's scissor cuts." Plagens says that "Bearden could hold together a bigger straight collage than just about anyone else, with the probable exception of late Matisse. Moreover, with his chromatic shards, Bearden constructed a visual narrative of the Black American experience that is finally the equal of the same epic tale told in music and literature." Plagens concludes his review by writing that Bearden's collages are "a major statement in American art."

Plagens acknowledges that Bearden never made it into the big history books as did his peers, such as Jackson Pollock and Yves Kline. He agrees with the authors of the exhibition's catalog that Bearden's being Black was "a likely factor." But the main reason was his style: "Bearden was simply out of step during the heyday of gargantuan abstract painting (the largest picture he ever made was a parlor-size 60" × 56").

Plagens notes still other biographical facts. Bearden studied math at New York University. Bessye, his mother, was an editor of the *Chicago Defender,* and played host to such prominent people as W. E. B. Du Bois, Paul Robeson, and Langston Hughes. Bearden was a jazz musician, and Billy Eckstine recorded the tune "Sea Breeze," which Bearden wrote. In addition to being a musician, we learn from Margaret Moorman, Bearden was also a fine writer. In an article on the artist, she quotes Bearden's friend Barrie Stavis, a playwright, saying that "Romie was a brilliant writer. Had he elected to write rather than paint, he would have left a legacy in writing as important and universal as the legacy he left us in paintings and collages."[20] Plagens informs us that for a while Bearden was a Social Realist, painted "pretty cubism" for a while, and went to Paris when Abstract Expressionism came in. He lived above the Apollo Theatre in Harlem in the early 1950s, and, according to Plagens, took up "a mild, Zen-ified version" of abstraction. He was awakened by the civil rights movement of the early 1960s, and founded Spiral, a Black artists group.

Elizabeth Alexander, in a review of Myron Schwartzman's biography of Bearden, provides a one-sentence summary of Bearden's subject matter: "His iconography was magically commonplace: trains seen through doorways, roosters, doves, saxophones, trumpets, washtubs, clouds." She also informs us that the family of Bearden's wife owned a home in St. Martin, the Caribbean, and claims that that landscape influenced him, as did the tiger lilies of South Carolina. She also writes that "the artist was a clever man, analytical and incredibly well-read, humble without being the least bit self-effacing."[21]

In a 1977 review, Nina french-frazier writes that Bearden's collages, "made from vividly colored paper cutouts and reading, like glowing Persian tapestries, as flat brilliant patterns and multiple intersecting planes, are peopled by two-dimensional, silhouetted, allegorical, masked beings identified by emblematic attributes."[22]

In a feature article in *Artforum* in 1984, Myron Schwartzman interprets Bearden as absorbing the legacy of the Cubists, Matisse, and Mondrian yet he "transformed the legacy into a Southern idiom, always stressing the ceremonial dimension in Southern life which gives it universality."[23] In addition to the influence of European artists, Schwartzman also writes, Bearden's "work stems from a creative conflict with an enormous range of predecessors: Dutch, French, Italian, Mexican, Japanese, Chinese and African." In a further interpretive statement, the

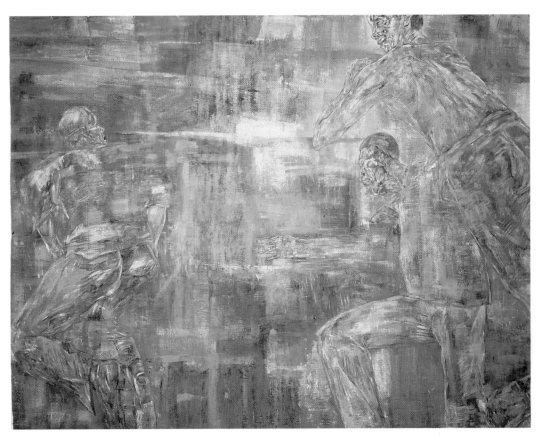

Color Plate 1
Leon Golub, *Night Scene I,*
acrylic on linen, 120" × 156",
1988. Courtesy of Josh Baer
Gallery, New York City.
Photograph: David Reynolds.

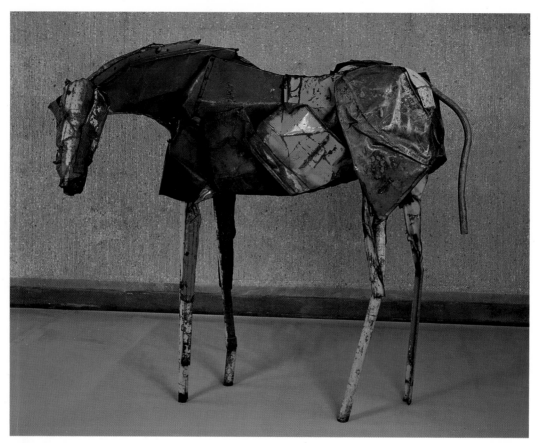

Color Plate 2
Deborah Butterfield, *Joseph,*
painted steel, 85" × 84" × 64",
1988. Courtesy of the Columbus
Museum of Art, Ohio: Gift of
Mary Nancy Davis.

Color Plate 4   ▶
Ann Hamilton and Kathryn Clark,
palimpsest, two part installation:
"Strange Attractors: Signs of
Chaos," newsprint penciled with
stories, beeswax tablets, a fan, a
vitrine, two cabbages, snails. The
New Museum of Contemporary
Art, New York City, 1989.
Courtesy of the artists.
Photograph: Kathryn Clark.

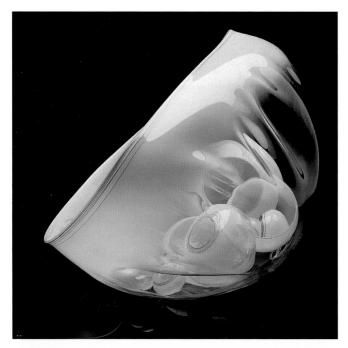

Color Plate 3
Dale Chihuly, *Alabaster Basket
Set with Oxblood Lip Wrap,*
18" × 27" × 21", 1991.
Courtesy of the artist.
Photograph: Claire Garoute.

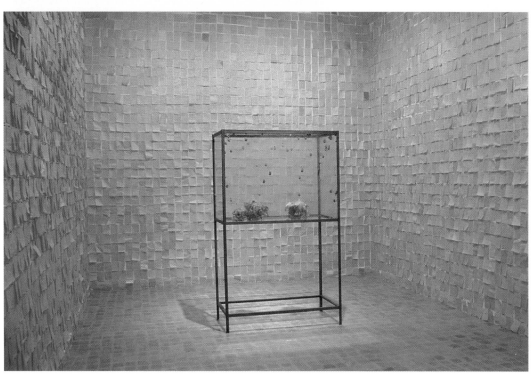

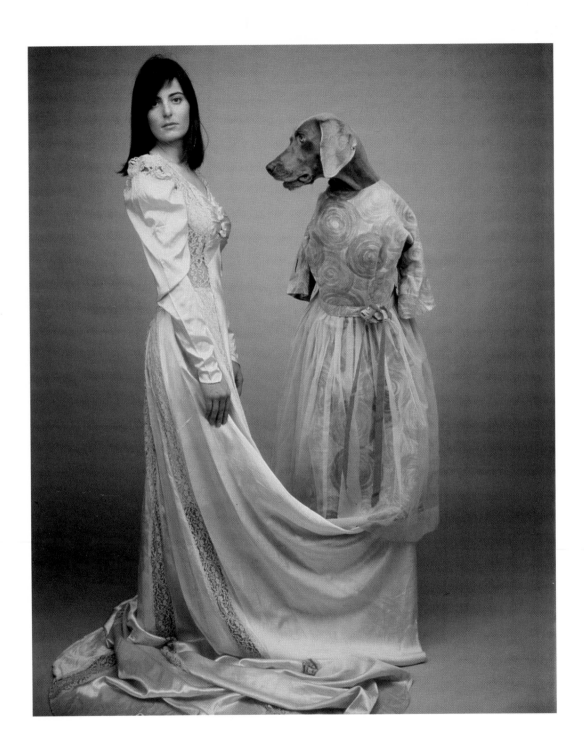

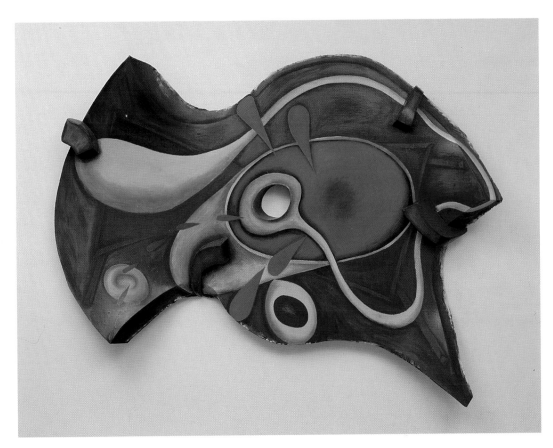

Color Plate 6
Elizabeth Murray, *My Manhattan,*
oil on canvas, 83¼" × 107¼"
× 16", 1987. Private Collection,
St. Louis, Missouri. Photograph:
Geoffrey Clements.

◀ *Color Plate 5*
William Wegman, *Arm Envy,*
20" × 24", Polaroid Polacolor ER
photograph, 1989. Copyright,
William Wegman, Courtesy of
Pace/MacGill Gallery,
New York City.

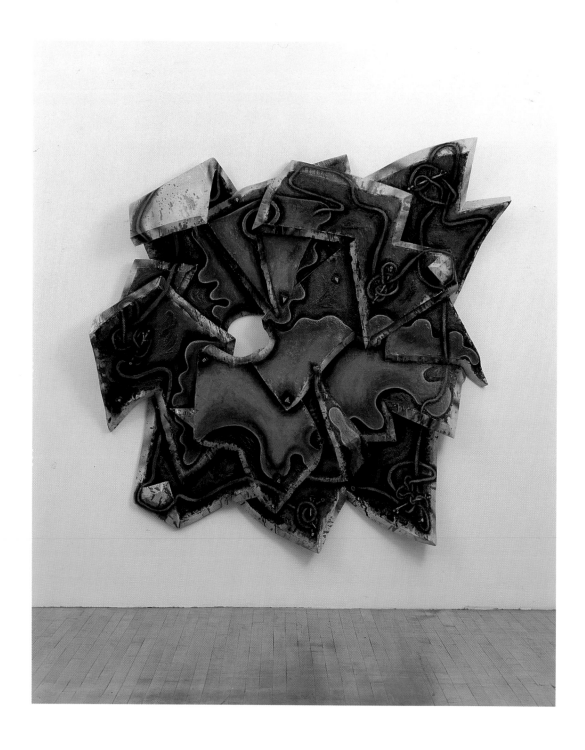

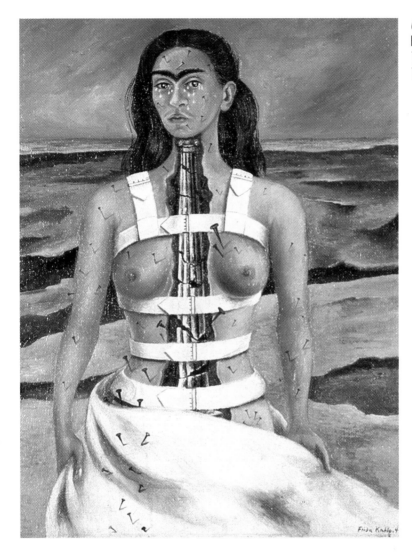

Color Plate 8
Frida Kahlo, *The Broken Column.*
1944. Oil on masonite.
15¾" × 12¼"

◄ Color Plate 7
Elizabeth Murray, *Terrifying
Terrain,* oil on canvas, 87" ×
90" × 10", 1983. Metropolitan
Museum of Art. Photograph:
James Dee.

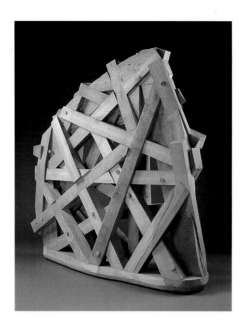

Color Plate 9
Martin Puryear, *Thicket,*
basswood and cypress,
67" × 62" × 17", 1990.
Seattle Art Museum. Gift of
Agnes Gund. Photograph:
Paul Macapia.

Color Plate 10
Romare Bearden, *Patchwork
Quilt,* collage and synthetic poly-
mer paint on composition board,
35¾" × 47⅞", 1970. The
Museum of Modern Art, New
York. Blanchette Rockefeller Fund.

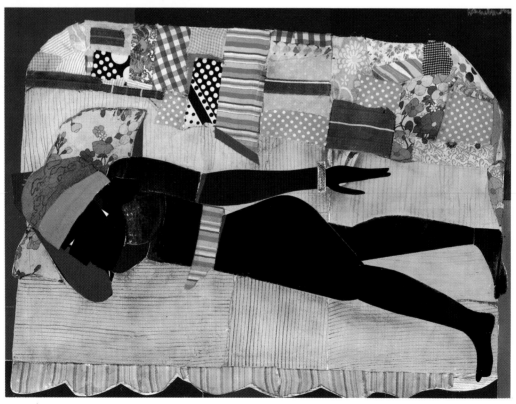

critic writes that "as a meditative human being, Bearden wishes to preserve the uniqueness of his own experience, and, by extension, part of America's experience, from demolition by modern technology and the pace of life it dictates." Schwartzman relates that in the 1960s Bearden painted his own papers before pasting them down on hard masonite and writes about two sets of artworks Bearden produced in the 1970s, "Of the Blues," a series of collages, and "Of the Blues/Second Chorus," a series of oils-on-paper, or monoprints. The critic tells us that the novelist Albert Murray wrote the catalog introduction for "Of the Blues" and virtually all of the titles of individual pieces in both exhibitions. About these works, Schwartzman writes that Bearden "was coming to exploit the possibilities of collage as an improvisational medium in a way that allowed him to unite a freer, more open approach to the canvas with his very subject matter, blues improvisation." The critic concludes by praising Bearden because "he has simply continued to grow by resynthesizing all his past work with each new modulation in style." Ellen Lee Klein reinforces this view in her review of a show late in the artist's life: "There seems to be a new kind of exuberance and an intensified richness in his palette and in his freely combined and applied media. This is an enchanting and personal show which reveals the kind of liberation that comes with maturity and experience."[24]

In the mid-1980s, the Detroit Institute of Art commissioned Bearden to produce a huge mosaic for its centennial. He made *Quilting Time*. Critic Davira Taragin found the mosaic medium and theme to be well matched: "It echoes the piecing together of the colourful bits of fabric while continuing the collage technique of building forms from small pieces of paper called tesserae. The juxtaposition of colour and line and the recurring themes of music and women make this piece a culmination of the artist's work over the past forty years."[25] Taragin's positive judgment of one of Bearden's large and monumental works goes against reservations Brenson and Plagens express regarding those large works. Nonetheless, Bearden's collages do attract the most critical attention. About them, Nancy Princenthal writes that although Bearden painted for thirty years before making collages, "The agility with which Bearden handles collage is undiminished; like his dauntless approach to sentimentality, his control of cut and torn paper recalls Matisse. So does his fluent use of saturated color."[26]

In summary, critics evaluating an artist's work sometimes attempt to decide which particular pieces of an artist's whole body of work are the best. The critics evaluating Bearden's works and cited here all agree that Bearden made good art, and they give reasons for their assessments; some then go on to argue that his collages are better than his paintings. Many of these critics provide biographical information about Bearden, and some claim that he could have been a successful musician and playwright. Some draw connections between the art of jazz and Bearden's art of collage. The critics also relate Bearden's urban and country experiences and discuss how he embodied aspects of both urban and rural situations in his work. Some praise him for capturing the Black southern experience and its rural roots, and others praise him for finding the pulse of the Black urban experience. With the help of biographical information, these critics formed interpretations of his work, and on the basis of their understanding of it, they went on to praise it. Thus description, interpretation, and evaluation are meshed in these examples of critical writings about Bearden.

Some critics followed the progression of Bearden's style and concluded that he kept refining his vision, staying within a style, and resisting what may have been a temptation to change styles radically, because his more economically successful counterparts in the art world at the time were being rewarded for such radical stylistic changes. Thus, his consistency is praised, especially in comparison to other art of his time.

EXAMPLES OF NEGATIVE JUDGMENTS

The judgments of most critics examined so far in this chapter have been generally positive, or have held only a few reservations. The following judgments are primarily negative and offer us other interesting examples to consider. They revolve around the paintings of David Salle. In a feature in *Art in America* on the painter, Eleanor Heartney disapproves of Salle's paintings because she sees them as sexist: The images of men in Salle's paintings "tend to embody the sphere of action, decision making amid societal constraint denied women. There are images of matadors (conquest and domination of brute animal force effected with the sexually charged sabre); iconic profiles of Abraham Lincoln (frequently positioned suggestively over portions of a female body, perhaps as comment upon our culture's discomfort with the idea that public figures have private lives); bone-weary workers or fist-waving agitators; and assorted pop-culture or otherwise clichéd male characters including Santa Claus, Donald Duck and Christopher Columbus." She also faults him for depicting Third World women as "other," in a *National Geographic* style.[27]

Heartney is not alone in rejecting Salle's paintings as sexist, and these other critics are more blunt in their rejections. David Rimanelli, in a review in *Artforum* of Salle's work, wrote that "a woman artist I know likened a visit to a David Salle exhibition to a gang bang."[28] Rimanelli characterizes Salle's work as "his trademark girlie pinup images" and "the flagrant beaver shots we have come to expect." The critic continues: "He makes fools of them [women] putting them through their paces as circus entertainers assembled for his amusement." Rimanelli offers the psychological conclusion that Salle's work is about "overcoming a desperate sense of masculine inadequacy by showing women—uh, excuse me, girls—as helpless and hopeless." In an earlier review in *Flash Art*, Laura Cottingham writes a two-paragraph dismissal of Salle's paintings. In the first, she faults them on formal grounds—"his assemblage technique is reductive of itself" and his work exhibits an "utter lack of draftsmanship."[29] Then, like these other critics, she also rejects the sexism of the work, writing that he has a

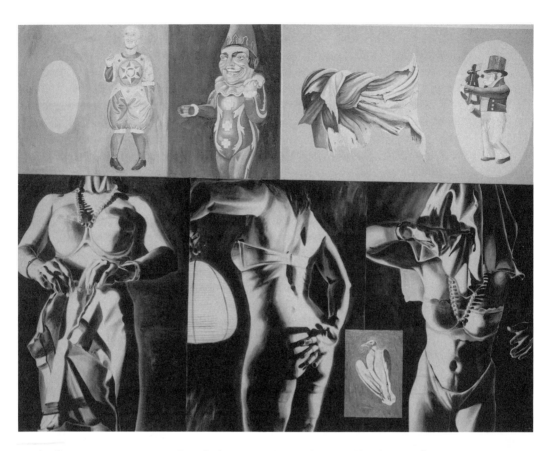

David Salle, *Sextant in Dogtown*, acrylic and oil on canvas, 96" × 126 1/4", 1987. Courtesy of Gagosian Gallery, NYC.

"mundane proclivity for sado-masochistic trappings. A crotch-intensive perspective holds Salle's eye most emphatically: panel by panel of female figures,
fetishized by posture or prop, create the dominant motif. Salle seems to insist on
a distinctively male heterosexual dialogue in painting: why else the repetitive
assault."

Just when it seems there may be a comfortable consensus among critics
about Salle's sexism, however, Robert Storr offers an objection. Writing in the
same magazine and the same issue as Heartney, just quoted, Storr claims "the
issues raised by David Salle's work cannot be reduced to the question of its representation of women."[30] He argues that "the real object of Salle's contempt is
not so much women and blacks per se as it is anyone who would insist that the
subject represented might in some way have a proprietary interest in their representation, or anyone who would presume to invest in pictures any residual belief
in the intrinsic identity of sign and meaning." Heartney forcefully objects with a
series of rhetorical questions whose answers are implicit: "Does an ostensible
refusal to embrace legible meaning ultimately become a moral issue? Can and
should decisively sexual subject matter be rendered in a manner that is free not
only of judgment but even of any implied value system? Does the reproduction
of imagery which objectifies women serve to expose, or does it rather exploit,
female subjugation within a patriarchal society? Is deconstruction of matter without some form of reconstruction enough?"

Storr disagrees with how other critics have been interpreting Salle's paintings. He sees them as being not about what they represent. He argues that Salle's
paintings challenge people who think they have any right over how they are represented. He also argues that Salle's paintings challenge anyone who might
believe there is any necessary connection between a sign and a meaning. Heartney
rejects Storr's argument as morally irresponsible. She raises moral rather than aesthetic criteria about Salle's paintings; she demands art that is morally responsible and art that clearly exposes sexism as a social evil. Conflicts over criteria,
such as this one involving moral and aesthetic issues, are explored more fully
later in this chapter.

OPPOSITE JUDGMENTS OF THE SAME WORK

In *The New Criterion,* a journal founded and edited by Hilton Kramer as a vehi-
cle for conservative writing about the arts, Jed Perl rejects a show he has not
seen, only read about: "I have been rather horrified to read about Vito Acconci's
recent work—some oversized brassieres that double as seating units, at the
Barbara Gladstone Gallery—in articles where these contraptions are discussed as
if they were part of a distinguished tradition. All traditions are not equal."[31] So,
in an effectively rhetorical fashion, Perl writes that he is "horrified" about
Acconci's work, and horrified that it is even being seriously considered by critics. It is below him and his sense of artistic tradition, and, although he has not

even bothered to see the show, he feels comfortable is dismissing it in print because of his ideological stance toward art. A. M. Homes has seen the show, however, and she writes about it very positively in *Artforum:* "Mammoth plaster, canvas, and steel-cable reinforced structures, Vito Acconci's four *Adjustable Wall Bra* pieces, 1990–1991, spanned the gallery with the sensual grace of a garment flung across the room to land half on the floor, half against the wall, bent, twisted and possibly still warm."[32] She refers to the "hysterical proportions" of the sculpted bras that she describes as being fitted with lights, seats, video, and the sound of music or a woman breathing. She praises Acconci for always challenging himself, his gallery spaces, and the viewers of his work. She likes that he "returns to the personal, the sexual and the taboo." She argues that he expands the associations of the bra as it has been reinvented in tandem with shifts in society's attitudes toward women's bodies. He creates a home for the body. She further writes: "On a recent afternoon, I snuggled into one, watched cartoons on the monitor and thought 'This is the life.' This *would* be the life, if only the cups had more padding. But even the discomfort is in keeping with Acconci's dialectic. Of course the seats are not comfortable; why would they be? Who ever heard of a comfy brassiere, a comfortable house, or a comfortable life for that matter?"

Perl's writing may be effective in that he may encourage others to adopt his point of view and discourage others from seriously considering this work of Acconci's, but it is not acceptable criticism. It is too dismissive. It is a pronouncement rather than an argument. It does not enlighten readers about the art in question. A reasoned rejection of Acconci's work by Perl would be better criticism. Perhaps if Perl had had the benefit of Homes's interpretation of the exhibition, he might be more accepting of it. But probably not. Sometimes critics agree to disagree, but it is better for their readers if they provide reasons for their disagreements.

APPRAISALS, REASONS, AND CRITERIA

Complete critical judgments are composed of appraisals of the work in question, reasons for the appraisal, and criteria on which the appraisals and reasons are based. "Ratings, reasons, and rules"[33] are another way of thinking about appraisals, reasons, and criteria. In the preceding section, Perl offers a clear appraisal (or rating) of Acconci's new sculpture: It's not worth his time. He does not, however, provide us with the reasons or criteria (rules) for this appraisal, although if we were to examine his whole article, his reasons and criteria would probably emerge. Rimanelli, also quoted earlier, disapproves of David Salle's paintings: His appraisal is clearly negative. His reasons for his negative appraisal are that Salle paints "girlie pinup images" and "flagrant beaver shots" and that "he makes fools" of women by representing them as "hopeless and helpless." Although Rimanelli does not state his criteria explicitly, we can easily infer that he believes art that depicts women should not degrade them. Several critics quoted earlier in the chapter wrote clear and complete positive judgments of Martin Puryear's sculptures. Neal Menzies praises Puryear's sculptures because they present "a variety of emotional states that range from light-heartedly playful to dangerously sinister and serious." His reasons are clear, and so is his criterion: Art is good when it expresses emotions. Carole Calo appraises Puryear as "one of the most exciting and influential sculptors working today." Her reasons are that he is independent, refuses to conform to the art marketplace, and overrides fashion—her implied criterion is that artists should be independent in their visions and not succumb to the pressure of what sells.

Criteria are rules for art making. They are "shoulds." They are "dos and don'ts." In critical writing, they are usually implied rather than stated explicitly by the critic. But they are usually easily uncovered as long as the critic provides reasons for his or her appraisals. Explicit, spelled-out criteria are more readily found in theoretical writings, aesthetics, or philosophies of art. Most of us carry around assumptions about what art should be: It would be a good critical exercise for anyone to attempt to be explicit about what he or she believes art should be or not be, do or not do.

DIFFERENT CRITERIA

Art is judged by many different criteria, and, although it is an oversimplification, these criteria can be separated into four categories, or theories of art: Realism, Expressionism, Formalism, and Instrumentalism.

Realism

A critic advocating Realism as the major criterion of art would hold that the world, or nature, is the standard of truth and beauty, and that the artist can do no better than try to accurately portray the universe in its infinite variety. Realism is as old as the ancient Greeks, backed by the authority and knowledge of Aristotle, rejuvenated during the Renaissance, and embraced at various times and places throughout the history of art. John Szarkowski, the recently retired and influential curator of photography at the Museum of Modern Art in New York, wrote that the basic premise of realism is that "the world exists independent of human attention, that it contains discoverable patterns of intrinsic meaning and that by discerning these patterns, and forming models or symbols of them with the materials of his art, the realist is joined to a larger intelligence."[34]

Expressionism

Szarkowski, quoted in the previous section on Realism, contrasts Realism and Expressionism, and writes this about Expressionism (although he uses the term *romantic*): "The romantic view is that the meanings of the world are dependent on our own understandings. The field mouse, the skylark, the sky itself do not earn their meanings out of their own evolutionary history, but are meaningful in terms of the anthropocentric metaphors we assign to them." Expressionism favors artists and their sensibilities rather than nature. Artists' inner lives are potent and their feelings about experiences are the source of their art. They use medium and form and subject matter to express their inner lives. It is their business to express themselves vividly so the viewer may experience similar feelings. Intensity of expression is much more crucial than accuracy of representation. Certainly Expressionists are sensitive to form, but whereas the Formalist sees art as being primarily about itself and other art, Expressionists embrace art about life.

The following is an example of the use of Expressionist criteria by Ken Johnson, commenting on paintings by Anselm Kiefer: "Kiefer is indisputably a master of the awesome effect. The enormous bulk of his works, the vast scale of their imagery, the elephant-skin surfaces, the grand allusions to history and mythology, the profound brooding on death—all this can combine to produce a thrilling experience."[35]

Formalism - Modernism   the FoRM, not the subj.

Formalism is a theory of "art for art's sake," and the term *formalism* should not be confused with *form*. All art has form. The theory of Formalism, however, asserts that form is the only criterion by which art should be judged. Formalists hold that aesthetic value is autonomous and independent of other values: According to them, art has nothing to do with morality, religions, politics, or any other area of human activity. In this view, the realms of art and social concerns are by their natures distinct, and the artist is alienated or separated from society.

The theory is new to art, introduced in this century, primarily through the writings of Clive Bell in the 1930s. To Bell it would not matter a hoot whether a crucifixion painting is of Jesus Christ or John Smith: It is not subject that counts, but form. For Formalists, narrative content in art is a distraction from the aesthetic and should be ignored, and politics as the content of art is anathema. Formalism was given new impetus in the 1950s and 1960s by the influential criticism of Clement Greenberg, who championed abstraction of certain sorts, particularly Minimalism. Formalist criticism grew up alongside New Criticism in literature and as a reaction against the excesses of biographical criticism and psychological criticism, and any other type of criticism that was thought to take primary attention away from the artwork or piece of literature itself.

Formalism may also be understood to be synonymous with Modernism. Formalism, or Modernism, may well be viewed by future historians and critics as *the* contribution of the 20th century, but today the theory is largely rejected as too limited in scope. Postmodernism is a rejection of Modernism; where these theories differ is one of the subjects of Chapter 5.

The following remarks in *Interview* magazine on the paintings of Ad Reinhardt exemplify the use of Formalist criteria: "The austere discipline of Ad

Reinhardt's work—the geometry of the early, experimental abstractions; the primary intensity of the monochromatic red, blue, and black paintings for which he became known—was a point of departure for the conceptualists and minimalists of the '60s and '70s . . . Looking over his career, you realize that it's not simply as an influential abstract artist that Reinhardt will be remembered. He is something of a myth—his work is a vital sign of this century's art."[36] In the following quotation, Gerrit Henry discusses Agnes Martin's paintings with Formalism in mind; the critic faults her work for being too concerned with form and leaving out feeling: "Martin's work was, as always, lovely to look at, and even delicious to contemplate, but its overbearing neatness . . . made it, on reflection, seem unsatisfying, even contrived. As with so much Minimal art, the search for perfection of an almost saintly sort excludes feeling and enshrines form. Where, as a popular song once put it, is the love?"[37] Perhaps Henry strictly adheres to Expressionist criteria and would say this about most Minimalist work, or perhaps he accepts Formalism but merely rejects this specific body of work.

Instrumentalism *- influence on society . message oriented*

For Instrumentalists, art serves values larger than the aesthetic and issues bigger than art. Instrumentalism rivals Realism in longevity. Plato argued that it is necessary to restrict the artist in the ideal state on the grounds that art affects human behavior. Art that produces undesirable behavioral consequences must be excluded, and art that yields good behavioral consequences should be produced for the benefit of the populace. Leo Tolstoy, the Russian novelist and theorist, upheld this view. For him, art was a force that should elicit the loftiest ethical behavior. For both Tolstoy and Plato, ethical and religious ideals determined aesthetic value. Marxist critics are Instrumentalist. Lenin argued that any art that does not serve the common cause should be condemned. For him, art was a tool, a shaper of political attitudes, and its function was social. An artwork's real value, Marxists insist, depends on its function in its social setting. Feminist criticism is largely Instrumentalist.

Instrumentalism plays prominently in much of today's art, particularly politically activist art. Douglas Crimp writes about the importance of considering audience when making art that is to influence change within society: "Success within the art world is not the primary goal of artists working within the context of AIDS activism, and communicating only to an art audience is a limited accomplishment. Thus, cultural activism involves rethinking the identity of the artist as well as the role of production, distribution, and audience in determining a work's significance."[38] Ann Cvetcovich, also writing about AIDS activism, stresses the need for persuasive art, arguing that if an artwork is only true and not persuasive, it will not be effective. AIDS activist artists must "not only provide information about safer sex, but eroticize it, acknowledging that telling people to use condoms may be useless if the presentation doesn't address the fear that safer sex interferes with sexual pleasure. AIDS activism thus questions not only whether the truth is represented but how truth is represented, and suggests that to be effective information must be both true and persuasive to its audience."[39]

Instrumentalist criteria often come into play when the work of underrepresented artists, such as that by African-American and women artists, is being criticized. Writing about the exhibition "Contemporary African Artists," Frances DeVuono argues "this was a long-overdue show. It was big enough and good enough to disabuse any remaining art chauvinists of the idea that contemporary art is the sole preserve of the developed nations of the West."[40] Similarly, Curtia James writes in *Artnews* that "in a show of three installations, Maren Hassinger, Beverly Buchanan, and Mel Edwards did a remarkable job of demonstrating the vitality of African-American artists to a society that is vastly ignorant of their achievements."[41]

Some exhibitions are conceived and mounted for instrumentalist ends, such as "Facing History: The Black Image in American Art 1710–1940," curated by Guy McElroy for the Corcoran Gallery in Washington, D.C.: "How did portrayals of blacks reflect the prejudices of the society at large? Were better artists able to transcend stereotypes, or, like their lesser-known peers, did they only propagate them further?"[42] In the exhibition catalog McElroy argues that "it's important for everyone—but especially for blacks and women—to become more sensitized to the insidious ways that images can work. That's the big point."

Other Criteria

These four major categories do not exhaust the range of criteria available to critics. Originality, for instance, is an honored criterion of recent art. A critic compliments the paintings of Susan Rothenberg, for example, because the artist has managed to do something new and different with a very used subject: "Until Rothenberg revived it in the mid-70's, the horse had fallen out of favor as proper subject matter for painting. Its connotations were classical, monumental and entirely too mythic for the late 20th century. Its ability to symbolize martial values and nobility of spirit had been rendered obsolete; as an esthetic device it seemed, at best, corny. But Rothenberg's horse paintings worked—in fact, they worked remarkably well."[43]

Craftsmanship is another criterion that is frequently used, and as we have seen in writings about the work of Puryear, his craftsmanship was praised because it was not excessive and fussy. Thus craftsmanship, at least for some critics, is not an absolute quality but a relative one, and they look for an appropriate amount of craft for the expression being made.

CHOOSING AMONG CRITERIA

The critics quoted in this book are not of a single mindset about criteria for judging art. Peter Plagens, for instance, has written that "political art ends up *preaching* to the converted—and preaching is the key word here."[44] Certainly, he is not an Instrumentalist. Eleanor Heartney seems more tolerant of Instrumentalist art, but she too has difficulty with it. In a review of an installation about the homeless by Martha Rosler, Heartney asks: "How, for instance, does the socially concerned artist avoid merely estheticising the victims of homelessness?"[45] Heartney ends up supporting Rosler's noble intent and attempt but concludes: "As it was, the gallery setting, with its preselected audience and social isolation, provided a constant reminder of the continuing gap between art and life. The real problems and the real solutions remained, and remain, out there—geographically only a few steps beyond the gallery door, but in practical terms, on another planet."

Donald Kuspit has also struggled with criteria for socially concerned art. In a review of Sue Coe's paintings, he writes: "Granted, the world is a rotten, inhumane place. Blacks are oppressed and brutalized, the meat industry manipulates us almost as much as the military-industrial complex, and the United States is a neofascist aggressor; yet it is not the message in Sue Coe's art that interests me. All of her characteristic complaints would be propagandistic dross if it wasn't for her visionary esthetic, which eloquently conveys the suffering she is at bottom obsessed with."[46] Thus, Kuspit accepts Coe's value positions, and accepts her Expressionism, but praises her for her use of form. Her intellectual insights are not enough, nor is her passion; but when her insights, passion, and aesthetic vision combine, Kuspit admires her work. "Coe, I think, is torn between a wish to communicate instantaneously to as large an audience as possible, and thus to use a public and invariably clichéd language, and a desire to make 'high' art, that is, art so dense with visual substance and subtle meaning that it cannot be exhausted at first sight. When she manages to balance these impulses, she takes her place among Expressionist masters, but when she makes images for 'the cause,' her works dwindle to militant cartoons, lacking even the saving grace of Daumier's wit."

Jan Zita Grover writes of a conflict over criteria with other critics on a state art's council while they were awarding grants to artists.[47] Grover was defending what she calls the "subcultural work"—the photographic work of Lynette Molnar entitled *Familiar Names and Not So Familiar Faces*. It is a series of photomontages of the photographer and her female lover stripped into existing reproductions, such as a Marlboro cigarette ad, and the Ward and June Cleaver family of "Leave it to Beaver." Grover writes that Molnar's "montage is deliberately not very convincing: it is quite obvious that the two figures have been imported from some other world and pastiched into these mainstream settings. The scale and repetitiveness of the same figures embracing in a variety of commercial settings enforce the artificiality of the insertion, producing a sense that this is an act of defiance, a clumsy and not altogether successful fusion of two different universes. Anyone living the life of an informed outsider will recognize that this is precisely the position we occupy—culturally and politically, if not economically. Molnar's work struck me as a clever objectification of both the aspiration and reality of the uncloseted lesbian." The other two jurors objected in terms of what lay within the frame—namely what they considered technical flaws, formal deficiencies. Grover defended the montages because "these seeming limitations became challenges and virtues, given the paucity and distortions of most images depicting lesbians." Another juror responded that "we're judging photographs, not social revolutions." Grover was working from within an Instrumentalist frame of reference while the others were appealing to Formal criteria such as craft.

With so many criteria, how is one to choose among them? The choices are difficult, but they must be made. One could hold an eclectic position and accept them all, but some of the criteria are contradictory or mutually exclusive. It would not be logically possible, for instance, to hold to both Formalism and Instrumentalism. Formalism holds art to be autonomous, a world unto itself, separate from the social world and outside of moral parameters. Instrumentalism insists that moral issues are very pertinent to art making. This is not to say that Instrumentalist critics would not have any formal demands on art. They would, but form alone would not be enough.

One might choose to be pluralistic and accept an artwork on its own grounds. That is, one would let the artwork influence which set of criteria should be used in judging it. A feminist work of art would be judged by Instrumental criteria; a formalist piece on Formal grounds; and so forth. The advantage to this position is that one would be very tolerant of a wide range of artworks. Many naive viewers of art hold only to Realist criteria and they very narrowly dismiss most of the art of this century. This is unfortunate. If they were taught a broader range of criteria, they might be able to enjoy a wider range of artwork.

Some critics, however, are informed about and have considered many criteria for judging art, but are still staunchly committed to a point of view, and will hold only one set of criteria. Some critics will remain Formalists, for instance, despite the severe limitations of Formalism, which postmodernist writers have made apparent. Any critic who assumes a single critical stance has the security of a single point of view and a consistent way of viewing art. The danger for them, however, is one of rigidity. For a student of criticism, it would probably be wise and beneficial to try on and try out many different criteria on many works of art before deciding which criteria to embrace.

Maintaining a distinction between preference and value can be liberating. That is, a work I like may not be as good as another artwork I don't like. I may understand that one work of art is better than another, but I may still enjoy the former more than the latter. I can like whatever I want to like. If we hold our preferences with confidence, then we might be in a better psychological position to critically and appreciatively attend to works that are beyond our range of tolerance.

It is also important not to confuse preference with value. Statements of preference are personal, psychological reports made by the viewer. Value statements are much stronger and need to be defended. There is no need to defend preferences. Aestheticians make the following distinctions: I may admire a work aesthetically that offends me religiously. I may buy a painting that is a poor investment, or profit from a painting I loathe. I may appreciate something but prefer to look at something else, even though I can acknowledge that its aesthetic value is inferior.[48]

Examining our preferences will yield insights into what is being valued and why. People writing criticism ought to be self-conscious of both their values and their preferences, so they do not confuse the two.

JUDGING ART: A SUMMARY

Critical judgments are much more than mere opinions. Judgments are informed critical arguments about the value of a work of art. Judgments should never be given without reasons, and they ought to be based on definable criteria. Judgments without reasons are both uninformative and nonresponsive.

Many aspects of art may be judged: how good is the exhibition; which is the best work in the exhibition; how good is the artist and what are his or her best works, or best periods; how good is a particular movement or style; how good an idea is the curator's for an exhibition; how good is the art of a decade or a century; of what consequences is this art socially and morally? Should any art be censored?

Usually critics judge artworks and not artists. It is logically and psychologically possible for people to both dislike an artist but value the artist's work, or to dislike a critic but agree with his or her critical positions. Some people, however, believe that judgments of artists (and critics) cannot and should not be separated from judgments of their work. Several positive comments about the personalities of artists are given in this book: Bearden is humble without being self-effacing, Wegman loves his dogs, Puryear is shy in public, and so forth. The belief seems to be that the character of the artist is instilled in the work.

Critics do not usually make judgments with eternity in mind. Judgments are usually tentative and open to revision. Critics know that the criticism they write is often the first words written about a work of art, and they realize they cannot afford to be dogmatic or doctrinaire in their judgments of it.

Critics judge art for an audience of readers, not for the artist who made the work, and they wish to persuade the readers to appreciate (or not appreciate) the work as they do and for their reasons. They would have us see as they see, have us enjoy as they enjoy.

Take mirror work from home -
write about it - begin to define criteria for judgement
go to gallery · write on piece you like
Come back - determine personal criteria for good art — each others work
↳ assignment -   pairs -

5
THEORY AND
ART CRITICISM

This chapter examines current art criticism by relating it to art theory. The criticism of any age is affected by and, in turn, affects aesthetic theory. Today criticism revolves around debates concerning Modernism and Postmodernism. The chapter is mostly about Postmodernism, art, and criticism, but Postmodernism makes sense only in relation to Modernism. Artistic Modernism, or Modern Art, arose from within cultural Modernity, a much larger and longer-lived phenomenon. Thus, the chapter first broadly sketches the Age of Modernity and contrasts it to Postmodernity, explains the aesthetic theory of Modernism, and makes Postmodernist art criticism more understandable through several extended examples of critics and artists influenced by and influencing Postmodernist theories of art, especially feminists and multiculturalists, including gay activists.

MODERNITY AND POSTMODERNITY

We are in an age referred to by many as Postmodernity. Postmodernity, according to some, has already replaced Modernity. The Age of Modernity is the epoch that began with the Enlightenment (about 1687 to 1789) and that, through such intellectual leaders as Isaac Newton, championed a belief in the potential of science to save the world. The age is also characterized intellectually by the discourses of philosophers such as René Descartes (1596–1650) and, later, Immanuel Kant (1724–1804), who believed that through reason scholars could establish a foundation of universal truths. Political leaders of Modernity also

science

reason +
truth

109

championed reason as the source of progress in social change, believing that reason can produce a just and egalitarian social order. Such beliefs fed the American and French democratic revolutions. Modernity proceeds through the Declaration of Independence, the French Revolution, the first and second World Wars, into our own day.

The major movements and events of Modernity are democracy, capitalism, industrialization, science, and urbanization, and its rallying flags are freedom and the individual. Scholars of Postmodernity Steven Best and Douglas Keller define modernization as a term "denoting those processes of individualization, secularization, industrialization, cultural differentiation, commodification, urbanization, bureaucratization, and rationalization which together have constituted the modern world."[1]

Not all theorists agree that Modernity is dead, or even that it is outmoded, but most Postmodernists do. Some scholars use the term *postmodern* descriptively; others use it prescriptively to urge the formation of new theories to deal with new times.

Scholars critical of Modernity cite the suffering and misery of peasants under monarchies, and later the oppression of workers under capitalist industrialization, the exclusion of women from the public sphere, and the colonization of other lands by imperialists and, ultimately, the destruction of indigenous peoples. Some social critics also claim that Modernity leads to social practices and institutions that legitimate domination and control by a powerful few over the weak many, even though Modernists promise equality and liberation of all people. Karl Marx, Sigmund Freud, and their followers have undermined Modernists' belief in the ability of reason to find truth by demonstrating that forces below the surface of society and psychological forces not bound by reason, are powerful shapers of society and individuals.

Proponents of Postmodernity say we have been living in the age of Postmodernity for about two decades, and some symbolically date its birth with the student riots in Paris in 1968, during which students, with the support of prominent scholars, demanded radical changes in a very rigid, closed, and elitist European university system. Proponents characterize the age as a period of rapidly evolving and spreading high-technology developments that are producing a new social order requiring new concepts and theories. There is no unified theory of Postmodernity. In fact, several different theories and theoretical directions, some of which conflict with others, are lumped together under the term. However, the following generalities can be made apparent.

Whereas Modernity is influenced by the rationalism of René Descartes, Immanuel Kant, and others, Postmodernity is influenced by philosophers such as Friedrich Nietzsche, Martin Heidegger, Ludwig Wittgenstein, John Dewey, and, more recently, Jacques Derrida and Richard Rorty. All of these thinkers are skeptical about the Modernist belief that theory can mirror reality. Instead they embrace a much more cautious and limited perspective on truth and knowledge, stressing that facts are simply interpretations, that truth is not absolute but merely the constructs of individuals and groups, and that all knowledge is mediated by culture and language. Whereas Modernists believe they can discover unified and coherent foundations of truth that are universally true and applicable, Postmodernists accept the limitations of multiple views, fragmentation, and indeterminacy. Postmodernists also reject the Modernist notion that the individual is a unified rational being. Descartes's dictum, "I think therefore I am," and, more recently, Jean-Paul Sartre's existentialist claim that the individual is free and undetermined, place the individual at the center of the universe. Postmodernists instead decenter the individual and claim that the self is merely an effect of language, social relations, and the unconscious; they downplay the ability of the individual to effect change or be creative.

These generalizations about Modernity and Postmodernity are mainly derived from Best and Keller, who also provide clear and detailed summaries of two important strands of theory contributing to Postmodernity that will be briefly examined here: Structuralism and Poststructuralism. Structuralism emerged in France after World War II, heavily influenced by the earlier semiotic theory of linguist Ferdinand de Saussure. De Saussure identified language as a system of signs consisting of signifiers (words) and signified (concepts) that are arbitrarily linked to each other in a way that is designated by the culture. Structuralists attempt to explain phenomena by identifying hidden systems. They believe that no phenomenon can be explained in isolation from other phenomena. They differ from previous scholars who explained things through historical sequences of events. Structuralists such as Claude Lévi-Strauss used linguistic analysis in anthropology, Jacques Lacan developed structuralist psychoanalysis, and Louis Althusser promoted a structuralist Marxism. Each of these structuralists in their varied disciplines sought to discover unconscious codes or rules that underlie phenomena. They sought to make visible systems that were previously invisible. They, like Modernists, strove for objectivity, coherence, and rigor, and claimed scientific status for their theories, which they believe purged mere subjective evaluations.

Poststructuralists, most influentially Jacques Derrida, Michel Foucault, Jean-François Lyotard, and Roland Barthes, attack the Structuralists for their scientific pretensions, their search for universal truth, and their belief in an unchanging human nature. Both the Structuralists and Poststructuralists reject the idea of the autonomous subject, insisting that no one can live outside of history, but Poststructuralists especially emphasize the arbitrariness of all signs. They stress that language, culture, and society are arbitrary and conventionally agreed upon rather than natural. Poststructuralists use historical strategies to explain how consciousness, signs, and societies are historically and geographically dependent. Poststructuralists also collapse the boundaries between philosophy, literary theory, and social theory. Postmodernists build on the semiotic projects of Barthes and others, who study the systems of signs in societies and who generally assume that language, signs, images, and signifying systems organize the psyche, society, and everyday life.

Poststructuralists believe Marx's emphasis on the power of economic relations too dogmatic and limited an explanation of historical and social development and seek to identify multiple forms of power and domination. In the political arena, according to Best and Keller, most Poststructuralists find Marxism to be obsolete and oppressive and no longer relevant for the Postmodern era, and instead advocate radical democracy.[2]

There is considerably more to Postmodernist theory, but it is much beyond the scope of this chapter, which deals more specifically with Modernism and Postmodernism in art and art criticism. Modernism, Modernity, Postmodernism, and Postmodernity are all interdependent, and a study of any one will help explain the others.

Postmodernism in art follows Modernism, or lives alongside it—many artists and critics continue the Modernist tradition. Postmodernists, however, reject Modernism. Postmodernism is more complicated than Modernism and, because in large part it is a denunciation of Modernism, the former cannot be adequately understood without an understanding of the latter. Thus, this chapter continues with a comparison of the two, then looks at the multiple influences on the encompassing, cumbersome, and influential ideological phenomenon called Postmodernism, and examines how it is affecting art and its criticism.

MODERNIST AESTHETICS AND CRITICISM

Artistic Modernism is more recent than philosophical Modernity. Artistic Modernism began during the middle or the end of the 19th century, or during the 1880s—depending on which scholar is consulted. Robert Atkins, for example, dates Modernism "roughly from the 1860s through the 1970s"[3] and writes that the term is used to identify both the styles and the ideologies of the art produced during those years. Although Modernism is now old and perhaps over, it was once new and very progressive, bringing a new art for a new age.

Modernism emerged amidst the social and political revolution sweeping Europe. Western European culture was becoming more urban and less rural, industrial rather than agrarian. The importance of organized religion in the daily lives of people was diminishing while secularism grew. Because the old system of artistic patronage had ended, artists were free to choose their own content. Their art no longer needed to glorify the wealthy individuals and powerful institutions of church and state that had previously commissioned their paintings and sculptures. Because it was unlikely that their art would flourish in the new capitalist art market, artists felt free to experiment, and made highly personal art. The slogan of the era, "art for the sake of art," is apt.

Modernists signified their allegiance to the new by referring to themselves as "avant-garde," thinking they were ahead of their time and beyond historical limitations. Modern artists were especially rebellious of restrictions put on previous artists by the art academies of the 1700s, and many avant-garde artists rebelled against the dominance of the art salons and their conservative juries in the late 1800s. Modern artists were generally often critical of the status quo and frequently challenged middle-class values.

Premodernists Jacques Louis David painted scenes from the French Revolution, and Francisco de Goya depicted Napoleon's invasion of Spain. Modernists Gustave Courbet and Edouard Manet turned their easels away from nobility and wealth to paint ordinary life around them. The Impressionists and Postimpressionists abandoned historical subject matter, and also turned away from the realism and illusionism artists had been refining in the West since the Renaissance.

Some Modernists, such as the Futurists in Italy during the 1920s, celebrated in their work the new technology, especially speed, while others, such as the Constructivists in the Soviet Union, embraced scientific models of thinking. The Abstractionists Wassily Kandinsky and Piet Mondrian embraced Spiritualism to offset the secularism of the modern era. Paul Gaugin, and later Pablo Picasso, sought solace and inspiration in non-Western cultures, while Paul Klee and Joan Miró "employed childlike imagery that embodies the yearning to escape adulthood and all its responsibilities."[4]

In 1770, the philosopher Immanuel Kant laid the philosophic foundation for artistic Modernism, and for the Formalism that grew up in the 1930s. Kant developed a theory of aesthetic response which held that viewers could and should arrive at similar interpretations and judgments of an artwork if they experienced the work in and of itself. When viewing art, people should put themselves in a suprastate of sensory awareness, give up their personal interests and associational responses, and consider art independently of any purpose or utility other than the aesthetic. An aesthetic judgment should be neither personal nor relative. The viewer should rise above time, place, and personal idiosyncrasies, reaching aesthetic judgment of art with which all reasonable people would agree. In 1913, Edward Bullough, an aesthetician, added the concept of "psychic distancing," reinforcing Kant's idea that the viewer should contemplate a work of art with detachment.[5]

In the 1920s, the theory of Modernism received a big boost from two British critics, Clive Bell and Roger Fry, who introduced what is now known in art theory as Formalism. Formalism and Modernism are inextricably linked, although the former is an outgrowth of the latter. Bell and Fry sought to ignore as irrelevant the artist's intent in making a work of art and any social or ideological function the artist may have wanted the work to have. Instead, the "significant form" of the artwork was what was to be exclusively attended to. Critic Robert Atkins[6] credits Bell's and Fry's critical purpose as being responsible, at least in part, for the early 20th century interest in Japanese prints and Oceanic and African artifacts. Their critical method of attending to art was meant to allow a crosscultural interpretation and evaluation of any art from any place or any time. Form was paramount, and attention to other aspects of the work—such as its subject matter or narrative content or uses in rituals or references to the ordinary world—were considered distractions and, worse, detriments to a proper consideration of the art.

During the 1930s, in the area of literary criticism, T. S. Eliot, I. A. Richards, and other writers developed "New Criticism," a Formalist approach to literature that paralleled Formalism in art. They wanted considerably more interpretive emphasis placed on the work itself—on the poem rather than the poet, for instance—and they wanted it to be analyzed according to its use of language, imagery, and metaphor. They were attempting to correct the then-current practice of critics placing too much emphasis on information outside of a literary work—for example, on a poet's biography and particular psychology, rather than on the actual text.

After World War II, Formalism became extremely important in the United States because of the work of Clement Greenberg, the most influential American critic of this century. With Formalist principles, Greenberg championed the Abstract Expressionism of Mark Rothko, Willem De Kooning, and Jackson Pollock in the mid-1940s through the 1950s. Greenberg particularly championed the work of Pollock, and the artist and critic in tandem are generally credited with moving the center of the high art world from Paris to New York. While regionalist painters such as Thomas Hart Benton and Grant Wood were painting the American scene, and while Social Realists depicted class struggles, the Abstract Expressionists championed the existential ideal of individual freedom, and committed themselves to psychic self-expression through abstraction. Shape, size, structure, scale, and composition were of utmost importance, and styles evolved out of enthusiasm for particular properties of paint. Abstract Expressionism gets much of its effect "from how paint in various thicknesses, applied by a variety of means, behaves differently and affects the finished work in different ways. Blobs of paint mean something different from drips or thin veils."[7]

With the backing of Greenberg and, later, fellow critic Harold Rosenberg, Abstract Expressionists and Color Field Painters and Hard Edged Abstractionists flattened their paintings under the Formalist principle that painting is two-dimensional by nature and that it ought not attempt three-dimensional illusions. Rosenberg declared that "a painting is not a picture of a thing; it's the thing itself."[8] He wanted artists "just TO PAINT." Barnett Newman, who painted huge minimally abstract paintings in the 1950s, wrote that the canvas should not be a "space in which to re-produce, re-design, analyze or express," and he rejected "props and crutches that evoke associations, and resisted the impediments of memory, association, nostalgia, legend, myth."[9] Frank Stella wrote, "My painting is based on the fact that only what can be seen there *is* there."[10] Minimalists, with their emphasis on reducing painting and sculpture to its bare essentials, were heavily influenced by the work of Newman, Ad Reinhardt, and David Smith.

Atkins credits Minimalism with being the first internationally significant art movement pioneered by American-born artists.[11]

During the 1960s, critic Michael Fried wrote extensively on Formalism, concentrating especially on Minimalist sculptors. However, as social forces in the 1960s sought to obliterate social boundaries, so art movements erased aesthetic boundaries. Joseph Beuys, the German Process Artist, was claiming that everyone was an artist, while Andy Warhol was claiming that everything was art. Movements such as Pop Art eventually rendered Formalism ineffective. Warhol's renditions of Brillo boxes and Campbell's soup cans demanded social and cultural interpretations rather than meditations on the significance of their form. Pop Art also relied on everyday life, a subject that was anathema to Formalists, and Pop Artists such as Roy Lichtenstein used comic book imagery to make art with important narrative content, a concept that Formalists wanted banished from painting. Pop Artists erased the boundaries between high art and low art, and between an elite and a popular audience, by placing their versions of comic strips, soup cans, and cheeseburgers in galleries and art museums.

Criticism of Modernism, its slogan of "art for art's sake," and its push toward minimal abstraction was growing. Tom Wolfe attempted to discredit Greenberg and Rosenberg and their abstract and minimalist movements with sarcastic wit in his entertaining short book, *The Painted Word.*[12] Wolfe mocked as a trivial idea the Formalists' insistence on the "flatness" of a canvas. In 1982, Wolfe wrote *From Bauhaus to Our House,*[13] this time concentrating on the glass box architecture of Modernism. In the book, Wolfe sarcastically dismisses the architectural principles and buildings of Mies Van Der Rohe, Le Corbusier, and the Bauhaus school of pre–World War II Germany, which had immigrated to the United States. Wolfe's book on architecture followed another influential critique of Modernist architecture by Charles Jencks, *The Language of Post-modern Architecture.*[14] Jencks pointed out that the utopian dreams of architects like Le Corbusier resulted in sterile skyscrapers and condemned public housing projects. Jencks called for a new architectural style based on eclecticism and popular appeal.

Arthur Danto credits Warhol with bringing about "the end of art."[15] By the phrase "the end of art," Danto refers to the logical end of a certain strain of art, namely Modernism. Danto describes Modernism as an internally driven sequence of "erasures" that took place over the course of decades and ended in 1964 with the exhibition of Warhol's *Brillo Box.* According to Danto, the history of Modernism since 1900 is "a history of the dismantling of a concept of art which had been evolving for over half a millennium. Art did not have to be beautiful; it need make no effort to furnish the eye with an array of sensations equivalent to what the real world would furnish it with; need not have a pictorial subject; need not deploy its forms in pictorial space; need not be the magical product of the artist's touch."

Many others agree that the history of Modernism is a history of "erasures." Modernist artists took apart the foundations of all that was special in previous art making. They abandoned beauty as the ideal of art—Picasso's Cubist rendering of women in *Les Demoiselles d'Avignon,* 1907. They dropped subject matter as essential—Jackson Pollock's "drip paintings." They stopped rendering three-dimensional forms on two-dimensional surfaces—Franz Kline's *Mahoning,* 1956, an approximately 6' × 8' oil on canvas, black-on-white linear abstraction. They eliminated the artist's touch—Don Judd's *Untitled,* 1967, consisting of eight cubes, made by commercial fabricators, of steel and car paint. They eliminated the need to have an art object itself—for Conceptual Artists of the mid-1960s and 1970s, the idea was more important than the finished work; John Baldessari, for example, exhibited only the documentation of a conceptual piece he made by placing the letters C-A-L-I-F-O-R-N-I-A in the actual landscape according to where these letters appeared on a map of California.[16] They eliminated the need to have an artwork be different from ordinary objects—soft sculptures of hamburgers and fries by Claes Oldenburg, and Andy Warhol's *Brillo Boxes,* 1964.

Danto specifically credits the *Brillo Boxes* with the end of Modernism because with it Warhol made the "philosophical" statement that one could no longer tell the difference between an ordinary object and an art object just by looking at it. To know that Warhol's *Brillo Box* was art and a Brillo box in the grocery store was not, one had to know something of the history of art, the history of the "erasures" that led to Warhol's ultimate erasure (or the death of art). One had to participate in a "conceptual atmosphere" and be familiar with some of the "discourse of reasons" afloat in an "art world."

Despite Danto's proclamation of the end of art, there obviously were and are many artists, with much energy, still making art, but it is the art of a new "pluralism" rather than art made under the dictates of mainstream Modernism. Danto sees "the end of art" as a liberation: "Once art had ended, you could be an abstractionist, a realist, an allegorist, a metaphysical painter, a surrealist, a landscapist, or a painter of still lifes and nudes. You could be a decorative artist, a literary artist, an anecdotalist, a religious painter, a pornographer. Everything was permitted since nothing was historically mandated."[17]

This is roughly the way that Danto and other mainstream critics and aestheticians see the history of Modern art. One art scholar may judge some artists to be major influences; another may see these same artists as less important. Fried, for instance, stresses the importance of Minimalist sculptors such as Judd and Robert Morris, while Danto finds the Pop artists, especially Warhol, to be most influential.

Others, notably Douglas Crimp, write a different history of Modernism, arguing that its demise was brought about by the invention of photography. Photography allowed the mechanical reproduction of images, including art images, thus eventually stripping away from the work of art its properties of uniqueness, originality, and location or place of origin. In reproduction, the artwork can be studied in libraries and living rooms. In reproduction, the artwork can be enlarged, cropped, and recombined with other artworks and images. That the artwork once was "original and authentic" is considered much less important.

What is considered important by Crimp and others is that any artwork made in any place in the world at any time can now be seen over and over again in a myriad of contexts.

The significance of the reproducibility of artworks by photographic means was first noted by Walter Benjamin in the 1930s. Benjamin was a member of the Frankfurt School, which also included Theodore Adorno, Herbert Marcuse, and other European scholars fleeing Hitler. These scholars, and now, more recently, Jürgen Habermas, developed what is known as Critical Theory, a form of Neo-Marxism that challenges dominant capitalist ideology, practice, and culture. Habermas particularly supports art that contributes to critical social discourse. Marxists accept Modernism's search for foundational truths, but are generally hostile to artistic Modernism's separation of art from life. The "Neo" in Neo-Marxism is a rejection of the strict and unwavering historical determinism and belief in the collapse of capitalism that Marxists once held. Currently, most Marxists accept the influence of culture on history and the ability of people to affect the future.

In Postmodernist terms, Danto's and other writers' renditions of Modernism are thought of as "stories." According to Derrida, all explanations of the world, including scientific explanations, are merely stories or "discourses" fabricated by people. Derrida holds that we never get to reality, only to what we say about reality; there is no truth, there is only discourse. Nevertheless, Danto's theory is compelling. It may be only discourse, or a story—but it may be a true story, certainly it is one to remember. It is convincing and makes sense of a myriad of stylistic changes that have taken place in art over the past 100 years, making these changes seem logical and linear in order. Like all stories, however, it draws our attention to certain characters and events and ignores thousands of other people who could have become major or minor characters. Danto's story of Modernism is set in Paris and New York: The rest of the world would be distracting. Danto's story ignores all aesthetic traditions except those of Western Europe and the United States. It is a story about modern Western culture, and it overlooks artists and artworks that do not fit its plot. Frida Kahlo is not a character in this story, nor is Romare Bearden. The art of most women is omitted, as is the work of artists of color, and indeed anyone who was making art with different intentions from those cited by mainstream critics and aestheticians.

We might have inherited a very different history of art than Modernism (others are currently being written). But we didn't. We inherited Modernism as a very influential, and limited, explanation of art of the past century. The predominant characteristics of Modernism are an optimism regarding technology; belief in the uniqueness of the individual, creativity, originality, and artistic genius; a respect for the original and authentic work of art and the masterpiece; a favoring of abstract modes of expression over narrative, historical, or political content in art; a disdain for kitsch in culture and a general disdain for middle-class sensibilities and values; and an awareness of the art market.

POSTMODERNIST AESTHETICS AND CRITICISM

Postmodernists set themselves apart from all or most Modernist beliefs, attitudes, and commitments. They present the art world with diverse aesthetic forms that break with Modernism, including the architecture of Robert Venturi and Philip Johnson; the radical musical practices of John Cage; the novels of Thomas Pynchon; films like *Blue Velvet;* performances like Laurie Anderson's; use of electronic signage by Jenny Holzer; Barbara Kruger's use of the linguist strategies of commercial advertising to make socially oppositional art in popular culture, "grazing" cable television with a remote control; and "spin doctors" positioning their presidential candidates in a positive way.

Sherrie Levine is considered a preeminent Postmodernist visual artist, and through an examination of one of her works we can gain entry into the morass of Postmodernist theories of art. Levine is most famous for "appropriating" artworks from the past, most often so-called masterpieces by such white male Modernist artists as the European painter Piet Mondrian and American photographers Walker Evans and Edward Weston (one of the most influential mentors of Modernist art photography). Levine copied ("appropriated") Evans's photograph and exhibited it as her own work of art under the title *After Walker Evans #7,* 1981. The very act of appropriating or borrowing or plagiarizing or stealing is a Postmodernist strategy that flouts the Modernists' reverence for originality.

According to Philip Yenawine, an educator at the Museum of Modern Art in New York, originality for Levine has to do with raising an issue rather than with inventing a new image. Her attitude, and that of other Postmodernists, "assumes that originality is impossible, anyway, given that there is nothing new under the sun. Therefore, invention and uniqueness are no longer essential in making art. Originality might, in their terms, be an egoistic grasping for individual recognition in a world that is ever more needful of the opposite—cooperation and integration."[18] Postmodernists remind us that the notion of originality is absent in most traditions of art, in the West and throughout the world. Throughout time most cultures felt no need to identify artists personally, even if they were especially gifted.

About Levine's *After Walker Evans #7,* Yenawine further explains that this image, reproduced here, is five or six generations of printing away from its original negative and exaggerates the by-products of reproduction: intensified whites and blacks and loss of subtle gradations from light to dark. We might look at this as distortion, but Yenawine examines it for the things gained, and interprets the most basic gain to be access because this particular image might have otherwise been unknown to us. Yenawine's point reinforces Crimp's, and Benjamin's before his, that the invention of photography has created havoc for Modernism. The original photograph, or any artwork, is not important. The reproduction brings the image to millions of us who otherwise would not see it at all because we would not travel to wherever Evans's photograph might hang. Levine scorns originality in her defiant and blatant copying.

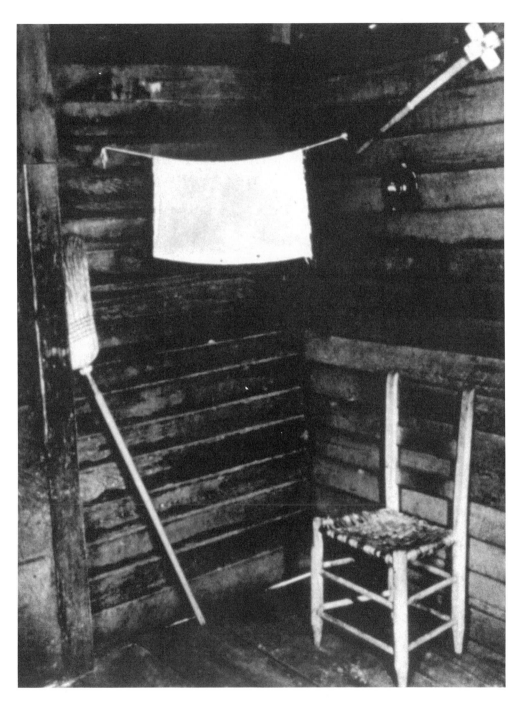

Sherrie Levine, After Walker Evans #7, black and white photograph, 14" × 11", 1990. Courtesy
of Marion Goodman Gallery, NYC.

Another quality that Yenawine finds more obvious in the reproduction than in the original is "pathos." Because Levine's reproduction has diminished the original photograph's fine print qualities, it encourages us to concentrate on the subject matter of the image. Evans's photograph is part of the large documentary project of photographing poverty in America that took place during the Depression. While doing this, Evans always gave great attention to compositional issues that are diminished in Levine's reproduction. Yenawine writes that "by reducing the formal perfection, we have left, then, something that is more a document of what Evans started with, perhaps made even more touching because of the heavy contrasts of black and white, the general dirtiness of the image itself. While we might be satisfied to see Evans's original image as a still life, here we are urged to wonder about the life of the person who sits in the chair."[19] Thus, Levine's *After Walker Evans #7* can be seen to illustrate other principles of Postmodernism—namely, that art ought not be separated from life, that art can and should refer to things other than art, and that art can and should be about more than its own form.

By using a camera to rephotograph a photograph, Levine is also eschewing the reverence previously given to painting, always considered the essential medium of Modernism, even though Minimalist sculptors attempted to challenge the primacy of paint on canvas.

By selecting the work of male artists, Levine questions the place of women in the history of art. By copying certain subjects of male artists, such as a photograph by Edward Weston of his son Brett Weston as a nude young boy, she also questions the role of the artist's gender when the audience views the work: If the nude torso of a young boy had been made by a woman artist, the implications would have been different than they are. The issue of gender and representation is a larger issue that will be explored in the following pages as we consider the role of feminist theory in Postmodernism.

As should be expected, not everyone is enamored with appropriations such as those by Levine. In one biting rejection, Mario Cutajar dismisses the practices of Levine and fellow Postmodernists like Jeff Koons, who appropriates crass three-dimensional commercial artifacts such as bunnies, has them made into stainless-steel replicas, and exhibits them as high art sculptures; and David Salle, the painter who freely and frequently paints others' imagery into his own. Cutajar writes: "The typical product of envy and resentment, postmodernism has extracted its vitality from parasitic critiques of far greater achievement, rationalizing the shabbiness of its own product by devaluing (deconstructing) the greatness of what is beyond the reach of its adherents."[20] He interprets the strategy of appropriation to be the strategy of adolescents trying to emerge from under the shadow of their formidable parents.

While acknowledging objections such as Cutajar's and those of others, with this example of a Postmodernist work of art by Levine, and fleeting references to the work of Koons and Salle, we can begin to draw some meaningful generalizations about the differences between Postmodernist art and Modernist art. Postmodernists do not merely follow Modernists chronologically, they critique them. Modernists throw off the past and strive for individual innovations in their art making; Postmodernists are generally content to borrow from the past and are challenged by putting old information into new contexts. Critics and theorists who support Modernism ignore the art of artists who are not working within the sanctioned theory of Modernism. Postmodernist critics and artists embrace a much wider array of art-making activities and projects. Modernists attempt to be pure in their use of a medium; Postmodernists tend to be eclectic regarding media, and freely gather imagery, techniques, and inspiration from a wide variety of sources, much of it from popular culture. Modernists generally disdain popular culture. Although Modernists are often enthusiastic about the times during which they work, they think themselves and their art apart from and above the ordinary events of their day. Postmodernists are skeptical and critical of their times, and, as we shall soon see when we deal with activist art, some Postmodernist artists are socially and politically active. Modernists believe in the possibility of universal communication; Postmodernists do not.

Whereas Modernists search for universals, Postmodernists identify differences. Difference, according to Cornell West, is concerned with issues of "exterminism, empire, class, race, gender, sexual orientation, age, nation, nature, region."[21] According to West, a new cultural politics of difference is determined to "trash the monolithic and homogenous in the name of diversity, multiplicity and heterogeneity; to reject the abstract, general and universal in light of the concrete, specific and particular; and to historicize, contextualize and pluralize by highlighting the contingent, provisional, variable, tentative, shifting, and changing."

In an article called "Beyond Universalism in Art Criticism," Karen Hamblen provides an overview of problems inherent in beliefs in the possibility of universal communication through art.[22] She explains that most scholars no longer believe that art objects can communicate without viewers having access to knowledge about the times in which they were made and the places in which they originated. Most critics no longer believe that they can interpret, let alone judge, art from societies other than their own without considerable anthropological knowledge of those societies. Most critics now believe that artworks possess characteristics and meanings based on their sociocultural contexts, and acknowledge that artworks have been interpreted differently in various times and places. Critics are now likely to consider personality differences, socioeconomic backgrounds, genders, and religious affiliations of artists and their audiences, whereas Modernist critics are much more likely to concentrate solely on the art object itself and believe that they can gain consensual agreement about their individual responses.

With the influence of Postmodernism, critics are much more attuned to viewers of art and how they respond to it, and they prize variable understandings of the same work of art. Wanda May, along with Hamblen, both scholars of art education, asserts that the Postmodernist goal is to "keep things open, to demystify the realities we create."[23] The rigid categories of Modernism "tend to make us more static than we are or wish to be." May adds that a Postmodern work is "evocative rather than didactic, inviting possibilities rather than closure." Craig Owens, drawing on the work of Barthes, explains a Postmodern distinction between considering literature, or any work of art, as either *work* or *text:* "Singular and univocal, the work is an object produced by an author; whereas the text is a permutational field of citations and correspondences, in which multiple voices blend and clash."[24] This is an important distinction and marks a big difference between newer and older kinds of criticism: Most contemporary critics, and all Postmodernist critics, hold that an artwork is indeed a text written by many people, providing viewers with many possible readings.

Lucy Lippard gives a clear and strong objection to the tendency of Modernists to withdraw from the world and ordinary viewers in their art making: "God forbid, the [Modernist] taboo seems to be saying, that the content of art be accessible to its audience. And God forbid that content mean something in social terms. Because if it did, that audience might expand, and art itself might escape from the ivory tower, from the clutches of the ruling/corporate class that releases and interprets it to the rest of the world."[25] She rails against what she calls the still-current Modernist taboo against what Modernists derogatorily refer to as "literary art," which encompasses virtually all art with political intentions. Critics and artists still influenced by Modernism are likely to denigrate social art as too "obvious, heavy handed, crowd pleasing, sloganeering." Lippard berates Modernists for rejecting Dada, Surrealism, Social Realism, Pop art, Conceptual art, performance art, video art, and all art with social concerns.

Barbara Kruger, a Postmodernist artist who appropriates and alters photographs and adds her own texts, is also a published critic who rejects the Modernists' fixation with distinguishing, in a hierarchical manner, high culture from low culture. The title of her article is telling: "What's High, What's Low—and Who Cares?" In the article she denounces such categories in general for their false authority, pat answers, and easy systems. She defends her rejection of distinctions between high and low art by arguing that art "can be defined as the ability, through visual, verbal, gestural, and musical means, to objectify one's experience in the world: to show and tell through a kind of eloquent shorthand how it feels to be alive. And of course a work of art can also be a potential commodity, a vessel of financial speculation and exchange. But doesn't popular culture have the ability to do some of the same things: to encapsulate in a gesture, a laugh, a terrific melodic hook, a powerful narrative, the same tenuously evocative moments, the same fugitive visions?"[26] In a related thought about Modernism's penchant for dogmatic statements and distinctions, Robert Storr writes: "Indeed if postmodernism means anything, it is an end to terminal arguments and the historical mystifications and omissions necessary to maintaining millennial beliefs of all kinds."[27]

Harold Pearse, a Canadian scholar of art education, succinctly draws significant distinctions among premodern, Modern, and Postmodern tendencies, and his thoughts summarize this section: "By dispossessing itself of the *premodern* tendency to repress human creativity to avoid usurping the supremacy of a divine creator, and the *modern* tendency to over-emphasize the originative power of the autonomous individual, the *postmodern* imagination can explore alternative modes of inventing alternative modes of existence."[28] Pearse explains that the model of the Modernist image of the artist as a productive inventor has been replaced by that of *the bricoleur,* or collagist, who finds and rearranges fragments of meaning. The Postmodern artist is the "postman delivering multiple images and signs which he has not created and over which he has no control."

FEMINIST AESTHETICS AND CRITICISM

**In 1985-86 the number of women given one-person shows
in New York City was one.**

This is the text of one of thirty posters produced between 1985 and 1990 by the Guerrilla Girls, an anonymous collective of women artists, art historians, and art administrators who have hosted panel discussions, attended symposia, appeared in *Vogue, Playboy,* and *Artforum* magazines, and on National Public Radio, and NBC television's "Night Watch." In all their public appearances, they wear miniskirts, high heels, and great hairy guerrilla heads. They also brandish phallic bananas. Membership in the Guerrilla Girls is held strictly secret to protect them from reprisals from the art establishment they challenge.

They produce their messages as stickers, posters, magazine advertisements, Christmas cards, and videotapes. One, directed at Jesse Helms, the vociferous opponent of "immoral" art such as that by Robert Mapplethorpe and Andres Serrano, says:

**Relax Senator Helms, the art world is your kind of place...
The majority of penises in major museums belong to Baby
Jesus.**

The Guerrilla Girls' Code of Ethics includes this satiric directive:

**A curator shall not exhibit an Artist, or the Artists of a
Dealer, with whom he/she has had a sexual relationship, unless
such liaison is explicitly stated on a wall label 8 inches from the
exhibited work.**

Another work asserts:

**For the 17.7 million-dollar cost of a single Jasper Johns
painting, a collector could buy one work each by 67 major
artists, including Mary Cassatt, Artemisia Gentileschi, Frida
Kahlo, Paula Modersohn-Becker, Louise Nevelson, and
Elizabeth Vigée-Lebrun.**

The Getty Museum and the New York Public Library now have in their permanent collections complete sets of 50 limited edition posters, labeled with a banana and signed with a lipstick kiss. Proceeds benefit future Guerrilla Girls activities.[29] A newer group of feminists, WAC (Women's Action Coalition), emerged in New York, and then in San Francisco and other cities, as local, direct action groups to raise women's issues in and out of the art world. When the group heard that the new Guggenheim branch museum was to open in lower Manhattan with an exhibition of Brancusi, Ellsworth Kelly, Kandinsky, and Carl Andre, the Guerrilla Girls and WAC organized a campaign and sent five hundred pink cards to Thomas Krens, Guggenheim director, saying: "Mr. Krens, Welcome to downtown. We hear your first show features four White Boys at the White Boys Museum. Lotsa luck." The Guggenheim revised its plans.

Describing the political work of the Guerrilla Girls and WAC is a good way to introduce the major contributions of feminism to current art theory. The history of recent feminism is older than some of us may realize: Simone de Beauvoir published *The Second Sex* in 1949, Betty Friedan's *The Feminine Mystique* came out in 1963, Kate Millet's *Sexual Politics* in 1970, Germaine Greer's *The Female Eunuch* in 1971, and Gloria Steinem founded *Ms.* magazine in 1972, over twenty years ago.

Feminist aesthetician Hilde Hein offers this caution to any summary of feminism: "Feminism is nothing if not complex."[30] She provides a brief historical overview of feminist art in Great Britain and the United States, recalling that Helen Frankenthaler and Bridget Riley in the 1950s and 1960s enjoyed great prominence in the art world, but their content was not feminist because it neither addressed the historical condition of women nor looked like art made by women. Until the end of the 1960s, most women artists sought to "de-gender" their art in order to compete within the male-dominated mainstream. By the 1960s, the counterculture no longer considered the mainstream to be ideologically neutral, and feminists recognized that the art system and art history had institutionalized sexism. Feminist artists such as Miriam Schapiro, Judy Chicago, and Nancy Spero exhumed women artists ignored in the past, and feminist historians began writing "revisionist" art histories to include the women artists who had been ignored. Many feminists dismissed the distinction between the crafts and high art as a male distinction, especially since women traditionally made craft items. Feminist artists in the 1970s began including decoration in their art. Other feminists produced autobiographical works in many media and cathartic, ritualized performances such as Mary Beth Edelson's *Memorials to the 9,000,000 Women Burned as Witches in the Christian Era.* During the 1980s, some feminist art took a conceptual bent—for example, Cindy Sherman's photographic investigations of female role playing in culture and Barbara Kruger's evocations of cultural domination through the graphic vocabulary of advertising. Feminist principles have currently become widely accepted and, in opposition to the purity and exclusivity of Modernism, feminists are calling for an expansive, pluralistic approach to

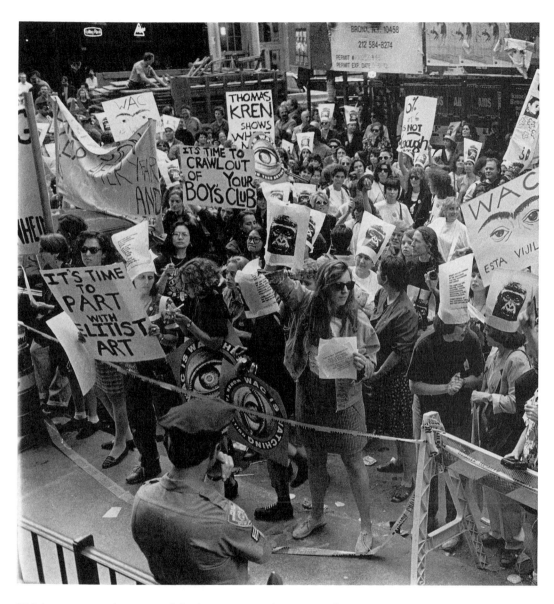

WAC demonstrates at the opening of the downtown Guggenheim, New York City, June 25, 1992. Photograph: Lisa Kahane.

art making, including the use of narrative, autobiography, decoration, ritual, and craft-as-art. Hein writes that feminists' acceptance of popular culture helped to catalyze the development of Postmodernism.

Hein's caution about the complexity of feminism and her brief historical overview provide an introduction to feminist art and criticism. Kristin Congdon and Elizabeth Garber, two art educators applying feminist views to the teaching of art criticism at all levels, provide further overviews. Their summary positions, given here, are supplemented and amplified by the work of other scholars of feminism, male and female.

Congdon summarizes recent feminism this way: "In the past twenty-five to thirty years the feminist movement has functioned to increase discussions about women's art and women artists. Dialogue centers on one or more of the following issues: (1) the recognition and establishment of women's art history; (2) the existence of gender differentiated approaches to artistic processes, products and aesthetic response; and (3) the development of non-hierarchical approaches to understanding and appreciating art."[31]

Garber offers four important distinctions. The first, and most important, is between sex and gender: "Sex is the biological trait we are born with: We are either male or female. Gender, on the other hand, is learned through socialization. Feminine and masculine traits are associated with gender, e.g., boys *learn*, through social expectations and modeling, to assert themselves and not to cry, while girls *learn* to express their emotions and to nurture others."[32] Congdon offers these examples of gender expectations: "While men are expected to excel in a particular arena, women are conditioned to be adequate in many areas. Boys learn independence, competition and organizational skills whereas girls focus on relationships with others which involve intimacy and a greater effort toward peaceful interchange and compromise."

Feminist theory is built on gender distinctions. Gender is a primary factor in how we perceive the world and understand art, but gender has been overlooked for centuries by aestheticians and critics who would want us to believe that we can approach art and experience neutrally. Some forty years ago, Simone de Beauvoir observed that "one is not born a woman; one becomes one"—she then went on to show how woman has been constructed as "Man's Other."[33]

Garber's second premise is that feminist theory is instrumental. That is, it works to change the way things are. It arises from the social and political goals of the women's movement. It seeks to alleviate the oppression of women. Garber asserts that "not all women artists are feminists; feminism is a chosen position." In Hein's words, "one becomes a feminist by declaration—not by birth or chance or out of habit." Hein goes on to explain that "contrary to a commonly held belief, feminism comes no more naturally to women than to men. Women are normally socialized to experience the world in accordance with male determined categories. Knowing themselves to be female, they nevertheless understand what that means in male terms, unless they explicitly take an oppositional stand and declare their right to self-determination." Feminist critics reject the notion that aesthetics and politics can be independent of one another. Some critics, however, still maintain that there should be a separation between art and politics. Hilton Kramer proclaims that feminism "tells us nothing about the qualities one should be studying in a work of art."[34] Hein counters the assertion that overtly political representations have no place in art by arguing that such critics "are failing to grasp the charge implicit in the feminist art that 'conventional' art is equally political, the politics being cast in that 'neutral' or masculinist mode that appears invisible." Despite objections such as Kramer's, most agree that a separation between art and politics *is* narrow and naive and obstructionist to intelligent critical discourse.

Third, according to Garber, "*Feminist* and *feminine* are not interchangeable terms. Feminine is a term assigned to women that connotes socially determined qualities of women such as delicacy and gentleness (these qualities are often assumed to be innate and to transcend historical eras) or inherent qualities such as generally smaller physiques than those of men." Feminism should always be understood as a political commitment to bring about change in a specific historical moment and to meet special needs that the lives of women dictate. Certainly, not all women artists are feminists in their work. Hein reminds us of the work of Riley and Frankenthaler, and Edward Gomez reminds us of the work of Susan Rothenberg and Jennifer Bartlett, two very successful contemporary painters in whose work gender has not been an explicit issue.[35]

Garber's fourth premise is similar to Hein's caution about the complexity of feminism. Garber agrees with those who hold that feminism is not a fixed set of principles or a single position or approach to understanding, but that it is varied and continues to evolve. Rosalind Coward emphatically makes a similar point: "Feminism can never be the product of the identity of women's experiences and interests—there is no such unity. Feminism must always be the alignment of women in a political movement with particular political aims and objectives. It is a grouping unified by its political interests, not its common experiences."[36] Hein also holds that feminists have not found a body of truths or a central dogma, but she credits feminists with reframing the questions. The list of problems feminists have abandoned as misguided are "the characterization of aesthetic 'disinterest,' the distinction between various art forms, as well as differences between craft and art, high and popular art, useful and decorative arts, the sublime and the beautiful, originality, and many puzzles that have to do with the cognitive versus the affective nature of aesthetic experience." This last point rejects splitting emotion from cognition, holding that they are essentially interrelated. Almost everyone agrees that the old problems, the older questions *are* outmoded and counterproductive to intelligent and inclusive criticism.

After making these general distinctions, Garber explicates the major themes and issues of feminism, beginning with a question often raised about whether there is a distinctive "female aesthetic" or a "female sensibility." She explains that feminists have taken different positions on this matter. Lucy Lippard identified qualities that distinguish women's art making from that of men's as "a central focus (often 'empty,' often circular or oval), parabolic baglike forms, obsessive line and detail, veiled strata, tactile or sensuous surfaces and forms, associative fragmentation, autobiographical emphasis." She says these qualities are found more often in the work of women than of men. Lippard cites as examples Georgia O'Keeffe's flowers with their vortices, Frida Kahlo's autobiographical paintings, and Miriam Schapiro's detailed pattern and decoration paintings of kimonos and houses. Lippard also speculated that she as a woman brings a different sensibility to looking at art: "I know that a certain kind of fragmentation, certain rhythms, are wholly sensible to me even if I can't analyze them."

The search for female sensibility as a universal quality of women's art was more important in the 1970s than it is now. Some feminists now argue that the insistence on a female sensibility reinforces characteristics socially assigned to the sexes and perpetuates too simple a dichotomy of opposites between male and female. Claims of a female sensibility circumscribe what and who women can be, and many feminists strongly reject limiting conceptions of women to any particular quality. Lippard abandoned her previous beliefs about female sensibility in 1984. Arlene Raven, however, recently defended the search, saying that a female sensibility was consciously introduced as the antithesis to imagery sanctioned by art history canons that related men's experiences and values as better than women's. Garber thinks such disagreements among feminists are healthy and can lead to "varieties of feminist aesthetics that represent chosen positions in the fight to end social, economic, intellectual, and spiritual oppression of women or that deconstruct stereotypic ideas about women's sensibilities."

Congdon argues that women have shared experiences that are binding: "Women are bound together by shared experiences which often include childbirth and child-raising and major responsibilities for homemaking and food preparation. They are also bound together by oppression. It *does* make a difference to women as a cultural group that one out of every three females in the United States is raped, that one out of every two wives is abused by her husband, that one out of every four female children is sexually abused; and that eighty percent of women who work outside of the home say that they have been sexually harassed on the job." She also argues that "everyone suffers from sexism. An oppressor may reap some benefits from an unjust position but that same oppressor must guard, continue to fight for, justify and distort reality in order to maintain the status quo. Energy expended in such negative ways is energy not spent in positive development." Congdon categorizes the work of Nancy Spero, Judy Chicago, Miriam Schapiro, Mary Beth Edelson, and Carolee Schneeman as dealing with issues that are uniquely female in women's experiences. She interprets the work of Barbara Kruger, Sherrie Levine, Jenny Holzer, Silvia Kolbowski, and Cindy Sherman as exploring topics of female experience as a social or psychological construct.

As noted earlier, Postmodernist critics reject the notion that an art object can communicate universally across time and space. Feminists also reject universal criteria as merely the tastes and values of a small segment of the population—usually male, white, and artistically and socially elite. Feminists ask why subjects of war are valued over mother-and-child or flower paintings. Recall from Chapter 2 that Deborah Butterfield was pleased that her renditions of horses were peaceful, as opposed to the warlike horses often rendered by male artists. Feminists also ask why quilting is called a "minor art." Congdon suggests that quilts have been unappreciated because they were made by women, just as jazz was underrated for so long because it was made by Black people. Postmodernists in general, and feminists in particular, argue against hierarchical distinctions in the arts. Congdon reminds us that Miriam Schapiro and Joyce Kozloff embrace the decorative arts in an effort to affirm women's contributions in history and to erode the distinction between high and low art.

Congdon cites several feminist scholars who argue that women think and act differently in the art world than their male counterparts. Carol Gilligan has found that that which is masculine tends to separate and that which is feminine tends to connect, and such attitudes have much to do with how men and women solve problems and define the world. Cheatham and Mary Claire Powell found that many of the women artists they studied "did not have as a characteristic goal the need to get to the top in a competitive isolated manner but to use art as a way of connecting to all things and creating more fulfilling lives." Sandra Langer claims that male artists strive to create the perfect art object while "a woman centered perspective replaces the dubious object and its mechanistic overtones with the more exciting and rewarding concept of experimentation. The right to fail, to be human, to keep on trying and growing is fundamental to feminism itself." Congdon cites others who argue that a woman's perspective can be noncompetitive, subjective, and bonding. Joanna Frueh studied art history texts and found their language to be associated with war, revolution, and conquest, in contrast to noncompetitive thinking: "Artists destroy pernicious styles, they engage in campaigns, skirmishes, military exercises, battles and conquests. We read about assaults, attacks, invasions and confrontations as well as rebels and revolutionaries." In contrast to this, feminist art criticism can be connective, inclusive, and nonhierarchical. Some feminist critics are quite content with their political and cultural actions to open doors and raise more questions than they answer.

Garber considers how feminist theory has contributed to our understanding of how viewers respond to images. She and other feminists credit John Berger, the British Neo-Marxist critic, with identifying the "male gaze" in his book and television programs, *Ways of Seeing*.[37] Berger's thesis is that the many nude paintings of women in Western art are made for the enjoyment of the male. The woman subject is presented as passive and available. Man is always assumed to be the ideal spectator, and the pictured woman is designed to flatter him. Man is the surveyor, woman the oppressively surveyed, reduced to an object of aesthetic contemplation, and thereby dehumanized. Jean-Paul Sartre, the existentialist philosopher, earlier made an observation very similar to Berger's about the male gaze. He wrote that the perceived object, aware of herself perceived, finds herself coerced to self-awareness as through the eyes of another, thus ceasing to be herself.[38] Images of women circulating in fine art and, especially, in popular films and advertisements provide what feminists call "paradigm scenarios" that shape our emotions, inform our ideas, and influence our actions. Images of women, positive and negative, help to construct and reinforce our emotional patterns and influence our worldly actions toward women and attitudes about them.

Hein characterizes the objectionable depictions of women in the high art tradition: "Along with loving and caressive exploration of women in intimate detail, they have been used to represent considerable violence toward and abuse of women. The grand tradition is full of rapes, abductions, mutilations, and hateful degradation of women. But these have not been authentic from a woman's perspective. By and large, they have been viewed through the lascivious, sentimental, or punitive eye of a man. Feminist artists face the challenge of recasting these same experiences *as they are undergone by women,* so as to reveal an aspect of them that has been ignored. In doing so, they expose both the politics and the gender bias of traditional art and risk rejection of their own work on the ground that it is not art within that traditional definition. What is distinctive to feminist art, then, is not that it is 'about' women, but that it is so in a way that is new, albeit using the same instruments as before."

Griselda Pollock names some of the images of women within popular culture that feminists are contesting—"the dumb blond, *femme fatale,* homely housewife, devoted mother, and so forth, which were judged in a vocabulary of absolutes: right or wrong, good or bad, true or false, traditional or progressive, positive or objectifying."[39] Pollock semiotically deconstructs a printed advertisement of how women are constructed. A high-gloss, airbrushed glamour photograph of a female model is carefully composed, constructed, and selected from many shots, and printed for mass circulation. With its carefully selected female body and lack of realized surroundings, the ad has a tradition, and evokes a "reality effect" for its appeal to fantasy. She argues that color, focus, texture, printing procedures, and airbrushing all constitute signifying elements that must be scrupulously decoded.

Jan Zita Grover considers representations of lesbians in the popular culture, asking: "Which representation has greater authority for you: the wanton woman in Victoria's Secret underwear or leather in *On Our Backs* or the jockettes in photographs of GAA softball players printed in a local bar guide or gay newspaper? Any of these? All? None?" She explains that "pulp paperbacks make explicit allusion to butch-femme dichotomies: what were popularly conceived as 'male' traits are attributed to one partner (short hair, tailored clothes, piercing stare, wiry, boyish build, dominating position above and behind partner), while the other is commonly depicted as exaggeratedly feminine (*en deshabille*—peignoir, brassiere or slip, frilly underpants—long hair, modestly downcast glance)." She asserts that "most of the social and sexual differences encoded in these illustrations say more about male illustrators'/editors'/readers' concerns with imposing marks of gender difference on the objects of their desire than they do about lesbian lives."

Grover asks an important second question, "not simply about which cultural institution's representations has authority or resonance or credibility, but *for whom*. For the Moral Majorian seeking proof for his contempt; for a parent of a gay seeking evidence that gay lives can be (almost) happy, (almost) normal; for a gay person living a closeted or isolated life, eager for evidence that others of her or his sex, class, race, sexual preference exist as openly gay; for a concerned straight person attempting to understand—to see—something about a gay friend's culture; for a gay or straight fantasy, turn-on, turn-off, daydream, nightmare."

Hein, Pollock, Grover, and other feminist, Postmodernist, and—as we shall next see—Multiculturalist writers try to deconstruct such images of the woman as the sexual object displayed in paint on canvases in museums, and the "dumb blonde" and "butch softball players" portrayed in popular culture. Feminists and Postmodernists in general see all images as part of discourse. They insist that images are not natural, but because they have been constructed so artfully and so often and are in such wide circulation, they falsely appear to be natural and true representations of how women are; thus, they very much need to be deconstructed, taken apart, dismantled. Much current politically engaged art and criticism purposely makes problematic that which we take for granted, and tries to make explicit that which is implicit and hidden in language and images.

Garber offers these further clarifying generalizations about feminism in contemporary art practice and theory.[40] Feminists are generally but not necessarily Postmodernists. Feminists draw on various theories and methodologies, such as psychoanalytic, semiotic, deconstructionist, and neo-Marxist, for political purposes to help them meet their social goals. Feminism is part of a broader political movement aimed at widespread social changes that affects women and, more recently, other Others—people of color, lesbians and gays, poor, and elderly. Women of color have made many recent and significant contributions to art and to criticism. As examples of art, Garber cites the photographs by Lorna Simpson, Carrie Mae Weems, Clarissa Sligh, and Celia Muñoz; the paintings by Santa Barraza; and the installations by Amalia Mesa-Bains. As examples of scholarship, Garber recommends the writings of Lowery Sims, Kellie Jones, Shifra Goldman, Amalia Mesa-Bains, and Coco Fusco. Last and very important, because of their social and political goals, feminists often emphasize lived experiences. Even when feminist scholars write theoretically and their work seems removed from lived experience, they, in fact, are often building bridges from theory to experience.

MULTICULTURALIST AESTHETICS AND CRITICISM

Fred Wilson is an artist who deals with museums and the ways they represent, fail to represent, and misrepresent racial and ethnic minorities. Wilson is born of African-American and Native American parents. In 1992, Wilson organized an exhibition entitled "Mining the Museum" at the Maryland Historical Society in Baltimore. In a *New York Times* review, Michael Kimmelman describes Wilson's exhibition as a critique of museums, writing that Wilson's installation "not only evokes the experiences of blacks and Indians in Maryland; it also suggests how those experiences have routinely been ignored, obscured or otherwise misrepresented at places like this one."[41]

Among the finely crafted and polished silver vessels that one would expect to see in a section of an historical museum labeled "Metalwork 1830–1880," Wilson placed steel shackles crudely forged and hammered for slaves. In a typical display of antique Victorian furniture, including a chair with the logo of the Baltimore Equitable Society, Wilson placed a whipping post. The museum has several oil paintings of locally famous and prosperous landowners with unnamed slaves in the background. Wilson researched one of the paintings, tracked down the identities of the pictured slaves, and then wrote their names in very large print on the gallery wall next to the painting. For another painting of wealthy white men, Wilson shone spotlights on the anonymous slaves in the painting and added audio tapes that pretended to speak what the slaves were thinking. With biting and effective humor that subverts the original function of glorifying the ruling class, Wilson renamed another painting *Frederick Serving Fruit,* to shift its meaning to a young Black boy who is shown serving his white master, the subject whom the painter intended to honor.

Kimmelman credits Wilson's work with bearing witness to injustice and writes that it reminds the visitors, once again, of the subjectivity of historical truth, precisely in an institution that assumes itself to be a dispenser of historical information. Based on Wilson's exhibition, museum educators prepared materials that asked visitors to consider any object in the museum by asking these questions, none of which would have been asked of an art object during the reign of Modernism:

> For whom was it created?
> For whom does it exist?
> Who is represented?
> Who is doing the telling? The hearing?[42]

These are provocative questions, especially because, as Karen Hamblen notes in a scholarly critique of the art museum, "one comes to a museum to appreciate, not to question."[43] When viewing art in a museum setting, we are not usually asking serious questions about why certain objects have been selected, who made these choices, why, who is best served by the choices, and which objects were *not* selected and why. Hamblen rightly argues that it is necessary to see our choices as proceeding from particular viewpoints, whether consciously held or not, that are themselves embedded in political motivations. The Guerrilla Girls and WAC ask us to raise the same questions, as has Foucault.

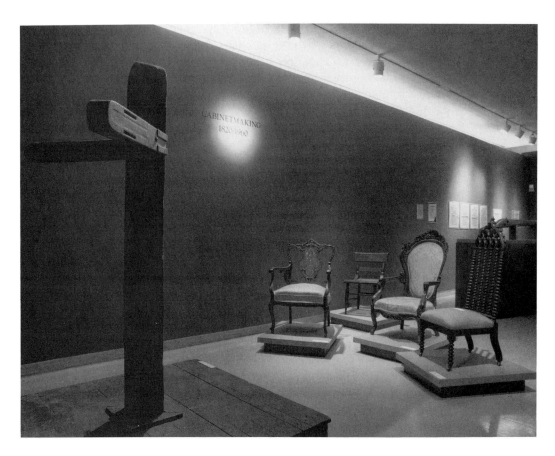

Fred Wilson, *Furniture with Whipping Post,* from the exhibition "Mining the Museum," 1992.
Courtesy of the Maryland Historical Society. Photograph by Jeff Goldman.

Wilson's gut-wrenching juxtapositions challenge the notion that appreciation is the proper attitude to hold in a museum when he confronts us with shackles next to tea pots and whipping posts next to armoires. Hamblen asks us to question the selection process involved in the collecting, preserving, and exhibiting of objects in museums, pointing out, as has Wilson, that such decisions have a problematic, political dimension that we have ignored too often and for too long. Hamblen notes that objects, by being placed in an art museum, automatically and instantly receive "an apolitical patina." The historical and ideological origins of art objects and artifacts are obscured and their chosenness is forgotten. We wrongly receive them as if they have an unquestionable correctness, a givenness, and we leave them with a sense of "that's the way things should be."

Whereas Modernist approaches to society tended to trust reason to bring about emancipation and social progress, Postmodernists see these attempts resulting in reductionist policies regarding differences among peoples and their oppression. Feminists, Postmodernists, and Multiculturalists recognize the plural nature of society and work politically for plurality, diversity, and individuality rather than conformity and sameness. Postmodernist critics and artists in a pluralistic American society are asserting in words and artworks that there are many repertoires of knowledge, several traditions, and different shapes of consciousness—despite the fact that, as Hamblen points out, only certain modes of consciousness are given institutional credence. Other traditions continue to exist alongside the traditions of the dominant culture but without the benefit of institutional sanctions. In museums and through art world discourse, particular and selected types of aesthetic knowledge and traditions are presented as correct. Rarely are these representative of the broad base of aesthetic preferences in a pluralistic society. Within a pluralistic democracy, diversity of expression, unpopular viewpoints, and minority rights are supposed to be protected and respected. Critics, scholars, and artists working to increase multiculturalist sensibilities are fighting the assumption that the Western European tradition of male superiority is of greater value than other traditions.

Hachivi Edgar Heap of Birds uses some Postmodernist strategies similar to Wilson's, but usually avoids the museums, taking his work directly to the streets. Like Wilson, Heap of Birds returns to what critic Mason Riddle calls "musty record books" for historical information that the dominant culture would like to suppress. In a 1990 piece on government property along the Mississippi River in downtown Minneapolis, Heap of Birds erected forty white aluminum signs with the names in blood red of forty Dakota Indians—first in Dakota, then in English—who were hanged after the 1862 United States–Dakota war. Thirty-eight of the execution orders were signed by President Abraham Lincoln, two by President Andrew Jackson. Riddle reports that some Minnesotans attacked the piece and she argues that their responses "reveal not only how fearful of (real) history many white people are, but also how powerful the piece is."[44]

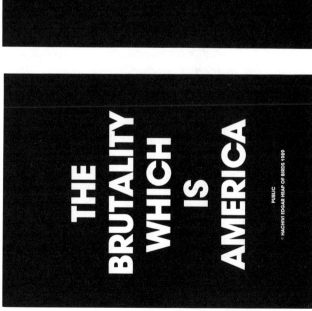

Hachivi Edgar Heap of Birds, *Public, Enemy, Care for Youth*, three stat photographs, 1989.

In 1990, in San Jose, California, Heap of Birds displayed a transit poster on the outside of a bus with these words:

SYPHILIS
SMALL POX
FORCED BAPTISMS
MISSION GIFTS
ENDING NATIVE LIVES

About his work and that of other artists who have been kept to the fringes of the art world, critic Meyer Rubinstein writes: "They are not using art to get a message across, rather, the getting across of the message is their art."[45] Since 1982, Heap of Birds has utilized abstract paintings; pastels on paper; ink on paper; and public works in the form of billboards, posters, and the Spectacolor Light billboard in Times Square in New York City. Heap of Birds received training in the traditions of his tribal elders on the Cheyenne Arapaho Reservation in Oklahoma, and has also pursued graduate studies in the United States and Great Britain.

About his use of traditional media—oil, pastels, and ink—for pieces that hang on gallery walls, critic Lydia Matthews writes that he "subverts any attempt to characterize this Native American artist as noble spirit, dangerous savage, or ravaged victim. Instead, Heap of Birds represents himself as a complex and fully dimensional individual working as an artist within a tribal community."[46]

David Bailey is a scholar working in England who uses semiotics and Poststructuralist theories to critique how minorities, especially Black people, are abusively misrepresented in the popular press through stereotypical representations. He writes that the stereotype "is commonly used to push people whom we do not value into still further subordinate positions. As soon as we think of people or groups whom we value, it is much harder to image them as stereotypical."[47] Bailey identifies three elements of a stereotype: *fragmentation* defines the whole group by one small aspect ("Blacks are inherently criminal"); *objectification* places the group outside of what is considered normal (the Black as exotic athlete); *name substitution* (nigger, kike, spic, yip, fag, gimp) by which a group is demeaned. Bailey tells us that stereotypes, like other forms of discourse, are not natural or inevitable; rather, they are socially constructed to serve the interests of the dominant group. Using techniques of psychoanalytic criticism, he explains that the notion that Blacks are exotic reinforces the position of white domination through the psychological constructs of otherness and difference, and a combination of desire and fascination. Blacks pose a threat to white society, yet within this fear is a desire and fascination with the physical, textural, and sexual physique of the Black subject's body.

Bailey contrasts two examples of media representations of Asians in British newspapers. An Air Lanka advertisement in a supplement of a London Sunday newspaper uses a color photograph of natives paddling long boats, with an inset of a female Asian model gazing at the reader with an inviting smile. The ad's copy is "A taste of paradise to Sri Lanka. Be dazzled with the people of Paradise." Bailey contrasts this ad with the paper's headline for a news story, "Asians still flooding in," about Asians and British immigration laws. Bailey identifies ambivalence in these two representations. First he identifies a sociopsychological fear of the Asian subject, an extreme xenophobia, fear and contempt, for strangers and foreigners "flooding the country." In the ad, however, Bailey identifies a desire for and fascination with Asian culture embedded within mythologies of exotic food ("a taste of paradise") and submissive women (the model's gaze, "be dazzled with the people"). Bailey concludes that "the logic of racist ideologies is such that it can naturalize representations and make it seem all right for the 'English' to go to Asia and flood it with a neo-colonialist mentality, yet it is not all right for Asians to come to this country (except to do low paid manual jobs)."

By means of his analyses of these Asian representations, Bailey presents another example of how words and pictures are not neutral. The power of words and images can be wielded only by those who have access to the means of representation and reproduction. This stereotypical imagery depends on the persons who constructed the ad and the headline—those who are part of or heavily influenced by the dominant culture and who reinforce racial stereotypes and contribute to the construction of demeaned "others."

The work of Michel Foucault, the late French historian of ideas (he did not want to be known as a *philosopher* because the term implies a search for foundational truths), is an important influence on Postmodernist criticism and particularly on gay activist art and criticism. Foucault's major contribution has been to show the authority and power of discourse—language and other representations—in general, and, especially, how discourse constructs gender and represents sexuality. Foucault warns that those in power assume the self-appointed task of upholding reason for and revealing truth to those whom they think are unable to see for themselves and who are not allowed to speak for themselves. Language can be descriptive, explanatory, controlling, legitimating, prescribing, and affiliating. Argument and reason can and have been used to silence and control others, and an unyielding insistence on rational discourse can silence or diminish those who think differently.[48]

Gay activist artists and critics are deriving strategies to use in their radical political activities from Postmodernist theories such as Foucault's. A new generation of gay activists calls itself *queer*, not *lesbian, gay,* or *bisexual*. The name *queer* is meant to confront both those who would have gays disappear into mainstream society through assimilation and any oppressors of gays. Lisa Duggan, in an article she aptly titles "Making It Perfectly Queer," explains that many gay militants have rejected "the liberal value of privacy and the appeal to tolerance which dominate the agendas of more mainstream gay organizations. Instead, they emphasize publicity and self-assertion; confrontation and direct action top their list of tactical options; the rhetoric of difference replaces the more assimilationist liberal emphasis on similarity to other groups."[49] The new politic poses anger instead of civility, flamboyance instead of respectability. Louise Sloan wants a "queer community of men, women, transsexuals, gay males, lesbians, bisexuals, straight men and women, African Americans, Native Americans, people who can see and/or walk and people who cannot, welfare recipients, trust fund recipients, wage earners, Democrats, Republicans, and anarchists that might be able to teach the world how to get along."[50] These and other writers have taken their theoretical direction, in part, from Michel Foucault, who convincingly demonstrated that homosexuality, indeed all sexuality, is socially constructed. That is, sexuality is something that we ourselves create.

New "queer theories" reject the humanly made dyad of the homosexual/heterosexual, with its valuing of the latter and condemnation of the former. Douglas Crimp, an influential critic and activist, writes that "the significance of so-called appropriation art, in which the artist forgoes the claim to original creation by appropriating already-existing images and objects, has been to show that the 'unique' individual is a kind of fiction, that our very selves are socially and historically determined through preexisting images, discourses, and events."[51] One strategy emerging from the theory is, as noted earlier, to reclaim offensive words like *queer* and *dyke* that have made people feel perverse, odd, outcast, different, and deviant, and to make the terms positive and confrontational. The names that recent activist groups have invented for themselves exemplify this point: ACT UP (The AIDS Coalition to Unleash Power), the Silence = Death Project, Gran Fury, Queer Nation, DIVA TV (Damned Interfering Video Activist Television), and LAPIT (Lesbian Activists Producing Interesting Television).

Gay activist artists confronting the crisis of AIDS have been quick to use the artistic strategies of Postmodernism, freely appropriating the styles of other Postmodernist artists such as Jenny Holzer, Barbara Kruger, and Hans Haacke. Crimp makes no apology for derivative and unoriginal work by "guerrilla graphic designers." Instead, he argues that "the aesthetic values of the traditional art world are of little consequence to AIDS activists. What counts in activist art is its propaganda effect; stealing the procedures of other artists is part of the plan—if it works, we use it." In contrast to Modernist criteria, Crimp writes, gay activist artists don't claim invention of their style or the techniques; they want others to use their graphics as well as make their own.

The graphic reproduced here is an advertising poster for New York City subways that was also used in a street demonstration confronting Cardinal O'Connor of the Catholic Church of New York City, who opposes any kind of safe sex education except for abstinence. The Cardinal opposes education for safe sex not only in Catholic schools, but also in public schools and in the AIDS health-care facilities in the city. Crimp asserts that "by advocating abstinence as the only means of prevention, O'Connor denies reality, denies lifesaving information, and endangers all our lives."

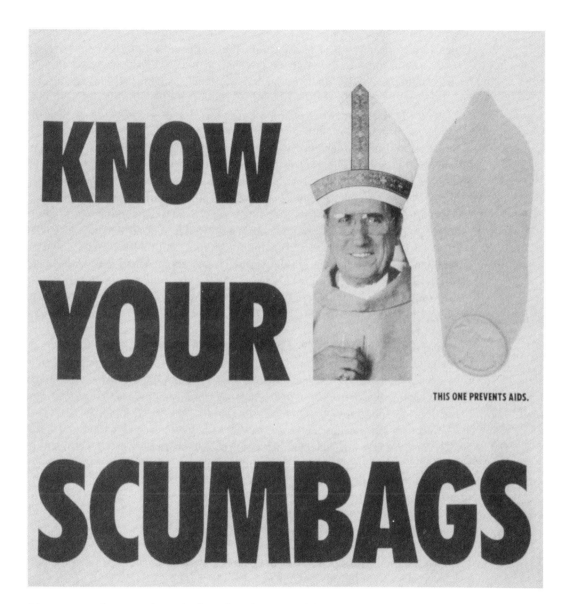

THIS ONE PREVENTS AIDS.

"Know Your Scumbags," graphic, Richard Deagle and Victor Mendolia, reproduced from <u>AIDSdemographics</u>, Douglas Crimp.

Like ACT UP, Survival Research Laboratories (SRL) is an activist collective of Postmodernist artists who mount spectacles of remote-controlled machine violence as a means to protest aspects of the dominant culture they find oppressive. For a machine that was to be covered with Bibles and designed to self-destruct in flames, SRL solicited donations for Bibles, saying: "Bibles can always be obtained for free from hotels, church organizations, libraries, the Gideon Society, thrift stores and your parents' house."[52] One of the artists described the planned performance as "the ultimate nightmare for the right wing religious male," and said it was designed to get at a whole range of issues such as population control, child pornography, the role of women in male-dominated culture, and "of course, the biblical angle of the misuse of the Bible by reactionaries."

As would be expected, not everyone in the art world is equally enthused about multiculturalism, all of its proponents, and its activist contingencies. Some scholars hold that there is a major fund of knowledge that all Americans should learn if they are to be considered culturally literate, and that there is a common cultural and aesthetic heritage in the United States about which everyone should be knowledgeable. Ralph Smith, a scholar of aesthetic education, writes that "the case for high culture and the cultivation of an appreciation of its masterworks are grounded in beliefs that would seem difficult to dispute. These beliefs are four: (a) there is a tradition of great art that is worth preserving and transmitting; (b) there are people (artists, historians, critics, educators) who care about this tradition and whose judgments are the best guides to artistic excellence that we have; (c) works of high culture are inestimable sources of intense enjoyment, gratification, and humanistic insight; and (d) such works are significant constituents of national pride and unity."[53]

Smith defends what has come to be called "the canon"—namely, those mostly Western artworks selected by some scholars as masterworks that ought to be studied by all who wish to be culturally literate: "What cannot be argued away is the existence of great art and the fact that it is great because it magnificently transfigures the commonplace. The criteria of greatness, moreover, are no mystery. They are incomparable artistic (technical) finesse, extraordinary capacity to provide high degrees of aesthetic gratification, and stature, the latter term implying the significant human values master-works individually express."

Multiculturalist opponents of the canon generally consider it much too narrow in scope, and hold it to be legitimating only certain types of art, while implicitly denigrating other types. Arguments of this sort often raise issues about the word and concept of *quality*: "What is in question is the way the word is used to compare, select and sort out art and artists. Some people in the art world claim that the word is simply a pretext for preserving the authority of the heterosexual white male."[54] Those on the right of the political and aesthetic spectrum tend to embrace the word *quality,* and those on the left to disdain it as a term used to exclude art. Despite opposition, a widening of the canon of what artworks ought to be considered seriously should be supported.

CONCLUSION

Artists and critics are informed by and contribute to the thought of their times. The many examples of uses of Postmodernist strategies by critics and artists given in this chapter are offered to make Postmodernist art and criticism, in all its complexity, clearer. No one-to-one correspondences between a theory and an artwork, or a theory and a piece of art criticism, are given, however—that would be too much of an oversimplification. This book is influenced by the Postmodernists' beliefs that an artwork does not have a single meaning and that multiple interpretations are beneficial. Thus, many critics are quoted about the work of a single artist. The more perspectives we can gain on a work of art, the richer and deeper will be our experience of that work. The chapter is aimed at helping the reader view new art and old art through new intellectual strategies, and read recent criticism with more confidence because of having some introductory knowledge of the underpinnings of Postmodernist ideas and practices.

6
WRITING AND TALKING ABOUT ART

This final chapter embodies the ultimate purpose of the book: To help you write and talk about art better than you were able to do before you read it. Many art critics have been quoted throughout so that you would have many positions to consider, several literary styles to read, different ideological positions among which to choose. You should now be in a position to develop a critical voice of your own. Do you want to further feminist criticism? Would you like to publish in the popular press and influence large numbers of people? Are there certain types of art or aesthetic issues about which you feel passionate and about which you want readers to know?

The chapter assumes that you are serious about learning and writing. If you are not, you are likely wasting your time and that of anyone who has to read what you write. Annie Dillard, the accomplished novelist, advises anyone who writes to "write as if you were dying. At the same time, assume you write for an audience consisting solely of terminal patients. That is, after all, the case."[1]

Each chapter has included a large number of references, and there is a lengthy bibliography at the end of the book. These references are provided in order to credit properly all the authors whose ideas were examined and, especially, to encourage you to read further. The quotations are brief and are used as examples to make various points. If you are intrigued by any of the quotes, pleased with the way someone writes, find the source in the library and read the critic's whole piece. Let these professional critics inspire your own critical thinking and writing.

Art critics are good models for those who want to engage in serious thought and writing about the art of our times. You probably identified with some critics, preferred some styles of writing, and feel closer to certain critical positions than to others—and now you can begin to articulate why. Because you have heard many voices, you are in a better position to further develop your own.

WRITING ART CRITICISM
Choosing What to Write About

If you are going to write art criticism, you have to have something to write about. You may be able to choose what you want, or you may have an assignment given by a professor or an editor. The critics quoted throughout the book work both ways: Some choose what they write about, others are given assignments or cover certain important exhibitions out of a sense of responsibility to their readers. It is usually easier to write about something you choose—you can avoid art you don't know enough about or aren't interested in. If you can choose, choose something you are passionate about or at least interested in. You might choose art that you love or art that you hate. You might choose art you know a lot about, or art you know little but want to learn more about.

If you are given an assignment by an editor or a professor that you are not interested in, ask for a change by suggesting more interesting alternative topics. Your professors may be more flexible than you think. Professors want students to learn, and if you can convince them that you can learn more from your chosen topic than their assigned topic, they may be willing to accept your proposal. If your request is denied, you need to motivate yourself. You might even examine your lack of interest as a premise for the piece. And once you investigate the assigned topic, your initial reactions might change. Your changed feelings could be an organizing theme of your writing: Begin by describing your initial disinterest and then explain how and for what reasons your feelings changed. If your initial disinterest doesn't change, you might write a piece that is primarily negative, giving convincing arguments for your position. The point is you want to be emotionally and intellectually involved and committed to what you are expressing. Do whatever helps you to motivate yourself to write honest and committed criticism.

Single Works of Art   Are you writing about a single work of art, an exhibition by one artist, or a group show of several artists? Each of these presents its own challenges. If the assignment is to write about a single work of art, then get to know that work of art very well. A single work of art is often part of a much larger body of work, and it is always embedded in a cultural context. The larger body of work and the culture in which it was made will inform you about that one piece.

Solo Exhibitions   Many of the critics quoted in this book were writing about exhibitions, often analyzing single pieces to support their larger thesis about an artist or the exhibition. Critics usually write about exhibitions or large bodies of work. Historians are more likely to concentrate on a single work of art, trying to determine who made it and when, or what it might have meant to the people who saw it during the time and in the place in which it was made and shown. The critics quoted in Chapters 2, 3, and 4 have concentrated on bodies of work made by such artists as Dale Chihuly, Deborah Butterfield, Romare Bearden, Frida Kahlo, and Martin Puryear. They had the advantage of being able to write about more than one work of art. It is an advantage because they had more to consider and could choose which pieces to examine and which to ignore. They didn't have to write about every piece or limit their comments to one artwork. They could compare and contrast several works by the same artist. However, they also had the challenge of making summary interpretive and evaluative statements about the lifelong careers of artists and whole bodies of work.

If you are writing about an exhibition by a single artist, you will probably want to provide an overview of the artist's accomplishments, pointing out stylistic similarities among the pieces that make the work distinctive. You might also consider whether the exhibition is a retrospective of a whole career of a living or deceased artist or an exhibition of works made during a particular period in the artist's career. You could determine if the artist's style changed over time, and, if so, describe how it evolved. Tell your reader if the work is by a professionally young or mature artist. Consider whether the work is a transition from or a continuation of a previous direction by the artist.

Group Shows   Group shows can be very challenging, depending on the number of artists in the exhibition. Some exhibitions may have fifty or more artists represented by one or two pieces each. Unless you are writing a very long paper or a book, writing about every artist and every piece would be impossible. Even to mention the names of all fifty artists would be too space consuming. You will have to choose which artists and which pieces to concentrate on. Here are some strategies that may help: You could look for interpretive themes that unite individual works; you could write about the best and the worst; you could describe the range of expression in the exhibition.

If the group show includes fewer artists, say six, then you would probably be obligated to write something about the work of each, concentrating on those you felt to be most important or most interesting. If the number of artists is up to ten and you have a limited word count, then you would probably mention all but, again, concentrate on a few. Explain why these particular artists were brought together at this time in this exhibition, how they were selected and by whom. Include the exhibition's title if it has one, and any explicit theme. If there is no explicit theme, make a conjecture about why these works are being shown together. Always inquire whether the exhibition curator has written a catalog, or provided some statement of explanation. If the artists themselves chose to show their work together, you can consider how the works relate to each other.

Include and comment on the written opinions of curators and artists when they are available. Consider interviewing artists and curators. Unless you are doing a news story, however, your writing should be more than just quotations of what the artists and curators think about the work. Use their thoughts to provide context, but keep in mind that it is your own point of view about what they say that is of interest and importance.

Describing

Remember from Chapter 2 that description is criticism, not merely a prelude to criticism. Your readers may never see the art you are writing about and your description may be their only access to it. You cannot count on having a photograph accompany your piece, but you always have your words. The main task in describing a work of art is to tell what it looks like. Describe accurately and with vivacity. Make the work come alive for your readers—give them a verbal image they can see. If you describe thoroughly and passionately, description may be all you need.

Chapter 2 discusses two major sources of descriptive data: internal and external. Internal information is based on what can be seen in the work itself and can be divided into three categories: subject matter, medium, and form. Subject matter refers to those recognizable people, places, or events in a work—the nouns of the work. The medium is the material of which the work is made. Form is how the artist shapes the subject with the medium. In nonobjective and nonrepresentational work, medium and form may be predominant with no identifiable subject matter. Chapter 2 includes good descriptive examples of writing from many critics on many different types of art forms from performance art to glassmaking. You may want to refer to these.

internal Sirc.

External contextual information includes data about the time in which the piece was made—its social and intellectual milieu—other works by the same artist, and works by other artists of the same period. You can also place the work within a setting for your readers. Describe the gallery, the general tone of the exhibition, the dates during which the work was shown, and the number of pieces in the exhibition. Provide accurate information about titles, sizes, media. Provide information about who curated the exhibition, and if the work is for sale and at what price range. If biographical information about the artist would be helpful to your readers, or helpful in defending your thesis about the work, then provide it. The test of what to include in description and what to ignore is relevancy. Relevancy refers both to what your readers need to know and to what you need to tell your readers so your thesis makes sense.

external

If you are assigned a descriptive paper by a professor, know whether you are expected to be descriptive only, or if you are allowed to color your descriptions with your preferences and values. If you are only to describe—not to make value judgments—then take care to avoid implied evaluations of positive or negative worth. If you are given free rein, let the reader know that you like (or dislike) the art. Also know if you can include external information.

Interpreting

Recall from Chapter 3 that interpretation of an artwork can be based on two types of information: internal evidence and external evidence. Internal evidence consists of what is in the work itself; it is drawn from a description of the work. External evidence consists of relevant information not within the work itself: the artist's other works; the artist's biography, including gender, race, age; and the social, political, and religious milieu of the time and place in which the work was made. If you are assigned an interpretive paper to write, ask whether your interpretation may go beyond what is in the work and include external sources.

The basic premise of interpretation is that works of art are about something. When you interpret, you present your understanding of the work in a way that is convincing, both by how you write and by the evidence you provide. You want to make the work as interesting to the reader as the work allows. Always present an artwork in its strongest rather than weakest light.

In a sense, all art is about other art—that is, influenced by and in dialogue with other art. At the same time, all art is affected by the culture in which the artist lives and, in turn, affects the culture in which it is shown. The interpretive goal is to make the art meaningful to your reader in terms of the art itself, the artist's other work, all art, and culture.

If you are writing about a new artist, you have advantages and disadvantages. One advantage is that any true thing you write is a contribution because you are one of the first to do so. A disadvantage is that you are starting the dialogue without benefit of an ongoing conversation about the artist. Much has already been written about an established artist, and your challenge in this case is to add something to the discussion.

If you are writing about the work of an artist who has already been written about, you can consult these other writings or develop your own interpretation. There are advantages and disadvantages to both approaches. Working on your own, without reading others' thoughts on the same topic, requires a certain amount of self-confidence and a willingness to take risks. If you trust yourself and trust that your insights are worthwhile, you will probably contribute to ongoing thought about the work. If you consult other writers, then you will need to go beyond what they have already written and contribute to the conversation. If you take the latter approach, you can add the points of view of these other critics to your own, thus giving your readers options among interpretations. And if you do take this course, be sure to fully credit all the others.

Throughout this book, we have examined several interpretive and ideological perspectives: psychoanalytical, semiotic, feminist, Neo-Marxist, Post-structuralist, Modernist, Postmodernist, and idiosyncratic worldviews. When you select art to write about, you might decipher the ideological basis of the artwork itself and adapt your criticism accordingly. If the art is clearly Postmodernist, for example, you can explain it in those terms and enlighten your reader about Postmodernist theory. If you disagree with the ideology of the art, first explain what it is and then resist the ideology with reasonable arguments.

Judging

Responsible judgments include a clear assessment of the worth of an art object, and reasons for the assessment based on reasonable criteria. Critics disagree about which exact criteria are appropriate for judging art. Types of criteria are Realism, Formalism, Expressionism, Instrumentalism, and combinations and variations thereof. As stated in Chapter 4, you need to decide which criteria or criterion you are going to use. You may let the art itself decide by which criteria it should be judged: If it is obviously a political work, for example, then Instrumentalist criteria would apply. If it is a Formalist work, then you might apply Formalist criteria to it. This is a generous and accepting approach that allows you a wide range of tolerance for many types of art.

You may, however, want to hold more narrowly to a particular set of criteria and judge all art, no matter what it strives to do, according to your chosen criteria. For example, because of the severe social problems in the world, you may want to measure all art by Instrumentalist criteria, favoring only that art which attempts to make the world a better place in which to live. Thus, you might reject Formalist work as socially irrelevant and a waste of human energy and natural resources.

These are difficult choices: You may err on the side of aimless and contradictory eclecticism, or narrow rigidity. Or perhaps you will be able to find some amicable middle ground.

When you judge art, you are not giving advice to artists but rather articulating to readers why you think something is good or not and on what basis. To judge is to risk the possibility of being demeaning to the artist by assuming a superior role or attitude. Such an approach will likely set you against artists, and them against you, in an antagonistic way. Antagonism is not in the spirit of good criticism. Criticism is meant to further rather than to end discourse about art; you want to further the discussion by inclusion rather than dismissive exclusions. Most often, critics' judgments are positive, informing readers why a work of art is meaningful and enjoyable. Resist finding minor faults in works of art—fault finding is petty—and argue for larger issues. Be generous to artists in your considerations of their art and enthusiastic for your readers. The spirit of this book is curiosity and the project of criticism is arousing curiosity and sometimes satisfying it.

Considering Assumptions

Infer the ideological basis of the art you are considering, and know and identify your own. What constitutes good art for the artist you are considering? What constitutes good art for you? Can you list your ten commandments of good art? Are there contradictions in your set? Are your assumptions and beliefs in consort with the art you are considering, or in conflict with them? Can you make both clear to your reader?

If the brief consideration in Chapter 5 of theoretical topics interested you, you would do well to take courses in aesthetics within a department of philosophy. You might also look into courses on recent literary theory and criticism, film theory and criticism, and women's studies, all of which are affecting art theory. You may have a penchant for writing feature-length articles of theoretical criticism rather than reviews of particular exhibitions. You may want to write social theory based on artifacts. Some critics are concerned with larger issues, and use works of art as examples of their theories. Others are content to write art journalism, or news about artists, rather than criticism. There is room for many approaches. Try several, find what you are comfortable doing, and do it as well as you can.

TECHNICALITIES AND PROCEDURES OF WRITING

Selecting a Style Manual

You can find style guides in libraries and bookstores. Style guides tell you how to footnote, how to present a bibliography, how to break your paper into sections. All journals and magazines have editorial styles that they follow. Your professor may require you to follow a certain style. If not, choose one of your own and follow it. Your selection can be arbitrary but you might first find what style is generally preferred in your major area of study. If you are a psychology major, the American Psychological Association (APA) has a style manual that you may want to obtain and use. If you are an English major, your professors may prefer the University of Chicago style, or the style of the Modern Language Association. Do not make up your own style—several have already been invented. If you plan on eventually writing a major paper, such as a senior thesis, a Master's thesis, or a doctoral dissertation, find out which style your department or advisor expects and practice using it for your shorter papers so that you become familiar with it.

Determining Word Count

Find out before you begin your project what length of paper or article you are expected to write. Do not even begin before you know. *New Art Examiner* wants reviews of less that 450 words. That might translate to only three or four para-graphs. A professor may want an end-of-term paper of twenty pages. You need to know the expected length and then make decisions accordingly. Some writers find it difficult to be succinct; others find it difficult to expand their thoughts over a number of pages.

Identifying Your Audience

Once you have decided on a topic, you have to decide on an audience, or con-sider the reader for whom you are writing. If you are writing for a specific pub-lication, make yourself familiar with that publication and with the range and type of writing it publishes. All magazines and journals have editorial staffs, and the addresses of their editorial offices are listed in the front matter of the publication. Sometimes this front matter material offers a statement of publication policies and procedures, such as whether they welcome unsolicited manuscripts. You may contact editorial offices by telephone or letter and ask if they have printed guide-lines for writers. You might even request a meeting or have a telephone conver-sation with an editor. You should not submit the same article to more than one publication at a time, or if you do, inform each editor that you have sent the arti-cle to other publications for consideration.

clarity of assig.

At this point in your career, however, you are probably writing to fulfill a course assignment for a professor who will give your paper a grade. If that is the case, know what the professor is looking for before you begin. Ask questions about the assignment so that you are clear about the professor's expectations. Sometimes professors think they are clear about what they are assigning but they're not—your questions may help them further clarify the assignment. You may ask what the professor considers a good paper and, conversely, a weak paper. When writing for a professor, he or she—the grader—is your most important audience, but you might well imagine writing for your classmates in the course. They are the readers against whom you will likely be judged by your professor.

Getting an assignment from a classmate is risky business—it makes you dependent on the classmate's understanding of what the instructor wants. It is bet-ter to go directly to the instructor. If you are writing for publication, seek advice and clarification from the editor.

Getting Started

<u>Get started the moment an assignment is given to you.</u> See the art as soon as you can and let it sink in over the days or hours you have before you start writing. If it is a single work of art, get a photocopy of it or sketch it and carry it with you. Think about it over coffee in the morning and whenever else you can. If it is several works of art, make instant photographs or sketches of them and include notes. Obtain from the gallery or museum an "exhibition checklist" if one is avail-able that lists artists, works, dates, and prices.

If you have choices, consider your options, then decide as early as you can what you are going to write about. If you can write about a number of artworks, or a number of exhibitions, look at the artworks and the exhibitions and choose the one that most interests you, or the one about which you have the most to say. Narrow your topic if you can, or determine your approach. If you can choose your topic, do so early, even if your choice is somewhat arbitrary. The more interested you are in the topic, the better time you will have writing about it. Remaining undecided may be merely an avoidance technique that will not help you. If you can't decide among options, make an arbitrary choice by flipping a coin and go with the results.

Determine for yourself or by asking your professor or editor if your criticism is to be based only on your own observations, or if you can use external sources of information. In other words, do you want and are you allowed to research what you are writing about? Research about contemporary art can take several directions. If the artist is somewhat or very established, other critics have already written about his or her work. You can search magazines and books for references to the work. If the artist has not been written about, you may choose to interview the artist, seeking to find out what he or she thinks about the work, where the ideas in the work originated, what he or she intended to express, and where the artist has been. If the artist is unavailable for an interview, he or she may have written an "artist's statement" to accompany the exhibition. The artist's insights are always interesting. Beware, however, of the intentionalist fallacy discussed in Chapter 3: The artist does not own the meaning of the work, and you should not let the artist dictate to you what the work means. Rather, take the artist's point of view about the work and test it against your own knowledge and intuitions.

Exhibition curators and gallery owners or directors also have information about the artists whose work they are showing, and they may be available for an interview. If you rely on their ideas, credit them in the text or in footnotes. Ultimately, however, no matter how many people you quote, you still have to present your own sense of the art to your reader.

If you choose not to do research, or are not allowed to, then you will rely on your own observations of the work and on your knowledge and life experiences to present your descriptions, interpretations, and judgments. The evidence in this case will be your own observations and your knowledge of art and of life.

Taking Notes

No matter what or for whom you are writing, take notes. If you are writing about new art by a new artist, observe the work very carefully, ask questions about it, think about it, and jot down your thoughts on paper, even if they seem random and unrelated. Note your first impressions and what triggers them. If you are writing about works of art in a gallery or museum, take many notes, more than you will need. Note everything that you find interesting and that you might use later when you are writing. If you do not take enough notes the first time, you may well have to return to the place where the work is hanging. With deadlines, this could be a problem—museums have limited hours and most aren't open on Mondays or you may find that the show has come down before you are through writing about it. If your note taking is thorough, you will probably have more notes than you can use. That is OK—it is better to have more than less information than you need.

If the work is by fairly prominent artists, there may be information on the artists' past works in the library. If you can find such information, you will be able to put new work into context with the older work. The *Art Index* is a useful reference for finding what has been written about artists or by critics.

Be sure your notes are accurate. If they are not, you will end up with factual errors and inaccurate descriptions that may lead to misinterpretations. Spell artists' names accurately, get the titles of the works correctly, and write down dimensions and dates carefully.

Avoiding Plagiarism

Sloppy note taking can lead to unintentional plagiarism. Plagiarism is taking someone's ideas and presenting them as your own, or taking someone's words and not putting them in quotation marks or citing who wrote them. Plagiarism is theft of ideas and words and is taken very seriously; it can have serious negative consequences to your career as a student and as a professional. When you take notes, be sure to put quotation marks around direct quotes so you know later that these are the exact words of another author; if you use them, keep them within quotation marks. If you are paraphrasing what someone else said, don't use quotation marks, but provide accurate bibliographical information, including author, publication and date of publication, publisher and place of publication if it is a book, and page numbers. If you take bibliographic notes in the format your style manual specifies, you won't have to correct them later when you use them in your footnotes and bibliography.

Making an Outline

Once you have gathered all the information and evidence for your writing, make an outline to organize your thoughts and formulate your argument. Outlines can be long, detailed, and very formal, or short and personal. It depends on the way you prefer to work. The purpose of the outline is to structure your critical argument. The outline should have three major sections: the introduction, which clearly states your major claim; the body of the paper, in which you build support to back your claim; and the conclusion, in which you forcefully draw your ideas together, conclude, and summarize your argument.

outline —
a sequence
leading to a
conclusion

a map

Your outline should be logical. Writing criticism is formulating arguments, and arguments are built on logic and evidence. Your outline is not just a series of steps, it is an ordered sequence of premises that lead to a conclusion backed by evidence. It is a map that shows you where you are going and how you are going to get there. Without such a map, you and your reader may wander about without direction, ending up with a lot of information that may be true but does not lead to a conclusion based on premises.

Once you have a sound outline, you can begin writing anywhere within the outline. You do not have to start at the beginning; you can start where you want, even with the conclusion. To build confidence and momentum, you might want to start with what you know best. An alternate strategy is to start with the hardest part; once you write it, the rest will be easy.

Writing

1st draft

Write your first draft, following your outline, in whatever order you are comfortable with. As you write this first draft, do not worry if you don't have the exact wording you want, or if you need to think about something longer or are missing needed research—just leave a blank space and move on. Return to the inadequate words or blank space later and make changes and additions. Don't get stuck in any one spot. Keep pushing forward. If you have to interrupt or stop your writing, leave your work knowing exactly what you will write next when you return to it, even if you leave a sentence or paragraph half finished. This way, you can start up right away and move forward immediately—you don't want to have to start over every time you return to your writing.

Early in your paper, maybe even in the opening sentence, state your major claim or the thesis of your paper. Each paragraph should have an organizing idea. Write logically and clearly so that one sentence leads to the next, and one paragraph leads to the following paragraph. Let your reader know your point of view about the art you are considering. If your paper is primarily interpretive, state the major theme you see in the work. If you are being judgmental, take a clear stand. Make a major claim that is clear and precise but also thought-provoking. All sentences and paragraphs should lead to your conclusion, which should be stated clearly at the end.

Consider the tone of your writing. Draw your reader into the art and into your ideas by expressing them in an interesting, evocative way. Being dogmatic will likely push your reader away. You might want the tone and pacing of your writing to match the tone and pacing of the artwork you are considering. Several of the critics quoted in this book matched their words to the work in poetic fashion; refer back to some of the writing about Chihuly's glass and Golub's paintings.

Rewriting

Consider your first draft as just that and plan on improving it. Always leave yourself time to think about what you have written, and to revise it. Never turn in a first draft. Leave yourself time to get away from your writing so that you can return to it with a fresh outlook and see it anew.

Check your first sentence to see if it will get your reader's attention. End strongly with a compelling closing sentence. Get rid of redundancies and avoid offering points that may be true but that are irrelevant and thus distracting from your major thesis. Be sure your argument is clear and flows logically. Check the tone of your writing so that it is consistent throughout and that you are pleased with it. Avoid sarcasm if you are judging art. Make sure your views are evident, but also make sure that you provide evidence for your positions. Polish your writing to get it just right. Be proud of what you are turning in to your professor or editor.

Common Errors and Writing Recommendations

The term *criterion* is singular, *criteria* is plural; *medium* is singular, *media* is plural. *Its* is possessive, *it's* means *it is*. *There* refers to a place, *their* is possessive. Examples of singular possessive are the *artist's* colors, *Pollock's* drips, *Plagens's* criterion; plural possessive is the *artists'* colors.

Avoid the passive voice and write in the active voice. Your writing will be more forceful. For example, active: Holzer programmed the LED display; passive: The LED display was programmed by Holzer. *voice*

Keep present, past, and future tenses consistent throughout your writing. Works of art are usually referred to in the present tense since they exist; exhibitions are often in the past tense since they are temporary. *tense*

Long sentences are not necessarily better than short ones. Whether long or short, make sure they are clear and easy to read. *use both* *sentences*

Delete any sexist language in your writing, and avoid using sexist pronouns such as *he* and *she*. When possible, use plural pronouns such as *they;* it is preferable to writing *he and she* or *s/he*. *pronouns*

Write colorfully but avoid inflated language. If you don't fully understand something, say so. Do not try to cover up with obtuse verbiage what you don't understand. Critics can allow for the mystery of art; they are not expected to understand everything concerning the new art about which they are writing. Invite your reader to help solve the problem you are experiencing with the work. *lang.*

Avoid qualifiers, or at least consider carefully before using them. Qualifiers such as *very* and *extremely* may weaken your writing rather than strengthen it. If you say that something is powerful, you do not need to say that it is *extremely* powerful. Too many qualifiers will make your writing seem gushy and will weaken your credibility. Avoid, too, qualifiers that make your statements too safe or too weak: *rather, little* (except regarding size), *pretty* (as in "pretty sure"), *somewhat*. *qualifiers*

If you can obtain and use reproductions (color or black and white) in your paper or article, do so. Be sure to provide the artist's name, title of the piece underlined, medium, dimensions, and date of execution, in this order. *reproduction*

Consider whether headings will clarify your argument for your reader. Consult your chosen style guide for types and levels of headings.

Editing

Being a good writer also means being a good editor of your own writing. An editor assumes the role of a reader. Read what you have written as if you were a stranger to it.

First read it from the point of view of someone who would agree with you. Imagine specific persons who might do so—your best friend, a brother or sister. Have you told them enough to allow them to visualize the art? Have you conveyed to them your enthusiasm for the art?

Then read it from the point of view of someone who would likely disagree with you. Have you presented your most convincing argument with sufficient evidence for your point of view? Will your intellectual adversaries have to admit, at least, that you presented a good argument, even though they might not accept your conclusion?

Once you have edited your paper and gotten it to where you are proud of it, ask someone else to read it and make suggestions for improving it. All writing that appears in print has gone through an editorial process. This book, for example, before it got to your hands, went through considerable editing. I proposed the idea for this book to an editor. Before she and her publisher gave me the go-ahead to write it, she sent my proposal to a handful of professors around the country who might use such a book if it were published. They recommended that the book be written, but offered suggestions they thought would make it better for their students.

As I wrote the book, I gave chapters of it to students in my criticism courses, and they commented on each chapter, pointing out sections they found unclear, and identifying typographical errors. I made the changes they recommended. I also asked a trusted colleague to read the whole manuscript, and others to read sections; they, too, offered valuable suggestions for changes, which I made. I then sent the manuscript to my editor, who sent it to another handful of professors to see if they would want their students to read such a book. They approved of it but suggested changes. I made revisions. The manuscript then was given to a professional copy editor, who made detailed suggestions for changes that would improve its clarity, eliminate redundancy, and enhance its literary style. A designer then set the manuscript in the typeface you see. At this point, the publisher asked me to proofread galleys of the whole text, looking for any errors; they also hired a proofreader to do the same. And after all this, there are probably still errors in the book—you may have already found some.

This laborious process of writing and editing is common. Read the acknowledgment sections of books on your bookshelf to see the variety of people authors credit and thank for their help. The point is that editing is important and you should go through the process with your own writing to help improve it. First, read your own work. Reading it aloud to yourself will help you find awkward phrases and incomplete sentences. Then, before you turn it in, have someone else read it. Choose someone in the class who knows the material and the assignment and ask him or her to read for substance—have this person assess the clarity of your writing, the logic of your argument, and the evidence you provide to support your conclusion. Then ask a roommate or a classmate to proofread it for spelling errors, poor grammar, and typographical mistakes, all of which hurt your credibility because they imply lack of respect, care, and concern for your reader and for how you regard your own work.

If writing is a problem for you and requires more help than a friend can provide, consider finding a tutor in the English department. Many universities have writing laboratories staffed with people who provide free help for students experiencing difficulties in writing. You might even consider hiring an editor.

Ask your professors if they will accept and comment on preliminary versions of your paper. If so, you can have the benefit of their opinions before you submit the final paper and they grade it.

Adhering to Deadlines

Because editing and making revisions take time, you will not be able to begin writing your paper an hour before the class period in which it is due. If you are a serious student who wants to write good papers, you must plan ahead to leave yourself enough time to revise. Every paper you turn in should be at least a second, if not a third, version.

Papers turned in late will likely lower your grade. Missing editors' deadlines is professionally irresponsible and will not win you future favors.

Using a Word Processor

If at all possible, buy a word processor of your own or use one in a library or computer center. The short amount of time it will take you to learn to write on a computer will save you many hours throughout your writing career. With word processing, you can make changes quickly. You can delete sentences, or move sentences and paragraphs to different parts of the paper. With a word processor you have a personal secretary that will type out your paper in perfect form in minutes. Word-processing programs have spell-checkers that find spelling errors, and a command that will accurately hyphenate your whole paper. Many writing programs also have grammar checks that will help you identify poor sentences. If your paper has footnotes, a word-processing program will allow you to insert new footnotes wherever you want them or to delete footnotes—and it will automatically renumber all of your notes. Programs are available to convert a paper written in one style into another style.

If you do not have access to a word processor, you will need to use a type-writer or hire a typist because all editors want typed copy, as do most professors. Retyping versions of papers is tedious, time-consuming, and expensive, thus making word processors all the more attractive.

Examples of Students' Writing

Eric Pickerill is an undergraduate majoring in art education at Ohio State University. He wrote the following paper in a criticism class for an assignment that asked students to judge the work of an artist of their choice, an exhibition at the Wexner Center for the Arts on campus, or an exhibition at the Columbus Museum of Art. The class had seen slides of *The Perfect Moment* and discussed Mapplethorpe's photography. During the class discussion, Eric held and defended a minority position, and later wrote this paper. I admire Eric for voicing his convictions, especially while faced with strong objections from his peers, and chose his paper as an example of good critical writing by a student because it is committed, forcefully argued, reasonable, and clearly expressed. This was the third assigned paper; the first had been a generally descriptive paper, the second, an interpretive paper.

Judging the Art of Robert Mapplethorpe

Eric Pickerill

Robert Mapplethorpe has created a new paradigm in the art world. He has torn down the walls of art and gone where no one has gone before. He has brought his images to society, and his images challenge the values and morals our society tries to uphold. I am referring to and judging only one aspect of Mapplethorpe's work—his most controversial photographs containing sexually explicit subject matter.

Mapplethorpe presents this work in a manner that is confusing to the viewer. He presents his sexually confrontational images in the pristine settings of galleries and art books. His photographs are very concerned with composition and form. In his photograph *Self-Portrait,* 1978, he has centered himself in a room, and shows a hardwood floor leading to a wall. He has draped a box on the floor with a white sheet. He has placed his left foot on the box and his other foot on the floor. Mapplethorpe's body leans forward towards the wall and away from the camera and extends to the right where his face looks to the camera and the viewer.

Mapplethorpe is obviously concerned with composition and form because of the lack of any distracting elements in the portrait and the presentation of the subject matter in an aesthetically pleasing manner: The lines of the floor lead to the main subject, who is manipulated with light, casting shadows that enhance the formal excellence of the composition.

Although the description so far is "clean," Mapplethorpe confuses the viewer by manipulating the subject matter to depict a sado-masochistic act. Mapplethorpe wears leather chaps with a cut-out seat and no pants underneath. He is also wearing a leather vest and boots. In his right hand he holds a bullwhip that protrudes from his anus and hangs to the floor.

Mapplethorpe has made a new paradigm in art by confronting society with images such as this one. His photographs are very pleasing formally in their making and presentation, but his subject matter often is of situations found in pornographic and sado-masochistic settings, such as magazines sold in adult bookstores. Because he presents his photography with formal excellence, we might say "It is art," but because his photography is often of sexually explicit images, we might say "It is pornography."

By bringing his images to the public, Mapplethorpe has caused controversy over this very issue: Are they art or pornography? Whichever they are, and they may be both since there is disagreement among one viewer and the next, Mapplethorpe has been successful in furthering the progress of moral decay. This has even been exemplified while writing this paper. Having the Mapplethorpe photograph in front of me, I have become immune to its subject matter, although when I first saw it, I was horrified at its explicit sexuality.

This decline in morality is brought about by immersion. The decline is witnessed in the effects of Mapplethorpe's self-portrait on the public through immersion. This portrait is shocking at first, but then I become consumed with the argument of art versus pornography, and after studying both the subject matter and form of the photograph, I become immune to what it shows.

The criteria for my judgment, that Mapplethorpe's images have furthered moral decay, is based in the root condition of humankind, forenamed "the sin condition." This condition is a separation between the living God, who is perfect and moral, and humankind, who is imperfect and immoral. This morality and perfection of God is witnessed in humankind's inability to meet God's standards; it is through the law of God that humankind becomes conscious of sin, for apart from this law, there is no sin. As this law reveals sin and immorality, it also stimulates it, because it is a natural tendency in humans to desire forbidden things. Therefore, we understand how Mapplethorpe's photographs have furthered moral decay because we are shocked, surprised, and drawn even closer to look into his images.

It took a little over ten minutes for my moral judgment to be tinted by Mapplethorpe's self-portrait. This portrait, along with others of his photographs, are among his most controversial. This is because it places society in a position of decision. Should America let its people be immersed in Mapplethorpe's images, which further moral decay?

The following paper is in response to the fourth paper assignment of the criticism course: Select a contemporary artist of your choice, find three critics who have written about the artist, and metacritically analyze their writings. When she wrote this paper, Kendra Hovey was a part-time, continuing education student (equivalent to a first-year Master's student), taking courses for enjoyment. Her undergraduate degree is in philosophy. She had had no previous criticism courses or art courses, but had had some photography courses. I think the clarity and sophistication of her thinking and writing need no further commentary.

Reading Criticism:
A Study of Three Critical Views on the
Photographic Work of Joel-Peter Witkin

Kendra Hovey

Theoretically there are as many different ways of looking at a work of art as there are pairs of eyes. A painting, a photograph, a body of artistic work is not subsumed under a singular interpretation. Art critics prove this again and again by offering a number of differing viewpoints on the same piece of work. To find importance outside the sphere of one's own personal opinion, critics' viewpoints should not be mere assertions, but statements supported by reasons—reasons that should find evidence in the work being discussed. If the critic takes an evaluative stance, the critic needs to address the "why it is" as much as the "it is."

As a reader of criticism, it is important to pay attention not just to the judgment of "good" or "bad" or to the declaration, "it means this," but to pay equal attention to the "whys" and "becauses." The following is a discussion of three different critics on the work of one photographer. In considering the photographic work of Joel-Peter Witkin, these three critics provide interpretations, some widely different, some similar; and judgments, some largely negative, others positive. Each has a sensibility and a set of criteria by which they see and judge. Confronted with three persuasive views it becomes evident that as a reader it is important to both examine the success of an argument and to recognize the chosen criteria of the critic.

In the opening sentence of her review of Witkin's work, critic Susan Kandel simultaneously expresses both interest and biting judgment: "There is something profoundly exhilarating about a show that is extravagantly awful." The review appeared in the November 1989 issue of *Arts Magazine* and the show was at the Fahey/Klein gallery in Los Angeles. The reviewer admits that this work, in appealing to a fascination with perversity and the "truly terrible," is "immensely satisfying," but clarifies that this is the singular purpose of the work. In other words, the circus has made an unexpected stop at the Fahey/Klein, but if it is art that you want to see, she suggests, go somewhere else.

One entered the gallery and confronted a prominently positioned wall plaque reading, "Joel-Peter Witkin is interested in working with pathologists and anatomists and anyone who is or knows about unique [sic] individuals who wish to be photographed," accompanied by Witkin's address in New Mexico; from that moment it was evident that the name of the game for Witkin was not art, but exploitation of the cheapest kind;

exploitation not merely of his subjects—hermaphrodites, pedophiles, deformed individuals, fetuses, cadavers, and animals—but of his voyeuristic audience, primed by the media to crave gratuitous sex and violence, and only too thrilled to find it in the lofty setting of the art gallery.

Kandel's interpretation of the work as a parade of the perverse is mirrored in her description of the work. Like a jaded circus huckster, she leads us on a tour of the freak show: "Here we find a topless woman with two chicken feet affixed to her nipples; around the corner, masked Siamese twins in negligees, and a man hanging upside down from his testicles; across the room, a pair of severed male genitals perched on top of two skulls." She describes Witkin's technique of "scratching into the negative and printing with tissues and toners" as a failed attempt to "endow his images with the museum-validated look of vintage 19th-century photographs." Kandel's judgment is clearly negative, her reasoning is that this work is misplaced, she refers to Witkin as "P.T. Barnum with an MFA" implying that the art world has been duped. Witkin's work is not art but "racy nothings" attempting to legitimate itself with "aren't we clever references to the heavyweights of art history." For Kandel it "doesn't work." "Big deal," she says.

In her review Kandel provides two reasons for her judgment. The first, already mentioned, is the subject matter itself. For Kandel this "art" is immediately redefined as exploitation. It is unclear whether this is because there is something intrinsically exploitative in any depiction of this subject matter or just in the artist's method of searching out the subject matter. A second reason she provides for its demotion to the merely exploitative is that this work seeks *only* to appeal to the voyeuristic desires of the viewer: "Witkin's images are so rooted in a desperate materiality that eschews all suggestion, all enigma—key tokens of the surrealistic quality Witkin hankers after, but perpetually fails to achieve." Because Witkin's work has content only for the corporeal, it fails as art. According to Kandel this work exists only for our curious senses which are "assaulted by greater and greater displays of the dreadful." Although her definition of "exploitation" is an unclear one, Kandel does make the point that art cannot be exploitative and still be called art. The criteria that kick these photographs out of the ranks of art are based in Kandel's own theories about what defines art. The reader, in assessing the critic's opinion, should consider both her interpretation and her criteria. Her definition of art certainly leaves open many unanswered questions, such as: Can any depiction of Witkin's cast of characters be considered art or is such a depiction inherently exploitative? Is any work that appeals only to the senses, "to materiality," not art? And, are depictions *only* of the pretty as opposed to the dreadful also not art?

In an April 1986 review in *Flash Art,* critic Alfred Jan agrees with Kandel's assertion that Witkin's images extend into the perverse: "[Witkin] engages in the esthetics of excess that defies conventional standards of good taste." Jan acknowledges a judgment of the work such as

Kandel's when he writes, "It would be tempting to write off all this Grand Guignol theatricality as self-indulgent sensationalist exploitation." Jan even agrees that Witkin is "playing on our voyeuristic curiosity toward the Other." Jan, however, disagrees with Kandel when he calls all this, "art-worthy."

What Kandel terms "racy nothings" Jan calls "powerful images." According to Jan, "Witkin heightens awareness about the human condition (with consensual agreements from his models) by exorcising our subconscious fears and desires." Jan opens up a slot for Witkin in the annals of art history by aligning his content of choice with that of known artists who were also "concerned with sacrilegious nightmares," adding that Witkin's method is "even more effective." He, unlike Kandel, finds Witkin's technique to be successful, saying it "gives the final result a look of faded antiquity." In these works Jan finds important content where Kandel finds none. By ascribing to Witkin a purpose, that of "invok[ing] the power equal to that of a vision or thought just before death," Jan is ascribing to this work an interpretation that recognizes content beyond just the material.

Jan judges the work favorably because it meets two of his implied criteria. The first is that it holds psychological content that "heightens awareness," the second is that it is full of personal vision. For Jan these photographs express the artist's sensibility, they "build a personal, if eccentric, world vision." Considering the writings of both critics, their individual criteria are not necessarily opposed (though Jan introduces an expressionist criterion, not mentioned by Kandel) yet each hands down a very different judgment. Kandel, negative; Jan, positive. The source of this difference is in their very different interpretations of the work. To Kandel it is only a freak show, to Jan it looks like a freak show but is also a valuable journey of awareness into the irrational and the unknown.

A third critic also introduces the issue of exploitation, but with a definition different from the one we may glean from Susan Kandel's review. Cynthia Chris is unconcerned with the issue of whether Witkin's work is or is not art. In her article "Witkin's Others" in the 1988 spring issue of *Exposure,* Chris gives a fuller meaning to the idea of exploitation and asserts that more important than its inclusion or exclusion in art, is its function in society. In a well-developed argument (admittedly she gets more time at the platform with 10 pages compared to Kandel and Jan's one), Chris states that Witkin's work is socially dangerous, and should be seen as such, because it displays the other as different and judges the other as "aberrant."

For Chris, these images are primarily about "representation," specifically, how the Other's "condition of being" is represented. "Witkin's photographs document his investigations of certain identities and practices; the transsexual, the androgyne, the fetishist, the sodomist, the masturbator, the homosexual, the masochist, and others whose sexuality is not encompassed by 'normal' heterosexuality." Ultimately, Chris says, the point of this investigation is to classify the listed behaviors as abnormal and thus allow the justification of their control. Witkin's images accomplish this by their method of portrayal which objectifies the models and those who share their characteristics, robbing them of both voice and point of view.

Chris describes Witkin's search for subject matter as a kind of anthropological pursuit, accusing him of reducing his subjects to a "shopping list" of attributes. She holds that Witkin suggests these people are of use only through their "unique interests and collections . . . physical characteristics . . . ranging from unusually large genitals to the wounds of Christ." He then renders them passive in his imagery. One way Witkin does this is by burying them in "textual overlays," thus making them only actors in Witkin's own re-interpretations of narratives from art history. Utilizing the symbol of blindness as "metaphorical castration" found in the tale of Oedipus, Chris argues that the masks pulled over the subjects' eyes and the negative scratchings that obscure their faces also serve this purpose of objectification.

> In effect, Witkin castrates his subjects; his scrawls on their faces are equivalent acts of violence. The eyes of the subject remain intact but the mask or the marks do interrupt access to the power of sight. No longer capable of looking back at the photographer, the model becomes effectively impotent, an object of the photographer's gaze. *Hermes* faces the viewer, but his ability to return the gaze, which is usually a feature of the frontal pose, is negated by the marks drawn over his eyes. He is left, literally, without a point of view.

The mask not only "robs the model" but "protects the viewer," it, like the distance of the camera from the subject, confirms a separation between the one who is depicted and the one who views: "The viewer can look at the model without illusion of participation." In the end, for Chris, these images are not about transsexualism or additional behaviors; they are "about our relationship to the transsexual-as-Other." To categorize persons in this way is a form of oppression, it opens the door for the "normal" to participate in the "management of individuals whose behavior is considered aberrant." Chris concludes:

> Witkin's crew of libertines . . . return to the status of documented, factionalized individuals who are to be corrected or controlled, divested of a voice, effectively castrated, diagnosed according to their perversions, and relegated to the mental institution, the prison, the redlight district, the freak show, the pornography industry, the gay ghetto, the closet, the art object— in short, to the margins of the culture into which all the oppressed are propelled—into the realm of the Other.

Chris' well evidenced and argued evidenced position relies a great deal on external information about the photographer's method of working, his personal life, and theories of oppression. Chris takes issue with the photographer, first, because of his search for subjects and second, because his viewpoint is from the outside. Like a "white actor in blackface" he temporarily plays out the role of his models' permanent lives and "like the white actor at the end of the minstrel show, Witkin washes off the Other." She accuses Witkin personally, as well as other photographers who have broached similar subject matter, for using "photography to visit the Other and to hold it up like a specimen at a safe distance. Neither speaks to us *as* the other, but always *about* the Other."

At the source of her argument is a theory about the relationship between representation and oppression. The reader should consider the source of her reasons with as much weight as the reasons themselves. One may agree with both her theory about oppression and her position that art is not immune to this type of evaluation, but still disagree with her negative assessment of Witkin by arguing for a different interpretation of the work, one that makes the case that these images are not of objects but of subjects.

The writings of these three critics contain a range of differing interpretations and evaluations of one body of work. Basic to these differences, are the different sets of criteria the critics use to see and to judge. Where Susan Kandel finds no real content, both Alfred Jan and Cynthia Chris find commentaries about sexuality and religion (and in Jan's case a view of the dark side of the subconscious). The technique of scratching and toning that according to Jan invests the work with a 19th-century aura is nothing but a ruse to Kandel, while in the eyes of Cynthia Chris it is a tool used to blind and castrate the Other. Alfred Jan basically dismisses the issue of exploitation by acknowledging the models' consent, for Kandel and Chris it remains a primary issue, though with Kandel we are led to assume that the exploitation would be excused if she found in the work deeper and more complex content. Chris on the other hand solidly refuses to excuse the objectification. Her perspective is that of an instrumentalist primarily concerned with the function art serves in society and its consequences.

Here we have a small collection of evidence illustrating the many different ways in which one piece of art can be viewed. Each critic hopes to convince us to join their side or, at least, to engage us in the discussion.

TALKING ABOUT WORKS OF ART

Casual Conversation About Art

Much of our talk about art occurs in casual conversations with a friend or someone we are close to. These conversations can be enlightening. You can express what you feel about a work of art, and get confirmation about what you see and what you say. If you trust the one you are speaking with, you can try out your ideas without fear of being ridiculed. You can hear what someone else has to say about the same work of art you have seen. Try to generate an interesting and enjoyable discussion and to keep the discussion going. Being a good conversationalist means being an attentive listener, encouraging someone to say more by showing them your interest in what they have to say.

Casual conversations about art are too often evaluative and dismissive: "I don't like it. Do you?" Try to extend the conversation by providing reasons for your opinions, and seek reasons from the person with whom you are talking. If you feel put down or that you are not being listened to, you will probably end the discussion; similarly, if you dismiss what your friend is saying, you will also probably end that discussion or, at least, turn it into an uncomfortable argument rather than a friendly and tolerant disagreement. Disagreements can be enlightening and enjoyable if they are conducted with mutual respect, with both parties listening to each other, and if reasons for the disagreement are explained.

Organized Talk About Art

Formal talk about art often occurs in art classes, and such talk is often referred to as a *critique*. Studio professors often hold critiques with a class of art students while their work is in progress, and also after the work is completed. The usual purpose of a critique is to improve the art being made. During critiques, artists are usually given a lot of advice, whether they want it or not, about how to change and improve their work. In this sense, critiques are different from published criticism. Critics do not attempt to improve the art about which they write. Nevertheless, critiques are a form of oral criticism that can be beneficial to artists and viewers alike, especially when they follow some of the principles of criticism presented in previous chapters.

Too rarely is work described during critiques. There is often an underlying and unidentified assumption that describing the work that is being critiqued is not necessary because it is there in front of everyone and everyone can see it. This is a false assumption. Everyone sees phenomena differently, based on their patterns of perception and their individual biographies. There is no one right way, and no complete way, to describe a complex work of art. Description depends to a certain extent on interpretation, and interpretation on description—and getting several descriptions from several individual viewers about the same work of art can be an enriching experience. If several viewers contribute their individual descriptions in their own chosen words, they can expand the group's perception of the work. If artists listen carefully to the several descriptions of their work, they can gain insights into what they have done and how others perceive it.

Too rarely is work interpreted during critiques. Usually everyone jumps over description and interpretation right to offering suggestions about how to improve the art—before they have even considered what it might be about. In critiques, interpretations are too often given by the artist whose work is being discussed. Then the critique is based on intentionalism and, specifically, the artist's intent. An artwork, however, does not necessarily mean what an artist means it to mean—it might mean more, or less, or something different. If artists insist that their art means only what they mean it to mean, then they are severely limiting the meaning of their own work. If the group allows artists to determine the meaning of their own works, then the group is denying its ability to add insights to those of the artists.

The focus of critiques is usually and predominantly the judgment of how good or bad the work is and how to make it better. Often the judgments are based on the artist's stated intent: "I tried to do this—how well did I do it?" Sometimes it is based on the teacher's intent: "I asked you to do this—how well did you do it?" Judgments based on intent, however, preclude judging the intent itself. If an artist's intent lacked merit to begin with, then, by achieving it, the artist still does not end up with a good work of art. Judgments based on intent tend to get very specific and ignore larger issues of criteria. A complete judgment ought to consist of a clear appraisal and reasons for that appraisal based on criteria. Several sets of criteria are discussed in Chapter 4.

Do you know your professor's criteria for good works of art? If not, you may well want to ask for them, and then to ask if you can vary from them, or if it would be better for you to follow them during the course.

One easy way to improve the intellectual quality of critiques and to expand the discussion to include more people and broader topics is to ask the artist whose work is being critiqued to remain a silent listener. This changes the usual critique by placing the burden of discussion on the viewers rather than on the artist, which is probably where the burden ought to be. It also precludes defensive and sometimes obstructionist statements by artists who feel put on the spot. The artists can stay in the background and take in what is being perceived about their work of art. They can check their intents against the group's perceptions. This could be a valuable experience for any artist.

Criticizing Works in the Public Domain

Discussing art with a group of viewers in a museum, gallery, or other public arena should take a different focus from the usual judgmental critique. The artist is not present and you are not trying to tell the artist how to make the art better. You are most likely there to experience art, to appreciate it, and to talk about your experiences. The motivation to describe and interpret should be stronger because the directive to judge will be weaker.

The museum or gallery setting probably offers several works of art by the same artist or different artists, so the invitation to compare and contrast what you see is implicit. Check the range of dates of when the pieces were made. Also note how the pieces are hung—which is next to which and to what effect; speculate on why these decisions were made. Look for the exhibition's title, and consider its theme. Attempt to infer the curator's criteria for selecting these particular works of art.

Remember also the questions in Chapter 5 raised about art by educators who suspect institutions of being too limited in what they select and what they sanction: For whom was it created? For whom does it exist? Who is represented? Who is doing the telling? The hearing?

General Recommendations for Good Group Discussions

These recommendations apply to both the studio critiques of art you and your classmates have and to group discussions at public sites.

Try to understand the work through your own unique perspective and then share your understanding with others. Don't censor yourself. It is your professor's job to moderate the discussion; you do not need to keep yourself in check. Professors often dread conducting critiques or group discussions of any kind because their students won't talk, and they end up in the uncomfortable position of having to give a spontaneous lecture.[2] When your professors, or perhaps tour guides in an art museum, ask what you think, they probably want to know and want you to talk. If they are merely asking a rhetorical question and really want to lecture, you will see that soon enough. In the meantime, accept the challenge of contributing to the discussion.

Try to limit yourself to one point per utterance, rather than two or three. Beware of saying "I have three points I'd like to make: First . . . ." It is difficult for anyone to follow more than one point at a time. Introduce a single point, and then at a later time introduce another.

Be honest with and kind to one another; otherwise, no one will want to talk for fear of being dealt with harshly. If you disagree with someone's position, say so, but respectfully. First acknowledge that you heard what the other said, agree with parts of the position, if you can, and then move the conversation forward. Always try to further a conversation rather than end it. Seek to find a word that will continue the conversation rather than wanting to have "the last word."

Avoid male tendencies to be right; avoid female tendencies to be dominated by males in the group.

Know that others in the group share your sense of vulnerability when you are speaking in public. A psychologically safe environment needs to be established to have a good discussion; if people in the group do not feel safe, they will try to hide rather than talk. You will be denied their insights and will contribute to the censorship of their ideas.

A sense of curiosity is more appropriate to criticism and to art than a constant penchant to judge. The major principle guiding both written and spoken art criticism is that criticism is an ongoing discussion: You can add to it. You are part of a community of interested observers of art. With your help, the community—whether a group of friends at a bar, a class in a college, or a number of publishing authors—can be self-correcting. That is, no one of us has the single and complete right answer about any work of art; but as a group we may eventually correct our notions and together achieve more adequate answers to complex problems of art than any one of us could achieve individually.

NOTES

PREFACE

1. These first two ideas are similar to goals for education stated more generally by R. S. Peters, a philosopher of education.

2. Deborah Ambush, Robert Arnold, Nancy Bless, Lee Brown, Malcolm Cochran, Alan Crockett, Susan Dallas-Swann, Arthur Efland, Ron Green, Sally Hagaman, Richard Harned, Bill Harris, Georg Heimdal, James Hutchens, K. B. Jones, Marcus Kruse, Peter Metzler, Lynette Molnar, Susan Myers, A. J. Olson, Stephen Pentak, Sarah Rogers, Richard Roth Larry Shineman, Amy Snider, Robert Stearns, Patricia Stuhr, Sydney Walker, Pheoris West.

3. Magdalena Abakanowicz, Vito Acconci, Dennis Adams, Terry Allen, Woody Allen, Gregory Amenoff, Laurie Anderson, Carl Andre, Benny Andrews, Eleanor Antin, Steven Antonakos, Arakawa, Diane Arbus, Siah Armanjani, John Armleder, Alice Aycock, Francis Bacon, Amelia Mesa Baines, John Baldessari, Miguel Barcelo, Steve Barry, Jenifer Bartlett, George Baselitz, Romare Bearden, Phoebe Beasley, Bernd and Hilla Becher, Lynda Benglis, Jake Berthot, Joseph Beuys, Ashely Bickerton, John Biggers, Ross Bleckner, Diane Blell, Nancy Bless, Mel Bochner, Christian Boltanski, Jon Borofsky, Louise Bourgeois, Nancy Brett, Marcel Broodthaers, Christopher Brown, Joan Brown, Roger Brown, Chris Burden, Daniel Buren, Selma Burke, Nancy Burson, David Byrne, Laurie Carlos, Maurice Casansky, Elizabeth Catlett, Electric Cats, John Chamberlain, Sarah Charlesworth, Judy Chicago, Dale Chihuly, Christo, Francesco Clemente, Chuck Close, Malcolm Cochran, Helen Codero, Sue Coe, Robert Colescott, Papo Colo, Clyde Connel, Houston Conwill, Tony Cragg, Richard Glaezer Danay, Julie Dash, Grenville Davey, Richard Deacon, Walter De Maria, Liz Diller/Rick Scofidio, Marcel Duchamp, Hartwig Ebersbach, Mary Beth Edelson,

David Elred, Kate Ericson and Mel Ziegler, Richard Estes, Jackie Ferrara, Karen Finley, Rev. Howard Finster, Eric Fischl, Janet Fish, Audrey Flack, Dan Flavin, Mary Frank, Helen Frankenthaler, Rupert Garcia, Jedd Garrett, Haile Gerima, Sam Gilliam, Renate Goebel, Leon Golub, Guillermo Gomez-Peña, Jose Gonzalez, Gran Fury, Nancy Graves, Spalding Gray, Eugene Grisby, Red Grooms, Group Material, Guerilla Girls, Philip Guston, Hans Haake, Dee Dee Halleck and Paper Tiger TV, Ann Hamilton, David Hammons, Keith Haring, Helen and Newton Harrison, Marin Hassinger, Alam Hausen, Edgar Heap of Birds, Michael Heizer, Eva Hesse, Joan Hill, Stuart Hitch, David Hockney, Nancy Holt, Jenny Holzer, Varnette Honeywood, Rebecca Horn, Oscar Howe, Richard Hunt, William Hutson, Robert Irwin, Alfredo Jaar, Neil Jenny, Bill Jensen, Luis Jimenez, Jasper Johns, Joan Jonas, Kirsten Jones/Andrew Ginzel, Lois Mailou Jones, Don Judd, Kabakov, Frida Kahlo, Amish Kapoor, Alex Katz, Mike Kelley, Anselm Kiefer, Silvia Kolbowski, Shishiko Kobuta, Joseph Kosuth, Jannis Kovwellis, Barbara Kruger, Suzanne Lacy, Wolfgang Laib, Artis Lane, Jacob Lawrence, Elizabeth Layton, Sherrie Levine, Samella Lewis, Sol LeWitt, Roy Lichtenstein, Maya Lin, Donald Lipski, Robert Longo, Truman Lowe, Mary Lucier, Robert Mapplethorpe, Agnes Martin, Gordon Matta-Clark, Allan McColum, Duane Michals, Kay Miller, Melissa Miller, Mary Miss, Linda Montano, Erroll Morris, Rae Morton, Robert Moskowitz, Elizabeth Murray, David Nash, Bruce Nauman, Tom Naykowski, Alice Neal, Odd Nerdrum, Maria Nordman, Jim Nutt, Claus Oldenberg, Pat Oleszko, Dennis Oppenheim, Nam June Paik, Tonita Peña, Beverly Pepper, Florence Pierce, Howardena Pindell, Jerry Pinkney, Adrian Piper, Sigmar Polke, Jackson Pollock, Richard Prince, Grandma Prisbee, Martin Puryear, Yvonne Rainer, Archie Rand, Robert Rauschenberg, Charles Ray, Gerhard Richter, Faith Ringgold, Aminah Robinson, Tim Rollins and KOS, Kay Rosen, Rachel Rosenthal, Martha Rosler, Charles Ross, Dieter Rot, Richard Roth, Susan Rothenberg, Ed Ruscha, Mahler Ryder, Betye and Alison Saar, David Salle, Cheri Samb, Juan Sanchez, Peter Saul, Raymond Saunders, Miriam Schapiro, Julian Schnabel, Carolee Schneeman, Sean Scully, James Seawright, George Segal, Allan Sekula, Richard Serra, Andres Serrano, Cindy Sherman, Lorna Simpson, Barbara Smith, Kiki Smith, Robert Smithson, Kenneth Snelson, Keith Sonnier, Nancy Spero, Haim Steinbach, Pat Steir, Frank Stella, Survival Research Laboratories, Antoni Tapies, Tony Tasset, TODT, Francesc Torres, William Tucker, James Turell, Cy Twombly, Alan Uglow, Vincent VanGogh, Bill Viola, Andy Warhol, Megan Webster, Carrie Mae Weems, William Wegman, Pheoris West, Pat Ward Williams, Todd Williams and Billie Tsien, Fred Wilson, Robert Wilson, David Wojnarowicz.

4. Brook Adams, Dennis Adrian, Lawrence Alloway, Dore Ashton, Kenneth Baker, Miquel Barcelo, Roland Barthes, Michael Berenson, John Berger, Rosemary Betterton, Peter Biskin, Richard Bolton, Arna Bontemps, Michael Brenson, Guy Brett, Linda Frye Burnham, Elizabeth Catlett, Germano Celant, Lyne Cook, Douglas Crimp, Arthur Danto, Joe Bob Davis, David Driskell, A. J. Fielder, Hal Foster, Peter Frank, Michael Fried, Joanna Frueh, Roger Fry, Suzi Gablik, Andy Grundberg, J. Hoberman, Bill Horrigan, Robert Hughes, Robert Irwin, Christopher Jenks, Ken Johnson, Max Kozloff, Hilton Kramer, Rosalind Krauss, Donald Kuspit, Vince Leo, Kim Levin, Lucy Lippard, Catherine Lord, Joseph Masheck, Thomas McEvilly, Stephen Melville, Annette Michelson, Keith Morrison, William Olander, Craig Owens, John Perreault,

Robert Pincus-Witten, Peter Plagens, Arlene Raven, B. Ruby Rich, Howard Risatti, Jonathan Rosenbaum, Martha Rosler, Jerry Saltz, Peter Schjeldahl, Allan Sekula, Jeanne Siegel, Roberta Smith, Susan Sontag, Robert Storr, Mary Stoppe, Paul Taylor, Brian Wallis, Stephen Westfall, Janet Wolff.

5. Morris Weitz, *Hamlet and the Philosophy of Literary Criticism* (Chicago: University of Chicago Press, 1964).

CHAPTER 1

1. Robert Rosenblum quoted by Deborah Drier, "Critics and the Marketplace," *Art & Auction* (March 1990): 172.

2. Rene Ricard, "Not About Julian Schnabel," *Artforum* (1981): 74.

3. Rosalind Krauss quoted by Janet Malcolm, "A Girl of the Zeitgeist-I," *The New Yorker,* 20 October 1986, 49.

4. Lucy Lippard, "Headlines, Heartlines, Hardlines: Advocacy Criticism as Activism," in *Cultures in Contention,* ed. Douglas Kahn and Diane Neumaier (Seattle, WA: Real Comet Press, 1985), 242.

5. Ricard, "Not About Julian Schnabel," 74.

6. Rosenblum quoted in Drier, "Critics and the Marketplace," 73.

7. Jeremy Gilbert-Rolfe, "Seriousness and Difficulty in Criticism," *Art Papers* (November-December 1990): 9.

8. Malcolm, "Girl of the Zeitgeist-I," 49.

9. Peter Plagens, "Peter and the Pressure Cooker," in *Moonlight Blues: An Artist's Art Criticism* (Ann Arbor, MI: UMI Press, 1986), 119.

10. Ibid., 126.

11. Ibid., 129.

12. Ibid.

13. Patricia C. Phillips, "Collecting Culture: Paradoxes and Curiosities," in *Breakthroughs: Avant-Garde Artists in Europe and America, 1950–1990,* Wexner Center for the Arts (New York: Rizzoli, 1991), 182.

14. A. D. Coleman, "Because It Feels So Good When I Stop: Concerning a Continuing Personal Encounter with Photography Criticism," in *Light Readings: A Photography Critic's Writings 1968–1978* (New York: Oxford University Press, 1979), 254.

15. Gilbert-Rolfe, "Seriousness and Difficulty," 8.

16. Linda Burnham, "What Is a Critic Now?" *Art Papers* (November–December 1990): 7.

17. Plagens, "Peter and the Pressure Cooker," 129.

18. Malcolm, "Girl of the Zeitgeist-I," 49.

19. Plagens, "Peter and the Pressure Cooker," 126.

20. Gilbert-Rolfe, "Seriousness and Difficulty," 9.

21. George Steiner quoted by Gilbert-Rolfe, "Seriousness and Difficulty," 10.

22. Pat Steir quoted by Paul Gardner, "What Artists Like About Art They Like When They Don't Know Why," *Artnews* (October 1991): 119.

23. Steven Durland, "Notes from the Editor," *High Performance* (Summer 1991): 5.

24. Ibid.

25. Lucy Lippard, "Some Propaganda for Propaganda," in *Visibly Female: Feminism and Art Today,* ed. Hilary Robinson (New York: Universe, 1988), 184–194.

26. Bob Shay quoted by Ann Burkhart, "A Study of Studio Art Professors' Beliefs and Attitudes about Professional Art Criticism" (Master's thesis, The Ohio State University, Columbus, OH, 1992).

27. Ibid.

28. Pheoris West quoted by Burkhart, ibid.

29. Tim Miller, "Critical Wishes," *Artweek,* 5 September 1991, 18.

30. Georg Heimdal quoted by Burkhart, "A Study of Studio Art."

31. Susan Dallas-Swann quoted by Burkhart, ibid.

32. Richard Roth quoted by Burkhart, ibid.

33. Kay Willens quoted by Burkhart, ibid.

34. Robert Moskowitz quoted by Gardner, "What Artists Like," 120.

35. Claes Oldenburg quoted by Gardner, "What Artists Like," 121.

36. Tony Labat, "Two Hundred Words or So I've Heard Artists Say about Critics and Criticism," *Artweek,* 5 September 1991, 18.

37. Lippard, "Headlines," 184–194.

38. Patrice Koelsch, "The Criticism of Quality and The Quality of Criticism," *Art Papers* (November–December 1990): 14.

39. Roberta Smith quoted in Drier, "Critics and the Marketplace," 172.

40. Rosenblum quoted in Drier, "Critics and the Marketplace," 172.

41. Wendy Beckett, *Contemporary Women Artists* (New York: Universe, 1988).

42. David Halpern, ed., *Writers on Art* (San Francisco: North Point Press, 1988).

43. Charles Simic, *Dime-Store Alchemy* (New York: Ecco Press, 1992).

44. Anne Beattie, *Alex Katz by Ann Beattie* (New York: Abrams, 1987).

45. Gerrit Henry, "Psyching Out Katz," *Artnews* (Summer 1987): 23.

46. Rosenblum quoted in Drier, "Critics and the Marketplace," 173.

47. *Newsweek,* 21 October 1991.

48. For a fuller discussion of the role of ideology in art criticism, see Elizabeth Garber, "Art Criticism as Ideology," *Journal of Social Theory in Art Education* 11 (1991): 50–67.

49. Deborah Solomon, "Catching Up with the High Priest of Criticism," *New York Times,* Arts and Leisure, Sunday, 23 June 1991, 31–32.

50. Garber, "Art Criticism as Ideology," 54–55.

51. Solomon, "Catching Up," 32.

52. Ibid.

53. Clement Greenberg quoted by Peter G. Ziv, "Clement Greenberg," *Art & Antiques* (September 1987): 57.

54. Ziv, "Greenberg," 57.

55. Tom Wolfe, *The Painted Word* (New York: Farrar, Straus, and Giroux, 1975).

56. Solomon, "Catching Up," 31.

57. Kenneth Noland quoted in Ziv, "Greenberg," 57–58.

58. Ziv, "Greenberg," 57.

59. Ibid.

60. Greenberg quoted in Ziv, "Greenberg," 58.

61. Ibid., 87.

62. The information on Lawrence Alloway is drawn from the work of Sun-Young Lee, "A Metacritical Examination of Contemporary Art Critics' Practices: Lawrence Alloway, Donald Kuspit and Robert-Pincus Wittin for Developing a Unit for Teaching Art Criticism" (Ph.D. dissertation, The Ohio State University, 1988).

63. Lawrence Alloway, "The Expanding and Disappearing Work of Art," *Auction* (October 1967): 34–37.

64. Lawrence Alloway, "The Uses and Limits of Art Criticism," in *Topics of American Art Since 1945* (New York: W. W. Norton, 1975).

65. Lawrence Alloway, "Women's Art in the Seventies," in *Network: Art and the Complex Present* (Ann Arbor, MI: UMI Press, 1984).

66. Lawrence Alloway, "Women's Art and the Failure of Art Criticism," in *Network: Art and the Complex Present* (Ann Arbor, MI: UMI Press, 1984).

67. Alloway quoted by Lee, "A Metacritical Examination."

68. Ibid.

69. Arlene Raven, *Crossing Over: Feminism and Art of Social Concern* (Ann Arbor, MI: UMI, 1988).

70. Ibid., xvii.

71. Ibid., xiv.

72. Ibid., xviii.

73. Donald Kuspit quoted in Raven, *Crossing Over,* xv.

74. Raven, *Crossing Over,* 165.

75. Ibid., 167.

76. Lucy Lippard, *Mixed Blessings* (New York: Pantheon Books, 1991).

77. Meyer Raphael Rubinstein, "Books," *Arts Magazine* (September 1991): 95.

78. Hilton Kramer quoted by Lippard in "Headlines," 242.

79. Lippard, "Some Propaganda," 186.

80. Ibid., 194.

81. Lippard, "Headlines," 243.

82. Coleman, "Because It Feels So Good," 204.

83. Kuspit quoted by Mark Van Proyen, "A Conversation with Donald Kuspit," *Artweek,* 5 September 1991, 19.

84. Smith quoted in Drier, "Critics and the Marketplace," 172.

85. Alloway quoted by Lee, "A Metacritical Examination," 46.

86. Ibid., 48.

87. Robert Pincus-Witten quoted in Lee, "A Metacritical Examination," 96.

88. Ibid., 97.

89. Ibid., 105.

90. Ziv, "Greenberg," 58.

91. Smith quoted by Drier, "Critics and the Marketplace," 172.

92. Joanna Frueh, "Towards a Feminist Theory of Art Criticism," in *Feminist Art Criticism: An Anthology,* ed. Arlene Raven, Cassandra Langer, and Joanna Frueh (Ann Arbor, MI: UMI Press, 1988), 58.

93. Ibid., 60–61.

94. Arthur Danto quoted by Elizabeth Frank, "Art's Off-the-Wall Critic," *New York Times Magazine,* 19 November 1989, 73.

95. Peter Plagens, "Max's Dinner with André," *Newsweek,* 12 August 1991, 61.

96. Edmund Feldman, "The Teacher as Model Critic," *The Journal of Aesthetic Education 7,* no. 1 (1973): 50–57.

97. Marcia Eaton, *Basic Issues in Aesthetics* (Belmont, CA: Wadsworth, 1988), 113–120.

98. Harry Broudy, *Enlightened Cherishing* (Champaign-Urbana: University of Illinois Press, 1972).

99. Morris Weitz, *Hamlet and the Philosophy of Literary Criticism* (Chicago: University of Chicago Press, 1964), vii.

100. Andy Grundberg, "Toward Critical Pluralism," in *Reading into Photography: Selected Essays, 1959–1982,* ed. Thomas Barrow et al. (Albuquerque: University of New Mexico Press, 1982), 247–253.

101. John Coplans quoted in Malcolm, "A Girl of the Zeitgeist-I," 52.

102. Ibid., 49.

103. Ibid., part II, 51.

104. Ibid., 52.

105. Ibid., 57.

106. Marina Vaizey, "Art Is More Than Just Art," *New York Times Book Review,* 5 August 1990, 9.

107. Eaton, *Basic Issues,* 122.

108. Kay Larson quoted by Amy Newman, "Who Needs Art Critics?" *Artnews* (September 1982): 60.

109. Mark Stevens quoted by Newman, "Who Needs Art Critics?" 57.

110. Harry Broudy, "Some Duties of a Theory of Educational Aesthetics," *Educational Theory* 1, no. 3 (1951): 198–199.

111. Chuck Close quoted by Gardner, "What Artists Like," 119.

112. Marcia Siegel quoted by Irene Ruth Meltzer, "The Critical Eye: An Analysis of the Process of Dance Criticism as Practiced by Clive Barnes, Arlene Croce, Deborah Jowitt, Elizabeth Kendall, Marcia Siegel, and David Vaughn" (Master's thesis, The Ohio State University, 1979), 55.

CHAPTER 2

1. Dana Shottenkirk, "Nancy Spero," *Artforum* (May 1991): 143.

2. Wendy Beckett, *Contemporary Women Artists* (New York: Universe, 1988), 16.

3. David Cateforis, "Anselm Kiefer," in *Compassion and Protest: Recent Social and Political Art from the Eli Broad Family Foundation Collection* (New York: Cross River Press, 1991), 46.

4. Waldemar Januszczak, "Is Anselm Kiefer the New Genius of Painting? Not Quite!" *Connoisseur* (May 1988): 130.

5. Michelle Meyers, "Robert Longo," in *Compassion and Protest: Recent Social and Political Art from the Eli Broad Family Foundation Collection* (New York: Cross River Press, 1991), 54–55.

6. Beckett, *Contemporary Women Artists,* 44.

7. Ruth Bass, "Miriam Schapiro," *Artnews* (October 1990): 185.

8. David Cateforis, "Leon Golub," in *Compassion and Protest: Recent Social and Political Art from the Eli Broad Family Foundation Collection.* Exhibition Catalog. Editors, Patricia Draher and John Pierce. New York: Cross River Press, 1991, 32–35.

9. Ed Hill and Suzanne Bloom, "Leon Golub," *Artforum* (February 1989): 126.

10. Rosetta Brooks, "Leon Golub: Undercover Agent," *Artforum* (January 1990): 116.

11. Robert Berlind, "Leon Golub at Fawbush," *Art in America* (April 1988): 210–211.

12. Pamela Hammond, "Leon Golub," *Artnews* (March 1990): 193.

13. Ben Marks, "Memories of Bad Dreams," *Artweek,* 21 December 1989, 9.

14. Robert Storr, "Riddled Sphinxes," *Art in America* (March 1989): 126.

15. Margaret Moorman, "Leon Golub," *Artnews* (February 1989): 135.

16. Joshua Decter, "Leon Golub," *Arts Magazine* (March 1989): 135–135.

17. Edward Thorp, "Deborah Butterfield," *Artnews* (April 1991): 154.

18. Donna Brookman, "Beyond the Equestrian," *Artweek,* 25 February 1989, 6.

19. Richard Martin, "A Horse Perceived by Sighted Persons: New Sculptures by Deborah Butterfield," *Arts Magazine* (January 1987): 73–75.

20. Kathryn Hixson, "Chicago in Review," *Arts Magazine* (January 1990): 106.

21. Marcia Tucker, "Equestrian Mysteries: An Interview with Deborah Butterfield," *Art in America* (June 1989): 203.

22. "Ceramics and Glass Acquisitions at the V. & A.," *Burlington Magazine* (May 1990): 388.

23. Andrea DiNoto, "New Masters of Glass," *Connoisseur* (August 1982): 22–24.

24. Robert Silberman, "Americans in Glass: A Requiem?" *Art in America* (March 1985): 47–53.

25. Gene Baro, "Dale Chihuly," *Art International* (August-September 1981): 125–126.

26. Ron Glowen, "Glass on the Cutting Edge," *Artweek,* 6 December 1990.

27. Linda Norden, "Dale Chihuly: Shell Forms," *Arts Magazine* (June 1981): 150–151.

28. David Bourdon, "Chihuly: Climbing the Wall," *Art in America* (June 1990): 164.

29. Marilyn Iinkl, "James Carpenter–Dale Chihuly," *Craft Horizons* (June 1977): 59.

30. Penelope Hunter-Stiebel, "Contemporary Art Glass: An Old Medium Gets a New Look," *Artnews* (Summer 1981): 132.

31. Peggy Moorman, "Dale Chihuly," *Artnews* (March 1984): 212.

32. John Howell, "Laurie Anderson," *Artforum* (Summer 1986): 127.

33. Ann-Sargeant Wooster, "Laurie Anderson," *High Performance* (Spring 1990): 65.

34. Kathryn Hixson, "Chicago in Review," *Arts Magazine* (November 1990): 123.

35. Kenneth Baker, "Ann Hamilton," *Artforum* (October 1990): 178.

36. David Pagel, "Still Life: The Tableaux of Ann Hamilton," *Arts Magazine* (May 1990): 56–61.

37. Sarah Rogers-Lafferty, "Ann Hamilton," in *Breakthroughs: Avant-Garde Artists in Europe and America, 1950–1990,* Wexner Center for the Visual Arts, The Ohio State University (New York: Rizzoli, 1991), 208–213.

CHAPTER 3

1. Kim Hubbard, "Sit, Beg . . . Now Smile!" *People Magazine,* 9 September 1991, 105–108.

2. Elaine Louie, "A Photographer and His Dogs Speak as One," *New York Times,* Thursday, 14 February 1991, B4.

3. Michael Gross, "Pup Art," *New York Magazine,* 30 March 1992, 44–49.

4. Louie, "Photographer and His Dogs."

5. Brooks Adams, "Wegman Unleashed," *Art News* (January 1990): 150–155.

6. William Wegman, *Cinderella* (New York: Hyperion, 1993).

7. William Wegman, *Man's Best Friend* (New York: Abrams, 1982); introduction by Laurance Wieder.

8. Martin Kunz, "Introduction," in *William Wegman,* ed. Martin Kunz (New York: Abrams, 1990), 9.

9. Peter Weiermair, "Photographs: Subversion Through the Camera," in *William Wegman,* ed. Kunz, 45.

10. Craig Owens, "William Wegman's Psychoanalytic Vaudeville," *Art in America* (March 1983): 101–108.

11. Robert Fleck, "William Wegman, Centre Pompidou," *Flash Art* (Summer 1991): 140.

12. Lewis Kachur, "Lakeside Boom," *Art International* (Spring 1989): 63–65.

13. Ken Sofer, "Reviews," *Artnews* (October 1987): 134.

14. D. A. Robbins, "William Wegman's Pop Gun," *Arts Magazine* (March 1984): 116–121.

15. Kevin Costello, "The World of William Wegman—The Artist and the Visual Pun," *West Coast Woman* (December 1991): 16.

16. Owens, "William Wegman's Psychoanalytic Vaudeville."

17. Jean-Michel Roy, "His Master's Muse: William Wegman, Man Ray, and the Dog-Biscuit Dialectic," *The Journal of Art* (November 1991): 20–21.

18. John Yau, "William Wegman," *Artforum* (October 1988).

19. Charles Hagen, "William Wegman," *Artforum* (June 1984): 90.

20. Martha C. Ronk, "Top Dog," *Artweek,* 3 May 1990, 16.

21. Jerry Saltz, "A Blessing in Disguise: William Wegman's Blessing of the Field, 1986," *Arts Magazine* (Summer 1988): 15–16.

22. Jeremy Gilbert-Rolfe, "Seriousness and Difficulty in Criticism," *Art Papers* (November–December 1990): 8.

23. Ibid., 10.

24. Robert Hughes, "A Sampler of Witless Truisms," *Time,* 30 July 1990, 66.

25. Gray Watson, "Jenny Holzer," *Flash Art* (March–April 1989): 120–121.

26. Peter Plagens, "The Venetian Carnival," *Newsweek,* 11 June 1990, 60–61.

27. Michael Brenson, "Jenny Holzer: The Message Is the Message," *New York Times,* Sunday, 7 August 1988, 29.

28. Candace Mathews Bridgewater, "Jenny Holzer at Home and Abroad," *Columbus Dispatch,* Sunday, 5 August 1990, sec. F, 1–2.

29. Grace Glueck, "And Now a Word from Jenny Holzer," *New York Times Magazine,* 26 May 1991, 42.

30. Ann Goldstein, "Baim-Williams," in *A Forest of Signs: Art in the Crisis of Representation,* ed. Catherine Gudis (Cambridge, MA: MIT, 1989), 34.

31. John Howell, "The Message Is the Medium," *Artnews* (Summer 1988): 122–127.

32. Diane Waldman, *Jenny Holzer* (New York: Abrams, 1989); exhibition catalog, Guggenheim Museum, New York.

33. Jenny Holzer, "Truisms," in *Blasted Allegories: An Anthology of Writings by Contemporary Artists,* ed. Brian Wallis (New York: The New Museum of Contemporary Art, 1987), 107.

34. Waldman, *Jenny Holzer,* 10.

35. Hal Foster, "Subversive Signs," *Art in America* (November 1982): 88–92.

36. Jenny Holzer, *The Survival Series,* Albright-Knox Gallery, 1991.

37. Holland Cotter, "Jenny Holzer at Barbara Gladstone," *Art in America* (December 1986): 137–138.

38. Deborah Solomon, "Celebrating Painting," *New York Times Magazine,* 31 March 1991, 21–25.

39. Robert Hughes, *Nothing If Not Critical* (New York: Knopf, 1990).

40. Jude Schwendenwien, "Elizabeth Murray," *New Art Examiner* (October 1988): 55.

41. Robert Storr, "Shape Shifter," *Art in America* (April 1989): 210–220.

42. Ken Johnson, "Elizabeth Murray's New Paintings," *Arts Magazine* (September 1987): 67–69.

43. Nancy Grimes, "Elizabeth Murray," *Artnews* (September 1988): 151.

44. Janet Kutner, "Elizabeth Murray," *Artnews* (May 1987): 45–46.

45. Gregory Galligan, "Elizabeth Murray's New Paintings," *Arts Magazine* (September 1987): 62–66.

46. Nelson Goodman, *Languages of Art* (Indianapolis, IN: Hackett, 1976).

47. Arthur Danto, *Transfiguration of the Commonplace* (Cambridge, MA: Harvard, 1981).

48. Richard Marshall and Robert Mapplethorpe, *50 New York Artists* (San Francisco, CA: Chronicle Books, 1986), 94.

49. Curtia James, "New History," *Artnews* (October 1990): 203.

50. Mark Van Proyen, "A Conversation with Donald Kuspit," *Artweek,* 5 September 1991, 19.

51. Pamela Hammond, "A Primal Spirit: Ten Contemporary Japanese Sculptors," *Artnews* (October 1990): 201–202.

52. Marcia Eaton, *Basic Issues in Aesthetics* (Belmont, CA: Wadsworth, 1988), 120.

CHAPTER 4

1. Peter Plagens, "Frida on Our Minds," *Newsweek,* 27 May 1991, 54–55.

2. Hayden Herrera, "Why Frida Kahlo Speaks to the 90's," *New York Times,* Sunday, 28 October 1990, 1, 41.

3. Joyce Kozloff, "Frida Kahlo," *Art in America* (May/June 1979): 148–149.

4. Kay Larson, "A Mexican Georgia O'Keefe," *New York Magazine,* 28 March 1983, 82–83.

5. Michael Newman, "The Ribbon Around the Bomb," *Art in America* (April 1983): 160–169.

6. Jeff Spurrier, "The High Priestess of Mexican Art," *Connoisseur* (August 1990): 67–71.

7. Georgina Valverde quoted in Robert Bersson, *Worlds of Art* (Mountain View, CA: Mayfield, 1991), 433.

8. Meyer Raphael Rubinstein offers another story in "A Hemisphere of Decentered Mexican Art Comes North," in *Arts Magazine* (April 1991): 70.

9. Angela Carter, *Frida Kahlo* (London: Redstone Press, 1989), Introduction.

10. Serge Fauchereau, "Surrealism in Mexico," *Artforum* (Summer 1986): 88.

11. Neal Menzies, "Unembellished Strength of Form," *Artweek,* 2 February 1985, 4.

12. Ann Lee Morgan, "Martin Puryear: Sculptures as Elemental Expression," *New Art Examiner* (May 1987): 27–29.

13. Nancy Princenthal, "Intuition's Disciplinarian," *Art in America* (January 1990): 131–136.

14. Carole Gold Calo, "Martin Puryear: Private Objects, Evocative Visions," *Arts Magazine* (February 1988): 90–93.

15. Colin Westerbeck, "Chicago, Martin Puryear," *Artforum* (May 1987): 154.

16. Judith Rusi Kirshner, "Martin Puryear, Margo Leavin Gallery," *Artforum* (Summer 1985): 115.

17. Joanne Gabbin, "Appreciation 26: Romare Bearden, *Patchwork Quilt,*" in *Worlds of Art* by Robert Bersson (Mountain View, CA: Mayfield, 1991), 450–451.

18. Michael Brenson, "Romare Bearden: Epic Emotion, Intimate Scale," *New York Times,* Sunday, 27 March 1988, 41, 43.

19. Peter Plagens, "Unsentimental Journey," *Newsweek,* 29 April 1991, 58–59.

20. Barrie Stavis quoted by Margaret Moorman, "Intimations of Immortality," *Artnews* (Summer 1988): 40–41.

21. Elizabeth Alexander, review of *Romare Bearden: His Art and Life,* by Myron Schwartzman, *New York Times Review of Books,* Sunday, 24 March 1991, 36.

22. Nina ffrench-frazier, "Romare Bearden," *Artnews* (October 1977): 141–142.

23. Myron Schwartzman, "Romare Bearden Sees in a Memory," *Artforum* (May 1984): 64–70.

24. Ellen Lee Klein, "Romare Bearden," *Arts Magazine* (December 1986): 119–120.

25. Davira S. Taragin, "From Vienna to the Studio Craft Movement," *Apollo* (December 1986): 544.

26. Nancy Princenthal, "Romare Bearden at Cordier & Ekstrom," *Art in America* (February 1987): 149.

27. Eleanor Heartney, "David Salle: Impersonal Effects," *Art in America* (June 1988): 121–129.

28. David Rimanelli, "David Salle," *Artforum* (Summer 1991): 110.

29. Laura Cottingham, "David Salle," *Flash Art* (May–June 1988): 104.

30. Robert Storr, "Salle's Gender Machine," *Art in America* (June 1988): 24–25.

31. Jed Perl, "Tradition-conscious," *The New Criterion* (May 1991): 55–59.

32. A. M. Homes, "Vito Acconci," *Artforum* (Summer 1991): 107.

33. Mary Jane Aschner, "Teaching the Anatomy of Criticism," *The School Review* 64, no. 7 (1956): 317–322.

34. John Szarkowski, *Mirrors and Windows: American Photography Since 1960* (New York: The Museum of Modern Art, 1978), 9.

35. Ken Johnson, "Anselm Kiefer at Marian Goodman," *Art in America* (November 1990): 198–199.

36. "Ad Reinhardt," *Interview* (June 1991): 28.

37. Gerrit Henry, "Agnes Martin," *Artnews* (March 1983): 159.

38. Douglas Crimp, *AIDS: Cultural Analysis/Cultural Activism* (Cambridge, MA: MIT Press, 1988), 18.

39. Ann Cvetcovich, "Video, AIDS, and Activism," *Afterimage* (September 1991): 8–11.

40. Frances DeVuono, "Contemporary African Artists," *Artnews* (Summer 1990): 174.

41. Curtia James, "New History," *Artnews* (October 1990): 203.

42. Guy McElroy, "Facing History: The Black Image in American Art 1710–1940," Corcoran Museum, Washington, DC.

43. Janet Bell, "Susan Rothenberg," *Artnews* (May 1987): 147.

44. Peter Plagens, "Max's Dinner with André," *Newsweek,* 12 August 1991, 60–61.

45. Eleanor Heartney, "Martha Rosler at DIA," *Art in America* (November 1989): 184.

46. Donald Kuspit, "Sue Coe," *Artforum* (Summer 1991): 111.

47. Jan Zita Grover, "Dykes in Context: Some Problems in Minority Representations," in *The Contest of Meaning,* ed. Richard Bolton. (Cambridge, MA: MIT Press, 1989), 163–202.

48. Margaret Battin, John Fisher, Ronald Moore, and Anita Silvers, *Puzzles About Art: An Aesthetics Casebook* (New York: St. Martin's Press, 1989).

CHAPTER 5

1. Steven Best and Douglas Keller, *Postmodern Theory: Critical Interrogations* (New York: Guilford Press, 1991), 3.

2. Best and Keller, *Postmodern Theory,* 24.

3. Robert Atkins, *Art Spoke: A Guide to Modern Ideas, Movements, and Buzzwords, 1848–1944* (New York: Abbeville Press, 1993), 139.

4. Atkins, *Art Spoke,* 176.

5. Karen Hamblen, "Beyond Universalism in Art Criticism," in *Pluralistic Approaches to Art Criticism,* ed. Doug Blandy and Kristin Congdon (Bowling Green, OH: Bowling Green State University Popular Press, 1991), 9.

6. Robert Atkins, *Art Speak: A Guide to Contemporary Ideas, Movements, and Buzzwords* (New York: Abbeville Press, 1990), 81.

7. Philip Yenawine, *How to Look at Modern Art* (New York: Abrams, 1991), 20.

8. Harold Rosenberg quoted by Howard Singerman, "In the Text," in *A Forest of Signs: Art in the Crisis of Representation,* ed. Catherine Gudis (Cambridge, MA: MIT Press, 1989), 156.

9. Barnett Newman quoted by Singerman, ibid.

10. Frank Stella quoted by Singerman, 157.

11. Atkins, *Art Speak,* 99.

12. Tom Wolfe, *The Painted Word* (New York: Farrar, Straus, and Giroux, 1975).

13. Tom Wolfe, *From Bauhaus to Our House* (New York: Farrar, Straus, and Giroux, 1982).

14. Charles Jencks, *The Language of Post-modern Architecture* (New York: Pantheon, 1977).

15. Arthur Danto, *Beyond the Brillo Box: The Visual Arts in Post-Historical Perspective* (New York: Farrar, Straus, and Giroux, 1992).

16. Atkins, *Art Speak,* 65.

17. Danto, *Beyond the Brillo Box,* 9.

18. Yenawine, *How to Look,* 124.

19. Ibid.

20. Mario Cutajar, "Goodbye to All That," *Artspace* (July-August 1992): 61.

21. Cornel West quoted by Thelma Golden in "What's White?" in *1993 Biennial Exhibition* catalog, Whitney Museum of American Art, New York City, 27.

22. Hamblen, "Beyond Universalism," 7–14.

23. Wanda May, "Philosopher as Researcher and/or Begging the Question(s)," *Studies in Art Education* 33, no. 4 (1992): 226–243.

24. Craig Owens, "Amplifications: Laurie Anderson," *Art in America* (March 1981): 121.

25. Lucy Lippard, "Some Propaganda for Propaganda," in *Visibly Female: Feminism and Art Today,* ed. Hilary Robinson (New York: Universe, 1988), 184.

26. Barbara Kruger, "What's High, What's Low—and Who Cares?" *New York Times,* Sunday, 9 September 1990, 43.

27. Robert Storr, "Shape Shifter," *Art in America* (April 1989): 213.

28. Harold Pearse, "Beyond Paradigms: Art Education Theory and Practice in a Postparadigmatic World," *Studies in Art Education* 33, no. 4 (1992): 249.

29. Susan Tallman, "Guerrilla Girls," *Arts Magazine* (April 1991): 21–22.

30. Hilde Hein, "The Role of Feminist Aesthetics in Feminist Theory," *The Journal of Aesthetics and Art Criticism* 48, no. 4 (1990): 285.

31. Kristin Congdon, "Feminist Approaches to Art Criticism," in *Pluralistic Approaches to Art Criticism,* ed. Blandy and Congdon, 15–31.

32. Elizabeth Garber, "Feminism, Aesthetics, and Art Education," *Studies in Art Education* 33, no. 4 (1992): 210–225.

33. Simone de Beauvoir quoted in Hein, "The Role of Feminist Aesthetics," 282.

34. Hilton Kramer quoted by Edward M. Gomez, "Quarreling over Quality," *Time,* Special Issue, Fall 1990, 61.

35. Ibid., 61–62.

36. Rosalind Coward quoted by Jan Zita Grover, "Dykes in Context: Some Problems in Minority Representations," in *The Contest of Meaning,* ed. Richard Bolton (Cambridge, MA: MIT Press, 1989), 169.

37. John Berger, *Ways of Seeing* (London: Penguin Books, 1972).

38. Jean-Paul Sartre quoted by Hein, "The Role of Feminist Aesthetics," 290.

39. Griselda Pollock, "Missing Women," in *The Critical Image,* ed. Carol Squiers (Seattle, WA: Bay Press, 1990), 202–219.

40. Personal correspondence with the author, February 22, 1993.

41. Michael Kimmelman, "An Improbable Marriage of Artist and Museum," *New York Times,* Sunday, 2 August 1992, 27.

42. Museum for Contemporary Arts, Baltimore, MD, 1992.

43. Karen Hamblen, "Qualifications and Contradictions of Art Museum Education in a Pluralistic Democracy," in *Art in a Democracy,* ed. Doug Blandy and Kristin Congdon (New York: Teachers College Press, 1987), 13–25.

44. Mason Riddle, "Hachivi Edgar Heap of Birds," *New Art Examiner* (September 1990): 52.

45. Meyer Raphael Rubinstein, "Hachivi Edgar Heap of Birds," *Flash Art* (November–December 1990): 155.

46. Lydia Matthews, "Fighting Language with Language," *Artweek,* 6 December 1990, 1.

47. David Bailey, "Re-thinking Black Representations: From Positive Images to Cultural Photographic Practices," *Exposure* 27, no. 4 (1990): 37–46.

48. May, "Philosopher as Researcher," 231–232.

49. Lisa Duggan, "Making It Perfectly Queer," *Art Papers* 16, no. 4 (1992): 10–16.

50. Louise Sloan quoted in ibid., 14.

51. Douglas Crimp with Adam Rolston, *AIDS Demographics* (Seattle, WA: Bay Press, 1990).

52. Walter Robinson, "Artpark Squelches Bible Burning," *Art in America* (October 1990): 45.

53. Ralph Smith, "Problems for a Philosophy of Art Education," *Studies in Art Education* 33, no. 4 (1992): 253–266.

54. Michael Brenson, "Is 'Quality' An Idea Whose Time Has Gone?" *New York Times,* Sunday, 22 July 1990, 1, 27.

CHAPTER 6

1. Annie Dillard, *New York Times Review of Books,* 28 May 1989, 1.

2. Terry Barrett, "A Comparison of the Goals of Studio Professors Conducting Critiques and Art Education Goals for Teaching Criticism," *Studies in Art Education* 30, no. 1 (1988): 22–27.

BIBLIOGRAPHY

Adams, Brooks. "Wegman Unleashed." *Art News* (January 1990): 150–155.

Alexander, Elizabeth. Review of *Romare Bearden: His Life and Life*, by Myron Schwartzman. *New York Times Review of Books,* Sunday, 24 March 1991, 36.

Alloway, Lawrence. "The Expanding and Disappearing Work of Art." *Auction* (October 1967): 34–37.

———. "The Uses and Limits of Art Criticism." In *Topics of American Art Since 1945.* New York: W. W. Norton, 1975.

———. "Women's Art and the Failure of Art Criticism." In *Network: Art and the Complex Present.* Ann Arbor, MI: UMI Press, 1984.

———. "Women's Art in the Seventies." In *Network: Art and the Complex Present.* Ann Arbor, MI: UMI Press, 1984.

Aschner, Mary Jane. "Teaching the Anatomy of Criticism." *The School Review* 64, no. 7 (1956): 317–322.

Atkins, Robert. *Art Speak: A Guide to Contemporary Ideas, Movements, and Buzzwords.* New York: Abbeville Press, 1990.

———. *Art Speak: A Guide to Modern Ideas, Movements, and Buzzwords, 1848–1944* (New York: Abbeville Press, 1993).

Baker, Kenneth. "Ann Hamilton." *Artforum* (October 1990): 178–179.

Bailey, David. "Re-thinking Black Representations: From Positive Images to Cultural Photographic Practices." *Exposure* 27, no. 4 (1990): 37–46.

Barnet, Sylvan. *A Short Guide to Writing about Art.* 3d ed. Glenview, IL: Scott, Foresman, 1989.

Baro, Gene. "Dale Chihuly." *Art International* (August/September 1981): 125–126.

Barrett, Terry. "A Comparison of the Goals of Studio Professors Conducting Critiques and Art Education Goals for Teaching Criticism." *Studies in Art Education* 30, no. 1 (1988): 22–27.

Bass, Ruth. "Miriam Schapiro." *Artnews* (October 1990): 185.

Battin, Martin, John Fisher, Ronald Moore, and Anita Silvers. *Puzzles About Art: An Aesthetics Casebook.* New York: St. Martin's Press, 1989.

Beattie, Ann. *Alex Katz.* New York: Abrams, 1987.

Beckett, Wendy. *Contemporary Women Artists.* New York: Universe, 1988.

Bell, Janet. "Susan Rothenberg." *Artnews* (May 1987): 147.

Berger, John. *Ways of Seeing.* London: Penguin Books, 1972.

Berlind, Robert. "Leon Golub at Fawbush." *Art in America* (April 1988): 210–211.

Bersson, Robert. *Worlds of Art.* Mountain View, CA: Mayfield, 1991.

Blandy, Doug, and Kristin Congdon, eds. *Art in a Democracy.* New York: Teachers College Press, 1987.

———. *Pluralistic Approaches to Art Criticism.* Bowling Green, OH: Popular Press, 1991.

Bloom, Suzanne, and Ed Hill. "Leon Golub." *Artforum* (February 1989): 126.

Bourdon, David. "Chihuly: Climbing the Wall." *Art in America* (June 1990): 164–166.

Brenson, Michael. "Is 'Quality' an Idea Whose Time Has Gone?" *New York Times,* Sunday, 22 July 1990, 1, 27.

———. "Jenny Holzer: The Message Is the Message." *New York Times,* Sunday, 7 August 1988, 29.

———. "Romare Bearden: Epic Emotion, Intimate Scale." *New York Times,* Sunday, 27 March 1988, 41.

Bridgewater, Candace Mathews. "Jenny Holzer at Home and Abroad." *Columbus Dispatch,* Sunday, 5 August 1990, sec. F, 1–2.

Brookman, Donna. "Beyond the Equestrian." *Artweek,* 25 February 1989, 6.

Brooks, Rosetta. "Leon Golub: Undercover Agent." *Artforum* (January 1990): 116.

Broudy, Harry. *Enlightened Cherishing.* Champaign-Urbana: University of Illinois Press, 1972.

———. "Some Duties of a Theory of Educational Aesthetics." *Educational Theory* 30, no. 3 (1951): 198–199.

Burkhart, Ann. "A Study of Studio Art Professors' Beliefs and Attitudes About Professional Art Criticism." Master's thesis, The Ohio State University, Columbus, OH, 1992.

Burnham, Lynda Frye. "Running Commentary." *High Performance* (Summer 1991): 6–7.

———. "What Is a Critic Now?" *Art Papers* (November/December 1990): 7–8.

Calo, Carole Gold. "Martin Puryear." *New Art Examiner* (February 1988): 65.

———. "Martin Puryear: Private Objects, Evocative Visions." *Arts Magazine* (February 1988): 90–93.

Carter, Angela. Introduction. *Frida Kahlo.* London: Redstone Press, 1989.

"Ceramics and Glass Acquisitions at the V. & A." *Burlington Magazine* (May 1990): 388.

Chambers, Karen. "Pluralism Is a Concept." *U&lc* (Fall 1991): pp. 36–40.

Cokes, Tony. "Laurie Anderson at the 57th Street Playhouse." *Art in America* (July 1988): 120.

Coleman, A. D. "Because It Feels So Good When I Stop: Concerning a Continuing Personal Encounter with Photography Criticism." In *Light Readings: A Photography Critic's Writings 1968–1978,* edited by A. D. Coleman. New York: Oxford University Press, 1979.

Compassion and Protest: Recent Social and Political Art from the Eli Broad Family Foundation Collection. New York: Cross Rivers Press, 1991.

Congdon, Kristin. "Feminist Approaches to Art Criticism." In *Pluralistic Approaches to Art Criticism,* edited by Doug Blandy and Kristin Congdon, 15–31. Bowling Green, OH: Bowling Green State University Popular Press, 1991.

Corn, Alfred. "Lucien Freud, *Large Interior, W. 9.*" *Artnews* (March 1990): 117–118.

Costello, Kevin. "The World of William Wegman—The Artist and the Visual Pun." *West Coast Woman* (December 1991): 16.

Cotter, Holland. "Donald Lipski." *Artnews* (October 1990): 184.

———. "Jenny Holzer at Barbara Gladstone." *Art in America* (December 1986): 137–138.

Cottingham, Laura. "David Salle." *Flash Art* (May–June 1988): 104.

Crimp, Douglas. *AIDS: Cultural Analysis/Cultural Activism.* Cambridge. MA: MIT Press, 1988.

Crimp, Douglas, and Adam Rolston. *AIDS Demographics.* Seattle, WA: Bay Press, 1990.

Curtis, James. "New History." *Artnews* (October 1990): 203.

Cutajar, Mario. "Goodbye to All That." *Artspace* (July/August 1992): 61.

Cvetcovich, Ann. "Video, AIDS, and Activism." *Afterimage* (September 1991): 8–11.

Danto, Arthur. *Beyond the Brillo Box: The Visual Arts in Post-Historical Perspective.* New York: Farrar, Straus, and Giroux, 1992.

———. *Transfiguration of the Commonplace.* Cambridge, MA: Harvard University Press, 1981.

Decter, Joshua. "Leon Golub." *Arts Magazine* (March 1989): 134–135.

Dery, Mark. "From Hugo Ball to Hugo Largo: 75 Years of Art and Music." *High Performance* (Winter, 1988): 54–57.

DeVuono, Frances. "Contemporary African Artists." *Artnews* (Summer 1990): 174.

Dillard, Annie. *New York Times Review of Books,* 28 May 1989, 1.

DiNoto, Andrea. "New Masters of Glass." *Connoisseur* (August 1982): 22–24.

Drier, Deborah. "Critics and the Marketplace." *Art & Auction* (March 1990): 172–174.

Duncan, Lisa. "Making It Perfectly Queer." *Art Papers* 16, no. 4 (1992): 10–16.

Durland, Steven. "Notes from the Editor." *High Performance* (Summer 1991): 5.

Eaton, Marcia. *Basic Issues in Aesthetics.* Belmont, CA: Wadsworth, 1988.

Editors. "Ad Reinhardt." *Interview* (June 1991): 28.

Efland, Arthur. *A History of Art Education: Intellectual and Social Currents in Teaching the Visual Arts.* New York: Teachers College Press, 1990.

Failing, Patricia. "Invisible Men: Blacks and Bias in Western Art." *Artnews* (Summer 1990): 152–155.

Fauchereau, Serge. "Surrealism in Mexico." *Artforum* (Summer 1986): 88.

Feldman, Edmund. "The Teacher as Model Critic." *The Journal of Aesthetic Education* 7, no. 1 (1973): 50–57.

———. *Varieties of Visual Experience.* 3d ed. Englewood Cliffs, NJ: Prentice-Hall, 1987.

ffrench-frazier, Nina. "Romare Bearden." *Artnews* (October 1977): 141–142.

Fleck, Robert. "William Wegman, Centre Pompidou." *Flash Art* (Summer 1991): 140.

Flood, Richard. "Laurie Anderson." *Artforum* (September 1988): 80–81.

Foster, Hal. "Subversive Signs." *Art in America* (November 1982): 88–92.

Frank, Elizabeth. "Art's Off-the-Wall Critic," *New York Times Magazine,* 19 November 1989, 73.

Frueh, Joanna. "Towards a Feminist Theory of Art Criticism." In *Feminist Art Criticism: An Anthology,* edited by Arlene Raven, Cassandra Langer, and Joanna Frueh. Ann Arbor, MI: UMI Press, 1988.

Galligan, Gregory. "Elizabeth Murray's New Paintings." *Arts Magazine* (September 1987): 62–67.

Garber, Elizabeth. "Art Criticism as Ideology." *Journal of Social Theory in Art Education* 11 (1991): 50-67.

———. "Feminism, Aesthetics, and Art Education." *Studies in Art Education* 33, no. 4 (1992): 210–225.

Gardner, Paul. "What Artists Like About the Art They Like When They Don't Know Why." *Artnews* (October 1991).

Gerrit, Henry. "Agnes Martin." *Artnews* (March 1983): 159.

Gilbert-Rolfe, Jeremy. "Seriousness and Difficulty in Criticism." *Art Papers* (November-December 1990): 8–11.

Gill, Elizabeth. "Elizabeth Murray." *Artnews* (October 1977): 168.

Gitlin, Michael. "Deborah Butterfield." *Arts Magazine* (February 1987): 107.

Glowen, Ron. "Glass on the Cutting Edge." *Artweek,* 6 December 1990.

Glueck, Grace. "And Now a Word from Jenny Holzer." *New York Times Magazine,* 3 December 1989, 42.

———. "The Pope of the Art World." *New York Times Review of Books,* 26 May 1991, 15.

Goldstein, Ann. "Baim-Williams." In *A Forest of Signs in the Crisis of Representation,* edited by Catherine Gudis. Cambridge, MA: MIT Press, 1989.

Gomez, Edward M. "Quarreling over Quality." *Time,* Special Issue, Fall 1990, 61–62.

Goodman, Nelson. *Languages of Art.* Indianapolis, IN: Hackett, 1976.

Grimes, Nancy. "Elizabeth Murray." *Artnews* (September 1988): 151.

Gross, Michael. "Pup Art." *New York,* 30 March 1992, 44–49.

Grover, Jan Zita. "Dykes in Context: Some Problems in Minority Representations." In *The Contest of Meaning,* edited by Richard Bolton. Cambridge, MA: MIT Press, 1989.

Grundberg, Andy. "Toward Critical Pluralism." In *Reading into Photography: Selected Essays, 1959–1982,* edited by Thomas Barrow, Shelley Armitage, and William Tydeman, 247–253. Albuquerque: University of New Mexico Press, 1982.

Gudis, Catherine, ed. *A Forest of Signs in the Crisis of Representation.* Cambridge, MA: MIT Press, 1989.

Hagen, Charles. "William Wegman." *Artforum* (June 1984): 90.

Halpern, David, ed. *Writers on Art.* San Francisco: North Point Press, 1988.

Hamblen, Karen. "Beyond Universalism in Art Criticism." In *Pluralistic Approaches to Art Criticism,* edited by Doug Blandy and Kristin Congdon, 7–14. Bowling Green, OH: Bowling Green State University Popular Press, 1991.

———. "Qualifications and Contradictions of Art Museum Education in a Pluralistic Democracy." In *Art in a Democracy,* edited by Doug Blandy and Kristin Congdon, 13–25. New York: Teachers College Press, 1987.

Hammond, Pamela. "Leon Golub." *Artnews* (March 1990): 193.

———. "A Primal Spirit: Ten Contemporary Japanese Sculptors." *Artnews* (October 1990): 201–202.

Handy, Elizabeth. "Deborah Butterfield at Edward Thorp." *Art in America* (April 1987): 218.

Hartney, Mick. "Laurie Anderson's *United States*." *Studio International* (April/May 1983): 51.

———. "Leon Golub." *Artnews* (March 1990): 193.

Heartney, Elizabeth. "Art and the Public." *Art Papers* (November-December 1990): 15–16.

———. "David Salle: Impersonal Effects." *Art in America* (June 1988): 121–129.

———. "Jenny Holzer." *Artnews* (March 1990): 173.

———. "A Little Too High Minded." *Artnews* (December 1990): 159.

———. "Martha Rossler at DIA." *Art in America* (November 1989): 184.

———. "Sue Coe." *Artnews* (December 1989): 158.

Hein, Hilda. "The Role of Feminist Aesthetics in Feminist Theory." *The Journal of Aesthetics and Art Criticism* 48, no. 4 (1990): 281–291.

Henry, Gerrit. "Agnes Martin." *Artnews* (March 1983): 159.

———. "Psyching Out Katz." *Artnews* (Summer 1987): 23.

———. "William Wegman." *Artnews* (April 1986): 154.

Herrera, Hayden. "Why Frida Kahlo Speaks to the 90's." *New York Times,* Sunday, 28 October 1990, 1.

Hill, Ed, and Suzanne Bloom. "Leon Golub." *Artforum* (February 1989): 126.

Hixon, Kathryn. "Chicago in Review." *Arts Magazine* (January 1990): 106.

———. "Chicago in Review." *Arts Magazine* (November 1990): 123.

Holmes, A. M. "Vito Acconci." *Artforum* (Summer 1991): 107.

Holzer, Jenny. *Survival Series.* Buffalo, NY: Albright Knox Gallery, 1991.

———. "Truisms." In *Blasted Allegories: An Anthology of Writings by Contemporary Artists,* edited by Brian Wallis, 107. New York: The New Museum of Contemporary Art, 1987.

Howell, John. "Laurie Anderson." *Artforum* (Summer 1986): 127.

Hubbard, Kim. "Sit, Beg . . . Now Smile!" *People Magazine,* 9 September 1991, 105–108.

Hughes, Robert. *Nothing If Not Critical.* New York: Knopf, 1990.

———. "A Sampler of Witless Truisms." *Time,* 30 July 1990, 66.

Hunter-Stiebel, Penelope. "Contemporary Art Glass: An Old Medium Gets a New Look." *Artnews* (Summer 1981): 132.

Iinkl, Marilyn. "James Carpenter—Dale Chihuly." *Craft Horizons* (June 1977): 59.

James, Curtia. "New History." *Artnews* (October 1990): 203.

Januszczak, Waldemar. "Is Anselm Kiefer the New Genius of Painting? Not Quite!" *Connoisseur* (May 1988): 130–133.

Johnson, Ken. "Anselm Kiefer at Marian Goodman." *Art in America* (November 1990): 198–199.

———. "Being and Politics." *Art in America* (September 1990): 155–160.

———. "Elizabeth Murray's New Paintings." *Arts Magazine* (September 1987): 67–69.

Jones, Ronald. "David Salle." *Flash Art* (April 1987): 82.

Joselit, David. "Lessons in Public Sculpture." *Art in America* (December 1989): 131–134.

Kachur, Lewis. "Lakeside Boom." *Art International* (Spring 1989): 63–65.

Kimmelman, Michael. "An Improbable Marriage of Artist and Museum." *New York Times,* Sunday, 2 August 1992, 27.

Kirshner, Judith Russi. "Martin Puryear, Margo Leavin Gallery." *Artforum* (Summer 1985): 115.

Klein, Ellen Lee. "Romare Bearden." *Arts Magazine* (December 1986): 119–120.

Koelsch, Patrice. "The Criticism of Quality and the Quality of Criticism." *Art Papers* (November-December 1990): 14–15.

Kozloff, Joyce. "Frida Kahlo." *Art in America* (May/June 1979): 148–149.

Kruger, Barbara. "What's High, What's Low—and Who Cares?" *New York Times,* Sunday, 9 September 1990, 43.

Kunz, Martin, ed. *William Wegman.* New York: Abrams, 1990.

Kuspit, Donald. "Sue Coe." *Artforum* (Summer 1991): 111.

Kutner, Janet. "Elizabeth Murray." *Artnews* (May 1987): 45–46.

Labat, Tony. "Two Hundred Words or So I've Heard Artists Say About Critics and Criticism." *Artweek,* 5 September 1991, 18.

Larson, Kay. "A Mexican Georgia O'Keeffe," *New York Magazine,* 28 March 1983, 82–83.

Lee, Sun-Young. "A Metacritical Examination of Contemporary Art Critics' Practices: Lawrence Alloway, Donald Kuspit and Robert Pincus-Witten for Developing a Unit for Teaching Art Criticism." Ph.D. diss., The Ohio State University, Columbus, OH, 1988.

Lewis, James. "Joseph Kosuth." *Artforum* (December 1990): 134.

Lichtenstein, Therese. "Artist/Critic." *Arts Magazine* (November 1983): 40.

Lippard, Lucy. "Headlines, Heartlines, Hardlines: Advocacy Criticism as Activism." In *Cultures in Contention,* edited by Douglas Kahn and Diane Neumaier. Seattle, WA: Real Comet Press, 1985.

———. *Mixed Blessings.* New York: Pantheon Books, 1991.

———. "Some Propaganda for Propaganda." In *Visibly Female: Feminism and Art Today,* edited by Hilary Robinson, 184–194. New York: Universe, 1988.

Louie, Elaine. "A Photographer and His Dog Speak as One." *New York Times,* 14 February 1991, B4.

Malcolm, Janet. "A Girl of the Zeitgeist—I." *The New Yorker,* 20 October 1986, 49–87.

———. "A Girl of the Zeitgeist—II." *The New Yorker,* 27 October 1986, 47–66.

Marks, Ben. "Memories of Bad Dreams." *Artweek,* 21 December 1989, 9.

Marshall, Richard, and Robert Mapplethorpe. *50 New York Artists.* San Francisco: Chronicle Books, 1986.

Martin, Richard. "A Horse Perceived by Sighted Persons: New Sculptures by Deborah Butterfield." *Arts Magazine* (January 1987): 73–75.

Matthews, Lydia. "Fighting Language with Language." *Artweek,* 6 December 1990, 1.

May, Wanda. "Philosopher as Researcher and/or Begging the Question(s)." *Studies in Art Education* 33, no. 4 (1992): 226–243.

McElroy, Guy. *Facing History: The Black Image in American Art 1710–1940.* Corcoran Museum, Washington, D.C.

McEvilley, Thomas. "New York: The Whitney Biennial." *Artforum* (Summer 1991): 98–100.

Meltzer, Irene Ruth. "The Critical Eye: An Analysis of the Process of Dance Criticism as Practiced by Clive Barnes, Arlene Croce, Deborah Jowitt, Elizabeth Kendall, Marcia Siegel, and David Vaughn." Master's thesis, The Ohio State University, Columbus, OH, 1979.

Menzies, Neal. "Unembellished Strength of Form." *Artweek,* 2 February 1985, 4.

Meyer, Raphael Rubinstein. "A Hemisphere of Decentered Mexican Art Comes North." *Arts Magazine* (April 1989): 70.

Miller, Robert. "Deborah Butterfield." *Artnews* (March 1987): 149.

Miller, Tim. "Critical Wishes." *Artweek,* 5 September 1991, 18.

Moorman, Margaret. "Intimations of Immortality." *Artnews* (Summer 1988): 40–41.

———. "Leon Golub." *Artforum* (February 1989): 126.

Morgan, Ann Lee. "Martin Puryear: Sculpture as Elemental Expression." *New Art Examiner* (May 1987): 27–29.

Newman, Michael. "The Ribbon Around the Time Bomb." *Art in America* (April 1983): 160–169.

Norden, Linda. "Dale Chihuly: Shell Forms." *Arts Magazine* (June 1981): 150–151.

Owens, Craig. "Amplifications: Laurie Anderson." *Art in America* (March 1981): 120–123.

———. "William Wegman's Psychoanalytic Vaudeville." *Art in America* (March 1983): 101–108.

Pagel, David. "Still Life: The Tableaux of Ann Hamilton." *Arts Magazine* (May 1990): 56–61.

Pearse, Harold. "Beyond Paradigms: Art Education Theory and Practice in a Postparadigmatic World." *Studies in Art Education* 33, no. 4 (1992): 244–252.

Perl, Jed. "Tradition-conscious." *The New Criterion* (May 1991): 55–59.

Phillips, Patricia C. "Collecting Culture: Paradoxes and Curiosities." In *Breakthroughs: Avant-garde Artists in Europe and America, 1950–1990.* Wexner Center for the Arts. New York: Rizzoli, 1991.

Plagens, Peter. "Frida on Our Minds." *Newsweek,* 27 May 1991, 54–55.

———. "Max's Dinner with André." *Newsweek,* 12 August 1991, 60–61.

———. "Peter and the Pressure Cooker." *Moonlight Blues: An Artist's Art Criticism.* Ann Arbor, MI: UMI Press, 1986.

———. "Unsentimental Journey." *Newsweek,* 29 April 1991, 58–59.

———. "The Venetian Carnival." *Newsweek,* 11 June 1990, 60–61.

Pollock, Griselda. "Missing Women." In *The Critical Image,* edited by Carol Squiers, 202–219. Seattle, WA: Bay Press, 1990.

Princenthal, Nancy. "Intuition's Disciplinarian." *Art in America* (January 1990): 131–136.

———. "Romare Bearden at Cordier & Ekstrom." *Art in America* (February 1987): 149.

Prud'homme, Alex. "The Biggest and the Best?" *Artnews* (February 1990): 124–129.

Raven, Arlene. *Crossing Over: Feminism and Art of Social Concern.* Ann Arbor, MI: UMI Press, 1988.

Reveaux, Tony. "O Superwoman," *Artweek,* 26 July 1986, 13.

Ricard, Rene. "Not About Julian Schnabel." *Artforum* (1981): 74–80.

Riddle, Mason. "Hachivi Edgar Heap of Birds." *New Art Examiner* (September 1990): 52.

Rimanelli, David. "David Salle." *Artforum* (Summer 1991): 110.

Robbins, D. A. "William Wegman's Pop Gun." *Arts Magazine* (March 1984): 116–121.

Robinson, Walter. "Artpark Squelches Bible Burning." *Art in America* (October 1990): 45.

Ronk, Martha C. "Top Dog." *Artweek,* 3 May 1990, 16.

Rosen, Michael. *The Company of Dogs.* New York: Doubleday, 1990.

Roy, Jean-Michael. "His Master's Muse: William Wegman, Man Ray, and the Dog-Biscuit Dialectic." *The Journal of Art* (November 1991): 20–21.

Rubinstein, Meyer Raphael. "Books." *Arts Magazine* (September 1991): 95.

———. "Hachivi Edgar Heap of Birds." *Flash Art* (November/December 1990): 155.

———. "A Hemisphere of Decentered Mexican Art Comes North." *Arts Magazine* (April 1991): 70.

Sofer, Ken. "Reviews." *Artnews* (October 1987): 134.

Saltz, Jerry. "A Blessing in Disguise: William Wegman's *Blessing of the Field,* 1986." *Arts Magazine* (Summer 1988): 15–16.

Schwartzman, Myron. *Romare Bearden: His Life and Life.* New York: Abrams, 1993.

———. "Romare Bearden Sees in a Memory." *Artforum* (May 1984): 64–70.

Shottenkirk, Dana. "Nancy Spero." *Artforum* (May 1991): 143.

Silberman, Robert. "Americans in Glass: A Requiem?" *Art in America* (March 1985): 47–53.

Simic, Charles. *Dime-Store Alchemy.* New York: Ecco Press, 1992.

Singerman, Howard. "In the Text." In *A Forest of Signs: Art in the Crisis of Representation,* edited by Catherine Gudis, 156. Cambridge, MA: MIT Press, 1989.

Smith, Ralph. "Problems for a Philosophy of Art Education." *Studies in Art Education* 33, no. 4 (1992): 253–266.

Smith, Roberta. "Outsider Art Goes Beyond the Fringe." *New York Times,* Sunday, 15 September 1991, 1, 33.

Solomon, Deborah. "Catching Up with the High Priest of Criticism." *New York Times,* Arts and Leisure, Sunday, 23 June 1991, 31-32.

———. "Celebrating Painting." *New York Times Magazine,* 31 March 1991, 21-25.

Spurrier, Jeff. "The High Priestess of Mexican Art." *Connoisseur* (August 1990): 67–71.

Storr, Robert. "Elizabeth Murray." *New Art Examiner* (October 1988): 55.

———. "Riddled Sphinxes." *Art in America* (March 1989): 126.

———. "Salle's Gender Machine." *Art in America* (June 1988): 24–25.

———. "Shape Shifter." *Art in America* (April 1989): 210.

Szarkowski, John. *Mirrors and Windows: American Photography Since 1960.* New York: The Museum of Modern Art, 1978.

Tallman, Susan. "Guerrilla Girls." *Arts Magazine* (April 1991): 21–22.

Taragin, Davira S. "From Vienna to the Studio Craft Movement." *Apollo* (December 1986): 544.

Thorp, Edward. "Deborah Butterfield." *Artnews* (February 1989): 138–139.

———. "Deborah Butterfield." *Artnews* (April 1991): 184.

Tucker, Marcia. "Equestrian Mysteries: An Interview with Deborah Butterfield." *Art in America* (June 1989): 203.

Vaizey, Marina. "Art Is More Than Just Art." *New York Times Book Review,* 5 August 1990, 9.

Valverde, Georgina. In *Worlds of Art,* by Robert Bersson. Mountain View, CA: Mayfield, 1991.

Van Proyen, Mark. "A Conversation with Donald Kuspit." *Artweek,* 5 September 1991, 19.

Waldman, Diane. *Jenny Holzer.* New York: Abrams, 1989.

Watson, Gray. "Jenny Holzer." *Flash Art* (March/April 1989): 120–121.

Wegman, William. *Cinderella.* New York: Hyperion, 1993.

———. *Man's Best Friend.* New York: Abrams, 1982.

Weitz, Morris. *Hamlet and the Philosophy of Literary Criticism.* Chicago: University of Chicago Press, 1972.

Westerbeck, Colin. "Chicago, Martin Puryear." *Artforum* (May 1987): 154.

Westfall, Edward. "Deborah Butterfield." *Arts Magazine* (February 1987): 107.

Wexner Center for the Arts. *Breakthroughs: Avant-Garde Artists in Europe and America, 1950–1990.* New York: Rizzoli, 1991.

Wolfe, Tom. *From Bauhaus to Our House.* New York: Farrar, Straus, and Giroux, 1982.

———. *The Painted Word.* New York: Farrar, Straus, and Giroux, 1975.

Wooster, Ann-Sargeant. "Laurie Anderson." *High Performance* (Spring 1990): 65.

Yau, John. "William Wegman." *Artforum* (October 1988).

Yenawine, Philip. *How to Look at Modern Art.* New York: Abrams, 1991.

Ziv, Peter G. "Clement Greenberg." *Art & Antiques* (September 1987): 57–59.

INDEX

191

Talk

Things happen in transition
   Comfort means decay - move on to risk something new
   1 - have idea of the concept - gestural, whimsical, process - rhythm of movement
   2 - being literate enough to recognize it
                                                      J. Pollock - stream of
   3 - clarity - simplicity   conciousness
            float
            energy beyond piece itself
      1 compositional element + repeated
   4 - creating dynamic

      " simple is harder than complicated "
      marriage of design + form

         repetition
         thought feeling + idea are the same

   critic must bring previous knowledge and thought -
   validity of opinion / judgement

      why laugh
      transition between the 2 works - lets the viewer have the
            opportunity to fantasize

      Does it work ? Is it believable ?

   5 - consistency   lyrical relationships between parts - unity

      communication of feeling - from nature
         natural

   sculptural or sculpture
      Everything is functional, some things are utilitarian

   Taoism -
   Boredom ⎱ engenders fantasy - frees you up from original ⎱ opens up possibility
   Failure ⎰   ⎰ of potential
   Frustration jars one out of comfort .   creates growth

control - fight to loose : realism
coffee cups

assimilate the environment   -   palm trees
beach eddies

art is a life style & process of interactivity

stressed
   innovation/moment of transition
   the dynamic movement in time & mass
   clarity & simplicity

Ted

should project from across a room

② have to learn all the rules - elements of design

① staying power - ability to endure in time - relevant to human race
    craftsmanship in design
    emotional response
    reaching into human soul + pulling something out

few in past 15 years -
Vietnam Memorial - one of the best

④ ~~relevancy~~

③ something different .   de Kooning - new use of space
                   Pollock - new applic. of paint
                   Oldenbourg - soft monumental commonplace

    " I don't want current it to influence my thinking "   . have to balance

⑤ do what is right for yourself

    I̲s   Postmodernism free from "bondage of traditional skills + teaching

New York   art crit ⌐ out of touch as main stream american
L A (Hollywood)   art cist ⌐

Santa Fe - 3rd (best in sales) more middle american

what I want to say - patterns expressing world around
after book - that didn't seem relevant
going back - drawing - taking tree + responding to it
finding of lang - Hebr. Gk Aramaic Eng - 3 great religions
  metaphors · gram transfer / backwards / relevant words.
  moved from realist
      to interpretation - more expression   Post Mod. infl. by arch.
      to message - fusion of form / message / expr.
        more